Knowing Fictions

Knowing Fictions

Picaresque Reading in the Early Modern Hispanic World

Barbara Fuchs

PENN

UNIVERSITY OF PENNSYLVANIA PRESS

PHILADELPHIA

A volume in the Haney Foundation Series, established in 1961
with the generous support of Dr. John Louis Haney.

Published by
University of Pennsylvania Press
Philadelphia, Pennsylvania 19104-4112
www.upenn.edu/pennpress

Printed in the United States of America on acid-free paper
1 3 5 7 9 10 8 6 4 2

Library of Congress Cataloging-in-Publication Data
Names: Fuchs, Barbara, author.
Title: Knowing fictions : picaresque reading in the early
modern Hispanic world / Barbara Fuchs.
Other titles: Haney Foundation series.
Description: 1st edition. | Philadelphia : University of
Pennsylvania Press, [2020] | Series: Haney Foundation series |
Includes bibliographical references and index.
Identifiers: LCCN 2020004067 | ISBN 978-0-8122-5261-3
(hardcover)
Subjects: LCSH: Picaresque literature, Spanish—History
and criticism. | Spanish fiction—Classical period,
1500–1700—History and criticism. | Skepticism in literature. |
Literature and society—Spain—History.
Classification: LCC PQ6147.P5 F83 2020 |
DDC 863/.30927—dc23
LC record available at https://lccn.loc.gov/2020004067

Para Mercedes García-Arenal,
que es toda una inspiración

And for my students at UCLA,
who helped me see how powerful
the picaresque remains

Contents

Introduction

Mi pluma y mi tintero me valen lo que quiero.

—Spanish proverb

From the *relación* to the captivity narrative, the Hispanic imperial project relies heavily on the first-person authority of genres whose authenticity undergirds the ideological armature of national consolidation, expansion, and conquest. At the same time, increasing pressures for religious conformity in Spain as across Europe require subjects to bare their interiority to external authorities, in intimate confessions of their faith. As it emerges in this charged context, the unreliable voice of the picaresque poses a rhetorical challenge to the authority of the witness, destabilizing the possibility of trustworthy representation precisely because he or she is so intimately involved with the material. The picaresque also limns itineraries beyond the metropole, transcending the limited range of foundational texts such as *La Celestina* and *Lazarillo de Tormes* to model alternative relationships to Spain and Spanishness from a distance. Via its imaginative geographies, it thus interrogates the conceptual and actual limits of nation and empire: while the texts themselves chart communities that transcend the nation, they also challenge the idea of a bounded polity from a transnational and imperial optic. *Knowing Fictions* shows, first, how the fictional serves as an early site of skepticism within Spanish letters, and second, how itinerant texts complicate both national and literary affiliations. It reveals the picaresque as both a writerly and a readerly strategy, problematizing truth and authority while implicating the broader textual apparatus of imperium in its fictionality and interestedness.

The picaresque is largely a retrospective critical construction, with Cervantes as an early and perspicacious adopter: not only is it famously debated and debatable, but there are as many examples of texts that might arguably be picaresques as those generally admitted to belong to the club.[1] As Claudio Guillén notes, "No work embodies completely the picaresque genre"[2]—and this seems to be even more true for the picaresque than for other kinds. Rather than reengaging this debate, my goal here is to examine the picaresque affiliations of complex, adjacent fictions—para-picaresques, if we were to imagine solid boundaries—as well as widely recognized picaresque texts, to examine the ideological work that they do. In their own moment and over a much longer history of reception, I will suggest, picaresques help to construct knowing readers, of the sort that Cervantes so often seems to address.

My readings build on Guillén's marvelously economic definition of the picaresque as "the fictional confession of a liar,"[3] to explore the historical and epistemological implications of the form. Beyond Guillén's useful construction of genre as "a problem-solving model," for writers, he also characterizes the picaresque as "a procedure for ordering the continuum of individual literary facts; and, as a critical perspective, perhaps fruitful at the moment of reading."[4] John Parrack extends Guillén's insights to argue that the picaresque "underscores its own narrative silences," inviting a particular "'game' of interpretation."[5] Parrack locates the picaresque's development in a historical context of print technology, increasingly widespread literacy, and the concomitant development of silent reading, all of which enable a more active—and even suspicious—reader. As the individual reading subject is granted more authority, Parrack argues, "picaresque discourse not only acknowledges but invites and requires interpretation as an active force to challenge existing systems of authority and textual 'truths.'"[6] *Knowing Fictions* proposes both a historical and a theoretical approach: it situates the picaresque in relation to imperial expansion and confessional suspicion, which render narrative authority singularly charged, and simultaneously proposes the form as a tool for reading. By venturing beyond the echt-picaresque, I explore what framing a text, rather than simply classifying it as picaresque or noting its inherent generic affiliation, can reveal.

Picaresque Framing

Some years ago I essayed the most radical version of this critical move, deliberately and perversely framing an English New World relation as a picaresque in order to complicate its construction of national and religious allegiances in a context of inter-imperial rivalry.[7] The narrative of "one Miles Philips, Englishman, one of the company put on shoare Northward of Panuco, in the West Indies by Mr. John Hawkins" covers events occurring from 1567 to 1582, and was published in Richard Hakluyt's *Principal Navigations of the*

English Nation (1589, 1598–1600). Hawkins's voyages of the 1560s launched the triangular trade between Europe, Africa, and the New World: the English took on human "marchandize" on the coast of Guinea, then sold the enslaved Africans in the Caribbean. On the third voyage, which was to prove so fateful for the young Philips, a storm forced the English ships into the port of Veracruz, New Spain, where the Spanish fleet largely destroyed them. Having lost most of his ships, Hawkins chose to abandon a portion of his crew to fend for themselves in New Spain while he tried to reach England with his remaining human cargo.

Richard Helgerson—whose insights in person and in print I sorely miss—argued that Philips's text asserts the emergence of an English identity that survives multiple trials—abandonment by Hawkins, wandering in the New World wilderness, interrogation by the Inquisition, the lure of Spanish riches.[8] Yet the narrative's retrospective quality and its deliberate re-presentation of its protagonist's adventures simultaneously cast that identity into doubt. My reading explores how the use of a Spanish literary frame—the picaresque—to analyze this English text serves to interrogate its construction of English identity, revealing the rhetorical maneuvers involved in performing and sustaining English national difference after the fact. For Philips is caught in a bind: his survival in New Spain clearly depended on his adaptability and even his ability to pass as a Spaniard, yet his reintegration into English society as he tells his story rests on proving that he remained distinctly English while among the enemy.

At the heart of Philips's account lies a harrowing interrogation of the ragged company of suspected "Lutherans" by the Inquisition, during which the English are asked to confirm their belief in transubstantiation and other Catholic dogma. Yet in narrating these events, Philips sidesteps his disavowal of reformed religion, and instead stresses the perilous alternative to acquiescence with his captors: "To which if we answered not yea, then was there no way but death."[9] While older or perhaps less pragmatic members of the crew die for their true beliefs, Philips serves five years in a monastery. The retrospective narrator must thread a fine rhetorical needle here, persuading his readers that whereas he needed to lie during the interrogation to survive, his present account of what transpired is completely trustworthy. We are meant to believe that his repudiation of Protestantism in New Spain was a necessary fabrication, yet the account we read is, if not heroic, at least fully authentic.

Framing Miles Philips's narrative as a picaresque is an extrinsic critical move: his account is not formally a picaresque, or even a literary text, nor do we have any evidence that Philips was familiar with texts such as *Lazarillo*.[10]

Yet as an "allegory of legitimation"[11] for a deracinated subject, the picaresque productively frames Philips's transatlantic narrative of vexed allegiances and protean transformations. The Spanish form elucidates this peculiar English narration of adventures in New and Old Spain both by revealing its distinct shape and by casting suspicion upon the narrator's claims. Thus a willfully perverse formal contextualization within a precise historical setting highlights the rhetorical maneuvers involved in performing and sustaining English difference, and reveals in the text ambiguities and hesitations that are occluded even by other literary referents, such as the epic, with which Helgerson frames the text.

In *Knowing Fictions*, I return to the Old World, tracing Mediterranean itineraries of diaspora, captivity, and imperial rivalry in a corpus that engages picaresque conventions to contest narrative authority. I focus on texts that fit uneasily within standard categories of genre and geography: in addition to Mateo Alemán's *Guzmán de Alfarache*—one of the few texts generally agreed by critics to represent the picaresque—I explore Francisco Delicado's *La Lozana andaluza*, the anonymous *Viaje de Turquía*, Cervantes's plays of captivity, and his various versions of the picaresque in the *Novelas ejemplares*. My canon is provisional rather than exhaustive: I offer it as a first sally beyond the lines of genre, a model for how reading with and through the picaresque might transform our understanding of a broad range of texts. My goal is not to lard the canon of the picaresque with runners-up and wannabes; I am less interested in how we delimit the form than in what we can do with it, mobilizing genre as a tool for our own reading. Intensive close reading in a picaresque vein, I argue, reveals connections and operations that cumulatively challenge not just social verities but their epistemological grounding. At the same time, although *Knowing Fictions* deals exclusively with texts explicitly engaged in literary play, I want to suggest how recognizing their strategies may prove useful in rereading historiographic materials often marked by similar ambiguities.

Critics have effectively charted the close connections between the picaresque as it emerges in the sixteenth century and the bureaucratic, legal, and inquisitional discourses of a vertiginously expanding and transforming Habsburg empire. As state and religious institutions required subjects to provide a narrative account of themselves, they produced not just subjects—in an early form of Althusserian interpellation—but also fictions. Yet even as witnessing becomes increasingly important as a guarantor of knowledge, the picaresque reveals that the compelled or interested stories of witnesses can be simultaneously more persuasive and less true. They are more authoritative, to be sure, given the narrators' proximity to the action, but also more interested, more evidently narrated for a particular reason and organized around deliberate emphases and omissions. Because they engage so closely the forms of knowledge authorized by experience, picaresques introduce doubt into the circuit of interpellation and subjectification.

I am intrigued by the possibilities of narration—whether in the first person or not—that problematizes first-person authority, revealing instead an unreliability born of intimacy and complicity. In the most straightforward version of this dynamic, the narrating *pícaro* demonstrates that across society things are not what they seem, especially when viewed from below, while his or her own narration remains fundamentally unreliable and self-serving. Yet beyond the *pícaro*'s own disenchantment with a society in which lying and stealing are widespread,[12] the picaresque sows doubt on narrative authority itself. From the equivocal immediacy of the exculpatory narrative that Lazarillo addresses to "Vuestra Merced," to Guzmán's dizzying alternation between moralizing and immorality, the knowing *pícaro*, cognizant of all the tricks of a narrator's trade, gives us a wised-up story. Whether narrated in the first person or not, the narrative foregrounds the *pícaro*'s point of view, and thus contrasts markedly with related genres, such as English "coney-catching" literature, that promise to expose the rogue. In the knowing fictions that concern me here, the immediacy that supports the *pícaro*'s claim to narrative authority—his or her central role—vies with an interestedness and partiality that undo that authority. Beyond the limited credibility that the reader might grant a marginal narrator—what Miranda Fricker might term the "epistemic injustice" of this testimonial transaction[13]—the unreliability of the narrative remains inextricable from its situatedness, its closeness to what is being narrated, often in the first person. Hence the picaresque functions as the vexed double of first-person narration that touts experience as the basis of authority, whether the New World *relación*, the Mediterranean captivity narrative, or even the confession. As a skeptical response to the outsize importance of first-person accounts, the picaresque reflects on the epistemological challenges of a particular moment and its outsize valorization of the witness.[14]

Beyond the unreliable first-person narrator, other forms in this early, wildly experimental era of prose fiction also challenge the reliability of the witness. Dialogue, which often includes long stretches of first-person narration, foregrounds problems of perspectivism, partiality, and situated truths, particularly in its portrayal of an intradiegetic audience that is often as complicitly interested as the narrator but with different goals in view. From *Lozana*, in which the narrator enters the story and contemplates an erotic encounter with his opinionated character, to the *Viaje de Turquía*, in which corrupt listeners hang on the captive's every word so they can learn how to lie more effectively, intimacy and opportunism erode narrative authority. Cervantes's kaleidoscopic exploration of picaresque variants in his *Novelas*—upper-class *pícaros*, two *pícaros*, dogs as *pícaros*—also probes what characters know and how they relay that knowledge, with the reader as voyeur, unacknowledged traveling companion, or even reluctant dupe. In all these cases, knowingness adumbrates the possibility of knowing.

At the same time, these are expansive texts: they explode the stifling small-town geography of *La Celestina*, and even the domestic itinerance of *Lazarillo*, with large-scale crossings to Italy, North Africa, the Ottoman Empire. Their events are relayed across the Mediterranean, while their narrators reveal how differently they operate in different spaces. Far-ranging picaresques foreground the challenges of relayed authority, calling our attention to the particular exigencies of trusting a narrator who describes what the reader has never seen or experienced, and who acknowledges the situatedness of his or her own telling. Their geographic expansiveness underscores the fragility of imperial and ideological mechanisms all too dependent on subjects' self-presentation. From the equivocal self-fashioning of Lozana or Guzmán in Italy to the recollected faith of the former captive Pedro de Urdemalas, an expanded world offers a more distanced, nuanced view of empire, and of the more flexible selves that might exist within it.

In this expansive version, the picaresque allows us to consider how narrative both renders and complicates the project of encompassing a larger world, one whose very dimensions make the authority of the witness at once crucial and untenable.[15] At the same time, it problematizes assumptions of access to the "little world," in John Donne's felicitous term, of subjectivity, interiority, and faith, reminding us that narrators who are uniquely positioned to relay their own truths often become less reliable the greater the stakes.[16] If the early sixteenth century featured the internalization of religious experience, through both Catholic movements that promoted a more intimate connection with God and the Protestant rejection of external marks of faith, it also saw the extensive policing of that experience, whether by an Inquisition suspicious of heterodoxy or by various state agents attempting to enforce a specific official religiosity. The externalization of what had become interior in compelled accounts of belief raises important questions about the narrating "I" whom the picaresque brings to the forefront. If intimacy or, even more problematically, self-interest compromises reliability, what is the basis for knowledge? How, in confessional accounts, can we distinguish knowing from knowingness?

Knowing Fictions focuses closely on a corpus of singularly self-aware texts, while reconstructing the intellectual and ideological contexts in which they operate. Although these texts seek particular effects as literature, they also evince and complicate larger debates about truth and knowledge in the period, from art history's exploration of the power of the image as guarantor of truth, to history of science's inquiries into the social construction of authority and the development of modern empiricism, to the broader historical examination of the epistemological and representational challenges of Iberian empire and metropolitan consolidation. In dialogue with these important developments across the disciplines, as well as with the burgeoning study of fiction and interiority, *Knowing Fictions* argues for the particular role of the literary as a locus of skepticism and resistance.

Witnessing and the Arts of Empire

The horizons of European exploration and conquest expanded exponentially in the late fifteenth and sixteenth centuries, from the early Portuguese voyages to Africa and India to the transformative encounter, first by Spain and soon thereafter by other Europeans, with the New World.[17] From late fifteenth-century narratives of travel to Jerusalem, still envisioning a latter-day crusade, to Columbus's imperial purview on the New World, witnessing became a key source of the traveler's textual authority. While the immediacy of first-person narration conveyed to readers the original proximity of experience, travelers, illustrators, and printers also developed multiple strategies to construct and support their accounts.

An important early collaboration, widely read across Europe, made the case for the visual as guarantor of travelers' authority. Bernhard von Breydenbach's *Peregrinatio* (1486), an account of his voyage to Jerusalem, foregrounds firsthand observation, bolstered in no small measure by the illustrations of the artist and engraver Erhard Reuwich, whom the aristocratic patron employed to record the experience. Above and beyond the narration, Reuwich records from observation the peoples and animals encountered en route (including, significantly, a unicorn), while rendering city views from an embedded, firsthand perspective. As Elizabeth Ross argues, Breydenbach enhances his narrative with Reuwich's visual authority, constructing a doubly powerful version of witnessing as the basis for knowledge.[18] The text traveled across Europe in a multitude of editions, with the reproduced images warranting its authority and authenticity.[19]

If the construction of authority was instrumental for an account of travel to Jerusalem, it would be all the more crucial for describing the Americas, a world never before contemplated in biblical or classical texts. However fitfully, eyewitness authority replaced that of preexisting texts, in what Anthony Pagden calls the "autoptic imagination."[20] New World accounts could not easily appeal to the extant canon of authoritative texts, or even build upon them, given that their matter had never previously been contemplated. Instead, "authority could only be guaranteed (if at all) by an appeal to the authorial voice," to "the inherent credibility of the 'I' who has 'been there.'"[21] "Esto que he dicho," claims chronicler Gonzalo Fernández de Oviedo, in his *Historia general y natural de las Indias*, "no se puede aprender en Salamanca, ni en Boloña, ni en París" ["What I have said cannot be learned in Salamanca, or in Bologna, or in Paris"].[22] The self-referential quality of autoptic authorization makes it both self-contained and self-sufficient, yet also renders it fragile. In the absence of external scaffolding for authority, everything rides on the narrator's reliability and probity.

As direct observation became a crucial guarantor of accuracy in describing the New World, visual artists supported the work of writers, as Reuwich had done for Breydenbach. As Pamela H. Smith notes: "The desire . . . to couple (artisanal) visual and (humanist) verbal accuracy with the communicative potential of images is often accompanied by what appears to be a new emphasis on first-person observation and autoptic proof, especially in an age when news out of the newfound world was arriving thick and fast. Images became an important way of recording, collecting, cataloguing, and witnessing the curious, the marvelous, and the particular."[23] In a famous instance of this desire to bolster narrative authority with visual confirmation, Oviedo laments that he does not have an artist with him to record the unfamiliar nature that he describes, "porque es más para verle pintado de mano de Berruguete u otro excelente pintor como él, o aquel Leonardo de Vince, o Andrea Manteña, famosos pintores que yo conocí en Italia" ["for it would be better to see it painted by the hand of Berruguete or another excellent painter such as he, or that Leonardo da Vinci, or Andrea Mantegna, famous painters whom I met in Italy"].[24] While maintaining the superiority of eyewitnessing over book learning, Oviedo nonetheless longs for visual supports for his narrative, from painters whom he has met personally and can presumably vouch for. Thus witnessing anticipates and invites empirical observation, yet circles back to established measures of authority—the artists are not only famous, but personally known to Oviedo.

Anxieties over what constituted sufficient narrative authority were magnified by the Iberian empire's widespread reliance on the written word. In Ángel Rama's hugely influential formulation, Spain has long been recognized as a "lettered" empire.[25] Explorers and conquerors wrote their own accounts, which notaries and chroniclers followed hard upon, in what historians describe as a "notarial culture" with specific textual models for relaying to the Crown and its representatives events that occurred far from the metropole.[26] While this textual bureaucracy, with its *relaciones*, *memoriales*, letters, and histories, helped establish and maintain the colonial regime, it also offered the means to individual advancement. First-person accounts of services rendered to the Crown, and individual achievements worthy of *mercedes*, or rewards, include not just the formal, codified genre of *relaciones de méritos y servicios*, but a much broader range of accounts of exploration, all of which are written, at least in part, to justify the narrator's actions and either claim rewards or avoid negative consequences. From Columbus to Cortés to Alvar Núñez Cabeza de Vaca, many of the most influential texts in the colonial canon offer accounts designed to excuse and promote their author. Influential histories of the New World, from Oviedo's *Historia general* to Bernal Díaz's belated *Historia verdadera de la conquista de la Nueva España*, to Inca Garcilaso de la Vega's *Comentarios reales de los incas*, also rely on the authority of the witness, often contrasting his or her own proximity to events with the distance—geographic, chronological, cultural—that hampered previous chroniclers.[27] As recent historiographies increasingly recognize, however, in these accounts "the actors themselves are supplying us with rather slick narratives in order to emphasize their personal integrity, the objectivity of the way they conduct official business, and the transparency of their motives."[28]

The challenge of authoritatively relaying new worlds was singularly productive in the literary realm, on both sides of the Atlantic. Mary Gaylord has shown how the proliferation of the "true history"—from *relaciones* to *historias*—produced a range of texts that flourish "on the frontiers between reality and fantasy," as they "paradoxically call into question, along with the verisimilitude of the places, people, and events they detail, the very authorial privilege they invoke."[29] Gaylord notes how fragile were the boundaries between fictional and historiographical accounts:

> The lived experience of astonishingly new worlds, and the urgent need of Spaniards in Europe and America to write about them, put the earnest historian and the literary liar in the same boat. Indeed,

> most early modern writers, whether of fiction or of history, wrestled with one and the same set of representational paradoxes. For both, after all, had to make things "never before heard or seen" present in the here and now of their audiences' imaginations. Both had to deal in and with things "not here": fiction, with scenes and characters that weren't here by definition, that didn't and never would exist outside the pages of books; contemporary history, with radically new scenes "not here," because dramatically increased physical distance precluded the widespread sharing of experience. . . . Each writer of history had to invent his own chain of witnesses and documents and to work actively to maintain his authority in the face of his readers' incredulity, of the possible appearance of other witnesses with other stories, or of chance turns of event that would require the rewriting of the entire narrative.[30]

Even in the absence of explicitly competing narratives, I suggest, narrative authority could be productively challenged by this sense of provisionality and partiality, particularly in texts that set out to interrogate the givenness of a narrator's claims.

My point in locating the picaresque within this context of competing accounts is not to suggest that it contrasts with the truth of the archive, but to signal, as Gaylord does so suggestively, the contiguities between what we now deem "literary" and "historiographic." Natalie Zemon Davis, in her influential *Fiction in the Archive*, alerted us to how powerfully fictionality operates within specific genres of the historical record, as petitioners to the courts shape and mold their narratives to particular ends.[31] More recently, Kathryn Burns has forcefully argued the need for historians to "look *at* our archives, not just through them," in order to recognize how "people's truths collided and competed" in the production of truth-effects and "textual fictions of agency."[32] The picaresque, as a mode not just of writing but of reading, allows us to recognize how situated, partial, and negotiated those truths are. If, as Burns argues, "Notarial records are . . . always in implicit dialogue with an imagined litigious future,"[33] the picaresque collapses that future skepticism into the reader's present, underscoring the difficulty of believing an interested witness, no matter how carefully his or her narrative has been codified.

By foregrounding interested knowing, the picaresque also ironizes the force of the captivity narrative, which claimed to be uniquely positioned to transmit information about religious and cultural others in an expanding empire.[34] As Lisa Voigt has demonstrated, narratives of captivity play a key role both in the turn to experiential authority in the period, and in the concomitant development of fictions that claimed to offer both truth and entertainment. Captives, Voigt argues, could offer themselves as privileged intermediaries whose knowledge, acquired among other peoples, could serve to support the imperial project.[35] Captivity narratives also served to solidify cultural identities and in particular religious difference, by foregrounding the immutability of the captive's faith even in the face of death. But if the captivity narrative invokes the martyrology, it must also finesse the narrator's actual survival through some sort of accommodation. Hence when the *Viaje de Turquía* foregrounds the unreliability of its narrator, a former captive, and the venality of his clerical audience, it challenges the authority of the witness and the religious hierarchies that captivity narratives ostensibly uphold. A narrator who knows too much—especially about a rival power or confessional other—can be as problematic as one who does not convince.

Inquisition, Interiority, and Fictionality

> Vuestra merced escribe se le escriba y se le relate el caso muy por extenso . . .
>
> [Your Grace writes you should be written to and the case related in great detail . . .]
>
> —*Lazarillo de Tormes*

Above and beyond the specific context of empire, critics have long noted the connections between the picaresque and those early modern discourses that serve to examine subjects or account for their actions. Perhaps the most influential account, by Roberto González Echevarría, links the picaresque with the *relación* as confessional modes before "the Law": "The individual conscience, which can and does err, writes to the embodiment of natural law (Lázaro to Your Lordship, Cortés to Charles V) to exculpate and recapture his or her legitimacy. This is the beginning of the Picaresque, and of the novel: the story of a new, civil individual, who writes on his own, subject to no myths and no tradition."[36] Robert Folger usefully expands upon González Echevarría's insight with detailed explorations, first, of *Lazarillo* as "a response to th[e] state-induced demand for autobiography,"[37] and second, with a survey of New

World texts actually prepared to satisfy official inquiry and seek recompense, as *relaciones de méritos y servicios*. David Gitlitz focuses on autobiographical confession to the tribunals of the Inquisition, noting: "the ingrained rhetorical strategies of disclosure and evasion, strategies of self-promotion and vindication, and habits of incessant self-monitoring with their associated hyper-consciousness of one's identity as a reportorial voice, so harrowed the psychic soil of Spain that the autobiographical genres easily took root."[38] Because intellectuals and *conversos* were constantly watched, Gitlitz argues, "survival required habits of thought which prepared one to give autobiographical account on demand."[39] Open-ended and deliberately vague, inquisitorial processes always welcomed—and often compelled—more stories.

Generative though these readings might be, they are primarily interested in the sources or origins of the picaresque, and treat it as largely mimetic of those genres. My argument picks up where Gitlitz leaves off: having noted the striking resemblances in the narrative strategies of the fictional *Lazarillo* and the inquisitional confessions as they attempt to satisfy their respective interrogators, he concludes, "Yet we—their wider public—perceive their inconsistencies and hypocrisies in ways that produce effects radically different from those the authors intended."[40] Gitlitz does not say what those effects might be, or how either authors or readers, as opposed to the narrators, of the literary texts might seek precisely those "radically different" effects. Literariness is clearly one of these: readers savor the irony, contradiction, and indirection of the picaresque in a way that would be obscene for the inquisitional confession. More importantly, knowing fictions inherently challenge the larger apparatus of interpellation that relies upon trust-worthy relation or confession. They rehearse and announce what cannot be said about the official discourses: that the latter rely on narratives riddled with interestedness, self-protective strategies, and deliberate omissions. Picaresque texts thus offer a critique of the structures of knowledge and control upon which the imperial project relies. Although they do not always leave evidence of their reception—many had limited or manuscript circulation—they can help us reconstruct a constellation of resistant, skeptical voices. As interested, partial responses to "the Law," knowing fictions reveal the literary as a site of contestation, from which the mechanisms of interpellation and subjectification can productively be challenged.

What might this contestation look like, beyond our own critical claims for the texts? Reconstructing reception is complex: as I have noted, many of these texts leave little evidence of their impact on readers. Literary history offers one kind of corroboration: Cervantes, who appears often in these pages, was himself an astute reader of picaresques—possibly the *Viaje*, certainly the *Guzmán*. His ironic response to picaresque narrators demonstrates that the challenge they pose was abundantly recognized in some quarters: thus the early modern writer provides evidence of what at least one early modern reader could take from the texts.

More broadly, modern scholars have begun to identify cognate phenomena that suggest we may need to revise our understandings of the policing of interiority in the early modern Hispanic world. In a recent study of inquisitional interrogations of would-be mystics, Dale Shuger shows the doubts that emerged as religious interiority became increasingly incompatible with the legal structures that attempted to control it. Shuger suggests that this dynamic, which long predates secularization, reveals the Inquisition's decline "from within": "the incompatibility of legal discourse and a post-Reformation language of mystic spirituality forced a separation of God and law, the withdrawal of God to private spaces, and the atrophying of an institution created to treat religious practice as a matter for public control."[41] What Shuger calls the "discernment of interiority"[42] presented problems akin to those posed by ironic texts: readers were required to assess the value of signs and opaque language that could point to diametrically opposed meanings, in what became for the legal process an impossible bind.[43] Paul Johnson, for his part, has recently traced the Inquisition's problematic attempts to read the sincerity of those who were accused of heresy and testified before its tribunals.[44] Attempts to codify a hermeneutics of authenticity based on forms of bodily expression coexisted with the increasing codification of gesture as performance in the world of the theater, where verisimilitude, rather than truth, was the goal. Inquisitorial attempts to develop an "emotional hermeneutics," in Johnson's term,[45] even as the theater was expanding its own gestural repertoire, suggest the complexity of basing certainty on the subject's own claims about his or her interiority.

On a similar front, scholars working on Spain and beyond have highlighted the vexed connections between fictionality and the investigation of interiority in early modernity. Enrique Fernández examines anxieties about interiority through what he calls "dissective narratives": texts, including novellas by Cervantes and María de Zayas, that appear to offer bodies up for scrutiny using anatomical methods, but which actually "practice a form of pseudo-compliance with interpellating authority" akin to the picaresque's.[46] In his study of the emergence of autobiography in early modern France, Nicholas Paige traces how a "naïve confidence in the readability of the human interior" gradually gives way to doubt about the possibility of such access, with autobiography as the "manifestly problematic promise to make identity readable."[47] All of these cognate investigations suggest how the picaresque might have engaged readers primed to recognize the epistemological challenges of reading intention and interiority.

While focusing on literary texts, the chapters that follow trace cognate problems to flesh out the historical resonance of each: the force of observation versus authority in medicine and the natural sciences; the vexed question of the (historical) captive's voice; and the slipperiness of credit as both a financial and a reputational category. *Knowing Fictions* thus returns to the intersection of inquisition, interiority, and fictionality to propose the newly distinctive form of the literary, and in particular the picaresque, as an emergent locus of skepticism in early modern Spain.

For a New History of Skepticism

Knowing Fictions dialogues with the recent work of Mercedes García-Arenal, Stefania Pastore, Felipe Pereda, and others on the intellectual consequences of forced conversion and religious polemics in Iberia. In a series of studies, these scholars have mapped out how orthodoxy is interrogated in texts and practices across Spain and its empire, from philosophical debates to religious images.[48] Many of these instances address the challenge of what one might term confessional opacity: the exterior invisibility of intimate convictions, on the one hand, and the dissimulation enabled by what García-Arenal calls "overlapping religiosities," on the other. Only a careful reading of what are often overdetermined and contradictory narratives can recover their complexity, and the historians doing this kind of work have called for a more sensitive reading of sources—a "linguistic turn" for the history of belief, in an effort to complicate the categories that the Inquisition sought to distinguish and keep apart.[49]

The stakes in identifying skepticism in early modern Spain and its empire are high. Pastore's work alerts us to the larger narratives reenacted when Spain and Italy, in particular, are largely omitted from key accounts of European skepticism: "Thus, on the one side we have Montaigne, Charron, Descartes, Spinoza and Locke, laying the foundations of a secularized culture that turned doubt and relativism into the keys to a new and modern culture that would eventually open its doors to the great age of the Enlightenment; on the other, a total void."[50]

Instead, Pastore contends that an important antecedent to the Spinozan "Marranism" that scholars identify as a source of modern, radical tolerance and skepticism in the Netherlands is the much earlier contestation of religious orthodoxy in sixteenth-century Italy. From the late fifteenth century, Spaniards in Italy, including but not just the Jews expelled in 1492, become synonymous with what is ironically termed the "peccadillo" of disbelief. "Marranos" in Italy, Pastore contends, contribute to the coalescing of religious doubt long before the Netherlands emerges as a locus for tolerance. Historiographical accounts that privilege the alliance between the Spanish crown and the papacy as Counter-Reformation defenders of the faith, she contends, often overlook the much richer and ambivalent history of Spanish disbelief in Italy. With frequent references to the literary, Pastore traces an alternative to the Counter-Reformation axis, recovering instead a world of intellectual questioning and disbelief.

Knowing Fictions moves from Spain to Italy and across the broader Mediterranean, identifying that questioning and disbelief in a specifically literary mode. From Zemon Davis to Burns to García-Arenal and Pastore, historians have increasingly argued for the need to attend to the fictional and the linguistic in order to reconstruct the fullest versions of early modern culture and its imaginaries. This study brings the literary to the table from a different angle, to suggest how self-consciously fictional texts intervene in their culture with an ironic force that interrogates the mechanisms of truth-telling. Picaresques are perhaps best known for foregrounding the situatedness of truth, reminding us how things look from below. The expanded corpus that I chart here is more radical: it reflects doubt about the reliability of knowledge itself as transmitted by any interested observer, and especially the first-person witness. As I suggest in my conclusion, this may be its most lasting effect, as it trains readers in discernment: how to ask the right questions of a text and read between its lines—how, in short, to read critically.

Chapter 1, "Imperial Picaresques: *La Lozana andaluza* and Spanish Rome," charts the limits of narrative authority in the Spanish exile Francisco Delicado's semi-anonymous *Retrato de la Lozana andaluza* (1528), his account of a Cordoban courtesan in Rome set just before the Spanish invasion of 1527, and his surprisingly proximate authored treatise on syphilis. *Lozana* ironically claims to *retraer*—to both paint and retract or recant—its syphilitic protagonist, in a highly self-conscious narration that foregrounds questions of authority and knowingness. As it chronicles the ravages of syphilis on the narrator and his subject, the text explores imperialism itself as a kind of contagion—a cosmopolitan disease that undoes them both. Delicado's version of the picaresque undercuts Spain's epic aspirations via erotic intimacy: his complicit narration, fully implicated in the borderlessness of its main character, can only render a debased Rome. On the eve of the Spanish invasion, the contaminated, picaresque account implicates the narrator while ironizing the imperial project that links Spain to the classical and contemporary city.

Delicado's brief contemporary treatise on syphilis, *El modo de adoperare el legno de India Occidentale* (1529), tantalizes with the promise of empirical certainty to supplement *Lozana*'s lacunae. The treatise confirms the *retrato*'s authorship, as the coy author of one text claims to have also authored the other. Where the fiction can only gesture toward epistemological certainty, the treatise foregrounds a medical and botanical accuracy born of experience. Yet the yoking of the two texts foregrounds the intimate connections between syphilis and empire as well as the interestedness of the observer, ultimately undermining the authority of the treatise rather than bolstering *Lozana*.

Chapter 2, "Picaresque Captivity: The *Viaje de Turquía* and Its Cervantine Iterations," explores the imbrication of humanist dialogue, travel account, and captivity narrative in the anonymous text of that name (1557/58), and its reprisal in Cervantes's *Persiles* (1616) and his *comedias* of captivity (pub. 1614). The *Viaje* presents a dialogue between three characters over two days, with a subsequent account of Constantinople and of Ottoman origins, also in dialogue form. Pedro de Hurdimalas, a former captive who has arduously made his way back to Spain, encounters his old acquaintances and agrees to share his experiences with them, though they will put his story to venal ends when recounting their false pilgrimages. In addition to the profoundly corrupt scene of telling, I explore what it means for the captive to be simultaneously an authoritative and an unreliable source. The intimacy of captivity, I suggest, complicates the mediating role of a narrator both privileged to know and arguably tainted by his knowledge. Marcel Bataillon dubbed Pedro "l'Ulysse espagnol,"[51] and indeed, the picaresque Pedro's narrative loudly advertises both its unreliability and its utility for the wily. In its relentless play with referentiality and instrumentalization of first-person authority, the *Viaje de Turquía* manages to ironize both travel and captivity narratives as they become versions of the picaresque. Beyond the famous episode of the false captives in the *Persiles*, Cervantes's *comedias* of captivity echo the *Viaje*'s irony by locating Spanish *pícaros* in Algiers and Constantinople. Their remarkable intimacy—both familiarity and erotic susceptibility—with Spain's religious others undoes the ideological distinctions that the captivity narrative strains to establish.

Volubly, even comically expressed on stage, the *pícaro*'s mix of self-interest and intimate knowledge qualifies the privileged position of the captive as narrator. Marked by its glib ventriloquizing, untenable justifications, and venal oaths, the *pícaro*'s voice in these *comedias* problematizes any authority that captivity might have afforded the narrator.

Chapter 3, "'O te digo verdades o mentiras': Crediting the *Pícaro* in *Guzmán de Alfarache*," examines perhaps the most canonical of picaresques, Mateo Alemán's confessional, first-person, two-part tour de force (1595, 1605). A consummately interested and unreliable narrator, Guzmán alternates between moralizing retrospectively as a *pícaro* now reformed and gleefully describing the exploits that required his reformation. His story makes patent just how easily narrative can supplant an unavailable or even indeterminable truth. If *Lozana* featured a less-than-fully authoritative narrator tussling with his ribald protagonist, *Guzmán* internalizes the struggle for authority in a single narrator and his imperfect attempts to convince the reader. As he crisscrosses the Peninsula and even tries his fortune in Italy, the *pícaro* uses distance to his advantage. He self-fashions easily and effectively, moving from the abject to the respectable and vice versa, in the process implicating not just the reader but the social mechanisms that served to authorize everything from identity and genealogy to the moral and financial credit granted to persons.

Chapter 4, "Cervantes's Skeptical Picaresques and the Pact of Fictionality," traces the author's engagement with the picaresque across the *Novelas ejemplares* (1613). In a range of picaresque fictions, Cervantes explores the connections between narrative authority, perspectivism, and skepticism. In "La ilustre fregona," a nobleman's irrepressible desire for the picaresque life ironizes exemplarity by emphasizing the idiosyncrasy of individual experience and taste. *Gusto* undoes any predetermined sense of self, offering instead new trajectories and alternative itineraries. "Rinconete y Cortadillo" and the dyad of "El casamiento engañoso/El coloquio de los perros" probe a broader readerly skepticism, extending beyond irony to epistemological questions of the truth of narratives and how they might be assessed. The tension between exemplarity and skepticism—the one offering models for behavior that presume belief, the other encouraging instead a productive doubt—results in a fully engaged fictionality as an alternative to the exemplary text.

Immersed in the challenges of Spain's internal consolidation and global expansion in the sixteenth century, knowing fictions offer a powerful reflection on the nature of authority and representation. Profoundly engaged with the epistemological and political challenges of conveying authority and determining truth, they interrogate how we know and what we know. In challenging the bonds that establish community, trust, and belief, knowing fictions also suggest the limits of any attempt to police those bonds, or get at the truth. They thus reveal fictionality as a locus of skepticism vis-à-vis the desire for certainty, offering opacity in response to interpellation and the tantalizing possibility of a resistant interiority.

Chapter 1

Imperial Picaresques

La Lozana andaluza and Spanish Rome

Francisco Delicado's *Retrato de la Lozana andaluza* (1528) is an extravagant text, wandering far and wide in its attempts to capture its slippery protagonist. Geographically capacious and narratively playful, *Lozana* tells the story of a Cordoban prostitute whose travels across the Mediterranean bring her to Rome and a community of exiled Jews and *conversas*. In its broad geographical sweep, Delicado's picaresque functions as a perverse counter-epic of one, as the imperial theater of Italy offers refuge to a protagonist who must leave Spain behind. Placing front and center what epic insistently marginalizes, Delicado offers a dark vision of empire: rather than celebrating conquest, the picaresque charts the messy reality that follows, from victimized exiles to a range of imperial subjects on the make and the diseases that they spread. In a world of constant circulation, whose violent exuberance exceeds the bounds of nation and empire, the *pícara* fabricates identities and alliances as necessary. Often chafing at her own depiction, she imaginatively relocates her own story within a canon of erotic texts. The narrator shares his protagonist's syphilitic condition, and strains to sustain any critical distance from his subject. Delicado's *retrato* thus replaces idealizing visions of imperial triumphs with a complicit narration as excessive and unbounded as its protagonist. As it chronicles the effects of syphilis on both the picaresque narrator and his subject, *Lozana* depicts imperialism as a ravaging, cosmopolitan disease. At the same time, the author's own contemporary treatise on syphilis (*El modo de adoperare el legno de India Occidentale, salutifero remedio a ogni piaga & mal incurabile* [Venice, 1529, with a possible first edition in Rome, 1527]) underscores the connections between empire and contagion, even as it attempts to offer an epistemological grounding for the *retrato*.

Lozana portrays an elusive subject in a lost world, forever changed by the 1527 Spanish invasion of Rome, constantly foretold in its pages. Although the text explores central questions of place and identity, its highly wrought, self-conscious narration undoes referential understanding, foregrounding instead problems of authority, knowingness, and the text's own worldliness.[1] The intimacy of the picaresque account implicates the narrator in its telling even as it ironizes the imperial project that links Spain to Rome: although this version is insistently, intrusively authorized, it lacks insight or critical distance. My reading first traces *Lozana*'s richly contradictory geographical and generic coordinates. I then examine how the text systematically deconstructs narrative authority, simultaneously registering the limits of omniscience and bringing the Auctor into a tantalizing intimacy with Lozana, who has her own ideas about how to render characters and canons. Finally, I trace the contagion of syphilis between *Lozana* and Delicado's contemporary treatise on the disease, to show how a highly skeptical picture of empire underlies the picaresque's erotics.

Although loosely mapped onto the life of its protagonist, the picaresque *Lozana* advances in fits and starts, with frequent hesitations and self-referential hiatuses, as meandering adventures stand in for any linear plot. Instead of chapters, the text is divided into "mamotretos," a term that connotes a gathering of loose papers, imperfectly organized, or, as the concluding "Explicit" would have it, "copilaciones ayuntadas" ("coupled compilations," with the pun on copulations).[2] Despite its ribaldry and its delayed rediscovery only in the mid-nineteenth century, *Lozana* has by now become virtually canonical, as critics recognize its sophisticated narrative games and complex depiction of marginality. At the same time, the text's own publication history challenges national and imperial boundaries, complicating any sense of it as a Spanish classic. The title page gives some sense of this complexity, framing the image of a ship of fools that carries Lozana and her lover Rampín from Rome to Venice with precise textual explication: "Retrato de la Loçana andaluza en lengua española muy clarissima. Compuesto en Roma. El qual Retrato demuestra loque en Roma passaua y contiene munchas mas cosas que la Celestina" [Portrait of the lusty/healthy Andalusian in the most famous Spanish tongue. Composed in Rome. Which portrait demonstrates what occurred in Rome and contains many more things than *Celestina*] (Figure 1). Place, language, and literary genealogy are incommensurable here: an Andalusian's story is composed in Spanish in a polyglot Rome, while the key point of reference for the text, as for its main character, is the Spanish masterpiece increasingly known as *La Celestina* (1499), translated into a multilingual and transnational setting. The ship emphasizes the geographic in-betweenness of a text on the move, even as the reference to *Celestina* gestures toward a deterritorialized canon. From its title page, the embarked *Lozana* translates the bounded concerns of the earlier text—tensions among classes and castes, the status of the marginal, the erotic as an index of disorder or corruption—into a broader Mediterranean and imperial context. *Lozana* is most interesting precisely for how it transcends the domestic parameters of its picaresque predecessor, even as it attempts to ride the coattails of its significant success in Italy.[3]

Whatever its generic categorization, *Lozana* begs the question of its national ascription: presumably written in Rome by the Cordoban cleric Delicado, largely in Spanish but with a good dose of Italian, it was first published semi-anonymously in Venice. The documentation on Delicado is scarce: in addition to the *Lozana*, he published a brief treatise in Italian for priests, *Spechio vulgare per li sacerdoti che administraranno li sacramenti in chiascheduna parrochia* (Rome, 1525), two treatises on syphilis, *De consolatione infirmorum*, now lost, and *El modo de adoperare el legno de India occidentale,* a belated account in Italian, Spanish, and Latin of an early treatment for the disease.[4] He also appears to have been active as a conduit for Spanish literature in Venice, serving as a corrector or editor for *Cárcel de amor* (Venice, 1531), the *Tragicomedia de Calisto y Melibea* (Venice, 1531), *Amadís de Gaula* (Venice, 1533), and *Primaleón* (Venice, 1534).[5] Much of what we know about Delicado comes from his own prologues to these editions, including the claim to have authored *Lozana* in the introduction to the third part of *Primaleón,* where he also recognizes his own use of "el comun hablar de la polida Andaluzia" ["the common speech of the lovely Andalucía"] rather than of a more standard "gramatica española."[6] At the same time, he includes in his editions of *Celestina* and *Primaleón* a guide to Spanish pronunciation. Both in his relationship to language and in his self-presentation, Delicado thus appears divided among attachments to Andalucía as a region, to an expansive Spain that he may or may not subscribe to, and to an Italy increasingly permeated by Spanish fictions as by its imperial reach. The effect is of an elusive historical author scattered among his texts, however large the "Auctor" looms in *Lozana.*

Delicado's canon-making and mediating functions foreground the potential of vernacular, imaginative prose as an alternative version of Spain in Italy, via a corpus of Spanish literature that upends decorum with erotic transgressions.[7] When a certain "Caballero" wishes to recommend Lozana to the

RETRATO DE
la Loçana: andaluza: en lengua española:
muy clarissima. Cōpuesto en Roma.

El qual Retrato demuestra lo que en Roma passaua y contiene munchas mas
cosas que la Celestina.

Figure 1. Title page, Delicado, *Retrato de la Loçana andaluza* (Venice, c. 1528). From the facsimile edition of the unique copy at the Osterreichische Nationalbibliotek, Vienna, published with permission of Tipografía Moderna/Artes Gráficas Soler, Valencia. Photo by Rhonda Sharrah.

Neapolitan ambassador, he praises her by locating her within a vernacular and amatory tradition of Spanish vernacular texts on love: "Monseñor, ésta es cárcel de Amor; aquí idolatró Calisto, aquí no se estima Melibea, aquí poco vale Celestina" (189) ["Your honor, this is the prison of Love, here did Calisto worship, here is Melibea scorned, here is Celestina worth little"].[8] Delicado's characters thus anticipate the corpus that he himself would promote through his editorial labors. Yet the ribaldry of *Lozana*, as of its most signal predecessor, *Celestina*, does more than simply disrupt expectations, offering instead an alternative picaresque canon that is both anti-exemplary and anti-imperial.

Despite the scarcity of sources, critics have surmised that Delicado was himself a *converso* who fled Spain sometime around the 1492 expulsion and sought refuge from the Inquisition in the priesthood.[9] Whatever the historical Delicado's origin, he gives his central character and his persona as Auctor/narrator a shared birthplace: both are Andalusian foreigners in Italy. The coincidence anticipates the dizzying play of self-referentiality that will characterize the text, as third-person narration breaks down into dialogue and the Auctor's direct exchanges with his characters. Paradoxically, the closer the Auctor gets to Lozana, the less reliable he appears, while she angles for control of her own story. As the text explores the implications of their shared Spanishness in light of the imminent invasion, the picaresque narration increasingly takes on the Spanish imperial project.

Knowing Narrators

In a series of paratexts, Delicado offers a playful reflection on narrative authority. Unlike *Celestina*, which largely sidesteps the problem of narration via its organization into dialogue and *autos*, *Lozana* returns often to the problem of authorial knowing and telling, mixing dialogue with narration in novel ways. *Lozana*'s interrupted, contested narration makes visible the interrelated stakes of narrative control, embeddedness, and sympathy that give the picaresque its particular power. Sidestepping teleological accounts that would make *Lozana*'s uneven form an accident of its early date, or of its author's limited possibilities, I want to recover the full complexity of *Lozana*'s narrative games—including but also beyond authorial intentionality.

The prologue, addressed to an "Ilustre señor," promises "que solamente diré lo que oí y vi, con menos culpa que Juvenal" (5) ["I will only say what I saw and heard, and be less to blame than Juvenal"]. Delicado's sly defense invokes a classical *exemplum* even as he claims eyewitness authority. Yet his referent is not mimetic but satiric, known for his acerbic take on life in the first imperial Rome, and its sexual foibles. Is Delicado less to blame because he relates only what he witnesses, or because in relaying it he is less biting than Juvenal? The tongue-in-cheek prologue immediately negates any claim that the text simply reports what the Auctor has witnessed:

> Y como dice el coronista Fernando del Pulgar, "así daré olvido al dolor," y también por traer a la memoria munchas cosas que en nuestros tiempos pasan, que no son laude a los presentes ni espejo a los a venir. Y así vi que mi intención fue mezclar natural con bemol, pues los santos hombres por más saber, y otras veces por desenojarse, leían libros fabulosos y cogían entre las flores las mejores. (6)
>
> [And as the chronicler Fernando del Pulgar says, "I will thus forget pain," and also for it will bring to memory many things that occur in our time, which do not honor those present nor serve as a mirror for those to come. And so I saw that my intention was to mix the natural with the flat, for the saints in order to know more, and also for relief, read fabulous books and chose the best among the flowers.]

The reference to Pulgar, royal chronicler for Ferdinand and Isabella, and also would-be defender of the *conversos*, introduces contradictory modes of telling. The national history to which Pulgar contributes is written to exclude *conversos* like Lozana (and possibly Delicado himself), yet here writing simultaneously memorializes and erases the pain of the excluded.[10] Delicado's irony works at multiple levels: as the editors point out, in the passage alluded to Pulgar actually notes that he *cannot* find consolation for old age in reading Cicero's treatise on the same (499). The solemnity further dissolves in light of the erotic polysemy of the passage, as Delicado packs his references to music and humanist commonplaces with sexual innuendo.[11] In fact, the Auctor, as a character in his own story, will have no direct contact with Lozana until Mamotreto XXIV, so his authority cannot be based on direct experience, whatever claims he makes here. His book must instead be more like those "libros fabulosos" that even the saintly pursue.

Even though the excursus into Lozana's origins will take us further than ever from the Auctor's direct experience of his character, the Argumento announces its interest in locating her precisely: "Decirse ha primero la ciudad, patria y linaje" (9) ["Her city, country, and lineage must first be told"]. The Auctor actually shares a Cordoban birthplace with Lozana, yet this serves primarily as an affinity, affording him no access to her early history. Nonetheless, the Argumento reiterates the prologue's claims for authority, forbidding anyone from adding to the self-sufficient text:

> Protesta el autor que ninguno quite ni añada palabra, ni razón, ni lenguaje, porque aquí no compuse modo de hermoso decir, ni saqué de otros libros, ni hurté elocuencia, porque "para decir verdad poca elocuencia basta," como dice Séneca; ni quise nombre, salvo que quise retraer munchas cosas retrayendo una, y retraje lo que vi que se debría retraer. (9)
>
> [The author insists that no one shall add or remove a word or a concept or any language, for I did not here compose a lovely way of telling, nor did I take from other books, nor steal eloquence, because "to tell the truth little eloquence suffices," as Seneca says; nor did I wish for a name, except that I wished to portray/retract many things by portraying/retracting one, and I portrayed/retracted what I saw should be portrayed/retracted.]

Bewilderingly contradictory, the passage undoes its own claims in the making. To underscore that he does not take from others, the narrator cites Seneca (yet another native of Córdoba), who writes eloquently on the irrelevancy of eloquence to truth. Severing the referential connection between name and truth, the Auctor refuses identification ("ni quise nombre"). The last two clauses, which might well function independently of his anonymity, instead appear linked to it, as though the refusal of a name were undone by the work of writing. The semantic multiplicity of *retrato*—Delicado's Italian import to the Castilian vernacular—makes it a particularly loaded signifier in the text.[12] Here, its multiple meanings expand the paradox of the synecdoche: by rendering one thing the Auctor would also render many, and yet for every portrait (*retrato*) he gives us, he also takes away (*retraer,* in its primary modern meaning).[13] The tension between rendering a portrait in words and withholding or withdrawing it alerts us to the many different levels on which this narration will operate.

The erotic polysemy of the *retrato* also complicates its verifiability, as when the narrator claims:

> Y porque este retrato es tan natural, que no hay persona que haya conocido la señora Lozana en Roma o fuera de Roma, que no vea claro ser sacado de sus actos y meneos y palabras; y asimismo porque yo he trabajado de no escribir cosa que primero no sacase en mi dechado la labor, mirando en ella o a ella. (9–10)
>
> [And because this portrait is so natural/faithful, there is no one who has known Mistress Lozana in Rome or outside Rome who will not see clearly that it is taken from her acts and moves and words, and also because I have labored not to write anything that I have not first worked out from my sampler/example, looking to her or at her.]

Natural alludes to the female sexual organs, or *natura*; thus to *know* Lozana and to recognize in the text's portrait her *meneos* establishes the reader's participation in the erotic economy of the text, rife with knowingness and polysemy. The portrait's accuracy, as well as the reader's verification thereof, implies complicity with this embodied and transgressive knowledge. Moreover, the narrator's own account of his careful work as he copies his version from a *dechado* (sampler/example) overlays the morality of the *exemplum* with the sexualization and effeminization of needlework. Given the narrator's full immersion in what he attempts to portray, and Lozana's own sexual currency, the invitation to evaluate the portrait that he extends here implicates the reader in the erotics of the text. There is no dispassionate place from which the portrait might be contemplated.

The narrator claims that his portrait will be recognizable to any who had seen Lozana in Rome, yet his construction of her early history ("ciudad, patria y linaje") remains unverifiable. Paradoxically, the Auctor has the most control over the story when his subject is furthest from her Roman incarnation and his supposed eyewitness experience, without the kind of resistance from the character herself that he will encounter later. His third-person narration is least interrupted as he relates that early history, which takes Aldonza, as she is originally known, from her birth in Córdoba and a sensual life with her family, to Granada with her widowed mother, to Seville and a *parienta* who seems poised to serve as her bawd. The girl soon flees with the Genoese merchant Diómedes, and agrees to accompany him on an extensive tour across the Mediterranean and beyond, "years, not months," to be spent "en Alejandría, en Damasco, Damiata, en Barut, en parte de la Soria, en Chiple, en el Caire, y en el Xío, en Constantinopoli, en Corintio, en Tesalia, en Boecia, en Candía, a Venecia y Flandes" (21). Her beauty and great success with all the merchants who frequent their house leads to her new name, Lozana (glowing, lusty, 20), which will become increasingly ironic as she contracts syphilis and loses her nose.

While she is already marked as Jewish or *conversa* by her culinary choices within Spain—she makes her *hormigos* with oil (15)—Lozana's travels across the Mediterranean establish her cosmopolitan difference: she acquires much recondite knowledge of beauty secrets, and is even deemed "universal" by one admiring nobleman (182). When Diómedes's father objects to the affair, he imprisons his son and has Lozana set adrift on the sea; only the intervention of a compassionate boatman saves her, the narrator explains, as he abandons her on shore instead.[14] By selling the single ring that she had been able to hide in her mouth, Lozana travels first to Livorno and thence to Rome. But just before bringing her within the Auctor's compass, the text problematizes his omniscience, simultaneously underscoring Lozana's interiority and rehearsing her fictions:

> Y viéndose sola y pobre, y a qué la había traído su desgracia, pensar puede cada uno lo que podía hacer y decir de su boca, encendida de muncha pasión. Y sobre todo se daba de cabezadas, de modo que se le siguió una gran aljaqueca, que fue causa que le veniese a la frente una estrella, como abajo diremos. (22, 25)
>
> [And finding herself poor and alone, and seeing to what her misfortune had brought her, each can imagine what she might do and say, consumed with great suffering. And above all she banged her head, so that a great headache came upon her, which was the cause of a star that appeared on her forehead, as we will relate below.]

The passage emphasizes Lozana's solitude, then invites the reader to fill in the unspecified words and actions born of her despair. Empathy stands in for omniscience: though none can actually hear or see Lozana on the beach, the narrator urges us to imagine what she would do or say, as though we would all agree on what was missing. Yet as soon as the narrator himself starts filling in the picture, he gets it strikingly wrong, anticipating Lozana's own fanciful account of how she got her syphilitic mark. Only a chapter later, Lozana will repeat the story of the "cabezadas que me he dado yo misma, de un enojo que he habido" (31) ["great bangs to my head that I have given myself, due to a vexation"]. Yet the "star" that supposedly results from these blows is actually the mark of syphilis on her body, and readily apparent as such to all who encounter her. The Auctor's alternative account as he reads Lozana thus signals either insufficiency, gullibility, or complicity. Whatever the case, his unreliability is patent, even if his motivation remains opaque. Moreover, given the foregrounding of syphilis as both the condition that the Auctor shares with his subject and his eventual claim to authority, his blindness appears willful, an early sign of how his intimacy with his material alters his narrative.

As Lozana takes over more and more of the text, we are confronted with the question of whose story this actually is, in terms not just of subject matter, but of narrative control of the material. While *Lozana* begins with narration, it gradually moves to dialogue: as soon as the protagonist arrives in the Roman quarter of Pozo Blanco (Mamotreto VI), where she finds some assistance, the narrator disappears entirely, to return only in Mamotreto XIV, and then gradually enter the story as a character. At first he remains invisible to Lozana and her lover/servant Rampín, who are sleeping off their first night of love. Amid the ribaldry the situatedness of the Auctor is increasingly thematized, staging the problem of his embodied narrative authority: not only can he not verify Lozana's early history, which he did not witness and she constantly embroiders, he is *de trop* as he attempts to convey what transpires in the background to the lovemaking. His first intervention in the dialogue describes a neighbor who prevents the lovers from sleeping:

> Auctor.—Allí junto moraba un herrero, el cual se levantó a medianoche y no les dejaba dormir. Y él se levantó a ver si era de día y, tornándose a la cama, la despertó, y dijo ella:
>
> —¿De dó venís?, que no os sentí levantar. (66)

> [Author: "Next door there lived a blacksmith, who was up at midnight and did not let them sleep. So he got up to see if it was morning, and, coming back to bed, woke her, and she said: "Where are you coming from, that I did not hear you get up?"]

Placed uncomfortably on stage to narrate, the Auctor relates an interruption even as his own voice interrupts. At the same time, his vantage point is reduced to the experience shared by his characters, minus their sexual satisfaction—the narrator as unsatisfied voyeur.

Mamotreto XVII turns precisely on the Auctor's frustrating proximity to the action, and his complicity with it.[15] During a hiatus in his writing due to a pain in his foot—a clear stand-in for the penis—the Auctor is visited by Rampín. Invited to join him and the whores at Lozana's house, the Auctor demurs, claiming that he will be criticized for voyeuristically seeking material:

> No quiero ir porque dicen después que no hago sino mirar y notar lo que pasa para escribir después, y que saco dechados. Piensan que si quisiese decir todas las cosas que he visto, que no sé mejor replicallas que vos, que ha tantos años que estáis en su compañía. Mas soyle yo servidor como ella sabe, y es de mi tierra o cerca de ella, y no la quiero enojar. (81)
>
> [I do not wish to go, for then they will say that all I do is watch and take note of what happens in order to write it down later, and that I make examples out of it. Don't they know, if I wanted to say all the things I've seen, I could render them even better than you, who have been with her for so many years. But I am her servant, as she knows, and she is from my land or close to it, and I don't want to upset her.]

In a highly eroticized version of *occupatio*, the "dechados" that the Auctor might take from Lozana cannot actually be told.[16] As in the Argumento, exemplarity is both feminized and ironized—what kind of example, after all, does Lozana offer?

Rampín urges the Auctor to find a cure in Lozana for what ails him, but he puts the young man off until another day. Instead, the Auctor claims to have all the material he needs already: the intimacy between him and his subject goes beyond even the sexual bond that links Lozana to Rampín. Intriguingly, that intimacy stems from their shared origins, in deference to which the Auctor claims he will not tell. As the text will only gradually reveal, this tension between the authority of the witness and a deeper connection born of what the Auctor shares with his character vexes the narrative throughout.

Part II begins with an epigraph that announces, at this late point, the Auctor's direct knowledge of Lozana, with all of the sexual innuendo that accompanies that knowing: "cómo el Autor la conoció por intercesión de un su compañero" (119) ["how the author knew/met her through a friend"]. The Auctor hears about Lozana's quick ascent from common whore to confidante, procuress, and healer to courtesans and their powerful lovers. He admires her wiles, even if his direct access to her is vexed by his own desire and his reticence due to their common origins. By Part III, Lozana has herself become a knowledge broker, a giant queen bee in the Roman *colmena* (211), pandering information as much as sex: “Y a todos mirar de qué grado y condición son, y en qué los puedo yo coger, y a qué se extiende su facultad, y ansí sacaré provecho y pagamiento, si no en dineros, en otras cosas” (212) [“And I will see of what class and condition they all are, and where I can catch them out, and what they are capable of, and from that I will profit and get paid, if not in cash, then in other things”].

In Lozana’s world, authority is a compromised and compromising business: when a potential client asks her to vouch for his potency to another woman, he threatens to rape her then and there to prove himself. Ultimately, however, Lozana exacts payment—a ring, no less—to relay the situation to the whore the man desires: “¡Por mi vida, señor, que como testigo de vista diré el aprieto en que me vi!” (194) [“By my life, sir, I will relay as a firsthand witness what a tight fix I found myself in!”]. Narrowly escaping rape, Lozana can only speak as a witness to the threat of his potency, from which she extrapolates. In the gaming house, meanwhile, gamblers ask her about their reputations, and she relays what people say about them, fleecing them in the process (196–97). Within the diegesis, there is no such thing as a disinterested portrait; instead, the picaresque witness is fully implicated in the unsavory business at hand.

Belatedly, Mamotreto LXII finally offers a direct dialogue between Auctor and character, as he visits Lozana and even suggests a liaison between them. The Auctor initially wants to make a son, but he is soon diverted by an alternative mode of reproduction, requesting pen and paper to take down his impressions of Lozana in the moment (215). Instead of dwelling on love, Auctor and character consider the problem of truth: he condemns women for their penchant for evil, while pontificating against superstition and urging Lozana not to believe in dreams or spells. She quickly corrects him, stressing that she herself does not believe everything that she says: “Para ganar de comer, tengo de decir que sé muncho más que no sé, y afirmar la mentira con ingenio por sacar la verdad. ¿Pensáis vos que si yo digo a una mujer un sueño, que no le saco primero cuanto tiene en el buche? Y dígole yo cualque cosa que veo yo que allí tiene ella ojo” (217) [“In order to eat, I have to say that I know much more than I actually do, and wittily confirm my lie, to get at the truth. Do you think that when I interpret a dream for a woman, I don’t first get from her what is in her gullet? And I tell her whatever I see she has set her eye on”]. For Lozana, belief is a means to a profitable end, especially as desire makes people credulous. There is no gullibility on her part, though there is plenty in her audience—a warning, perhaps, to both the Auctor and his readers. The grandstanding Auctor hardly seems a privileged reader of his subject at this point, as she educates him on how to tell a story most effectively. His fullest access to his subject only confirms her slipperiness: narration, Lozana insists, is a profitable negotiation.

Jarringly, the passage soon shifts from picaresque trickery to prophecy:

> Mirá el prenóstico que hice cuando murió el emperador Maximiliano, que decían quién será emperador. Dije: "Yo oí aquel loco que pasaba diciendo oliva de España, de España, de España," que más de un año turó, que otra cosa no decían sino "de España, de España." Y agora que ha un año que parece que no se dice otro sino "carne, carne, carne salata," yo digo que gran carnecería se ha de hacer en Roma. (217)

> [Look at the prophecy I made when the emperor Maximilian died, when they wondered who would be emperor. I said: "I heard that crazy man go by saying the olive of Spain, of Spain, of Spain" for over a year, for all they said was "of Spain, of Spain." And for a year now it seems that all they say is "meat, meat, salted meat," and I say that a great butchery will be done in Rome.]

Lozana applies the opportunistic guess of the charlatan to the privileged register of imperial augury, undercutting the retrospective dynastic prophecy traditionally offered by epic (and even by such satiric versions as Ariosto's *Orlando Furioso* [1516/1521/1532]). Her second prophecy warns of the bloody immediacy of war, in what will become the running motif of an ending repeatedly foretold. Amid the sustained questioning of the truth of narratives, the Spanish invasion serves as a disquieting undercurrent of historical foreboding, confirmed by the time of *Lozana*'s publication, that paradoxically authorizes the text's various imperfect narrators. As with so many of Lozana's tricks, her prophecies are successful because she provides in them convincing approximations of the truth, much as the narrator himself claims to do.

Lozana herself has much praise for her Auctor, even if she pretends not to be able to place him, as when she asks his friend Silvano: "Decime, por mi vida, ¿quién es ese vuestro amigo que decís que ayer hablaba de mí? ¿Conózcolo yo? ¿Reísos? Quiérolo yo muncho, porque me contrahace tan natural mis meneos [illegible]" ([illegible]) ["Tell me, by my life, who is that friend of yours whom you say was talking about me yesterday? Do I know him? You laugh? I love him well, because he counterfeits my moves and acts so naturally"]. To demonstrate just how well her author knows her, Lozana reviews intimate and highly sexualized moments: his putative authority depends on his absolute immersion in her bawdy existence. The Auctor, she explains, relates "cómo hablo con mi criado. . . . Y cómo yo lo hago dormir a los pies, y él cómo se sube poco a poco, y otras mil cosas que, cuando yo lo vi contrahacerme, me parecía que yo era" (229–30) ["how I talk to my servant. . . . And how I have him sleep at my feet and he climbs up by and by, and another thousand things, so that when I saw how he counterfeited me I thought it was me"]. Thus Auctor and character uneasily share authority in this dizzyingly reflexive text. Somewhere between counterfeit and conflation, their constant negotiation of carnal and other forms of knowledge makes it difficult to find any purchase for narration. There is, if anything, too much information, implicating narrator as well as reader in a voyeuristic exchange that Lozana both conjures and commands.

Spain in Rome, Spain as Rome

The problem of narrative authority in *Lozana* is further complicated by the positionality of Auctor and character, and by the text's own vexed relation to Spain. Delicado explores throughout how allegiance to *natio*—in the sense of ethnos as well as the relatively new notion of Spain—and to the land of one's birth outdoes commitments to the truth, as personal and communal loyalties pervert any account. This proves particularly important in a cosmopolitan city where each must speak up and step up for his or her own, and where prostitutes of all nations are frequented by "amigos de su nación" (108) ["lovers of their nation"]. At the same time, when Spain makes its way into the text in an account of the Auctor's origins, Lozana challenges the pieties of Spanish imperial aspiration, to foreground instead her favorite, highly ribald Spanish texts (236). Confronted with visions of a classicized Spain, however imperfect, Lozana counters with her resolutely erotic canon.

Importantly, Lozana's Rome is already permeated by Spanish venality, even though the actual Spanish invasion lies in the future. Spain sends to Rome both its most unsavory and its least favored characters: penniless soldiers, multitudes of prostitutes, corrupt clergy and the parasites they attract, as well as persecuted religious minorities,[17] to join whatever corruption Rome already flaunts. This picaresque Spanish Rome qualifies *Lozana*'s constant thematization of pride in and allegiance to the nation. Instead of the imperial *translatio* by which Spain would become the heir to classical Rome, the picaresque foregrounds the inextricable role of Spain and Spaniards in the debased contemporary city.

Janus-like, *Lozana* looks backward to the great program of Roman improvements undertaken by Julius II and Leo X, and forward to the reviled invasion by Charles V's mercenaries, deflating both. To Julius's rhetoric of a new golden age and *renovatio imperii* as justifications for a temporal Christian empire, the text counters with an account of louche sexualities and a venal clergy.[18] To the cultural magnificence of Leo's spectacular public entertainments, *Lozana* juxtaposes private corruption and sexual excess. Well before the Spanish invasion, Rome is characterized by its excesses.[19] No *caput mundi*, whatever papal propagandists might say, it is instead the *cola mundi*, as the slanderous Pietro Aretino would note once he had put some distance between himself and the city.[20]

Prostitution characterized what was a city of immigrants long before the Spanish invasion, for much of the Roman population in the early sixteenth century was impermanent: in 1526–27 only a quarter of the city's inhabitants were native Romans, while 60 percent came from other regions of Italy and the rest were foreigners.[21] In this context, the ambiguity of Aretino's *Cortigiana* speaks volumes—does its title refer to a courtesan, or to the comedy of the court itself, revealed in all its tawdriness and constantly for sale?[22] By invoking the courtesan Rome, *Lozana* both undoes the papal vision of renewed imperial grandeur and questions the Spanish imperial project that looms over the future of the city.

The Auctor's friend Silvano attributes the corruption of Rome to its cosmopolitanism as he denounces the excesses of the city: "Aquí, a decir la verdad, los forasteros son muncha causa, y los naturales tienen poco del antiguo natural, y de aquí nace que Roma sea meretrice y concubina de forasteros" (130) ["And here, to tell the truth, foreigners are to blame, and the naturals/those born here have little of their ancient nature, and hence Rome is the whore and concubine of foreigners"]. Yet the sexual pun on *natura/naturales*, which introduces female sexuality even into the purported classical antithesis to modern Rome ("antiguo natural"), undoes the neat opposition between then and now, or between a purely indigenous and a corruptly cosmopolitan city.

Delicado also connects Roman corruption to the city's cosmopolitan character when he portrays Lozana's welcome by Spanish compatriots. Her arrival in Rome is greatly eased by the mutual recognition in the diverse community of Jews and *conversas* of Pozo Blanco, prostitutes who recognize her as one of their own—"*de nostris*" (35)—while recalling their own connections to Spain: "¡Por vuestra vida, ahí tenemos todas parientes!" (27) ["By your life, we all have relatives there!"]. This diasporic *natio* of exiles from Spain offers a more powerful connection than religion, ethnos, or geography alone.[23] Yet Lozana's embrace of her origins is strategic, not to say opportunistic. At times she is said to renege on them: "dice que no tiene tierra, que ha sido criada por tierras ajenas" (96) ["she says she has no country, that she has been brought up in foreign lands"], while one of her interlocutors in Pozo Blanco imagines her adopting identities of convenience: "ésta en son la veo yo que con los cristianos será cristiana, y con los jodíos, jodía, y con los turcos, turca, y con los hidalgos, hidalga, y con los ginoveses, ginovesa, y con los franceses, francesa" (38) ["I see this one with the Christians shall be Christian, and with the Jews, Jewish, and with the Turks, Turkish, and with the nobles, noble, and with the Genoese, Genoese, and with the French, French"]. The Auctor, conversely, reminds both the reader and his character of their shared origin at every turn, claiming, "Como vos sabéis, os quiero yo muncho por ser de hacia mi tierra" (213) ["As you know, I am very fond of you because you are from my country"]. Although their common link to Spain, and to Córdoba in particular, may grant the Auctor greater access to Lozana, it also qualifies what can and should be told, as he reminds us (81).

Through his constant invocations of Spain, the Auctor attempts to offer an alternative to the picaresque rootlessness of Lozana, although he is as displaced as she is. Yet her ribaldry constantly destabilizes any authority over his character that their shared Spanishness might afford him. Perhaps the most interesting episode in this negotiation is the *mamotreto* devoted to the Auctor's own place of birth, narrated by his friend Silvano. The interlude calls attention to itself by replacing the Auctor with yet another narrator figure, who dialogues with Lozana over several *mamotretos*. His longest intervention is an extensive account of the Auctor's actual origins not in Córdoba, as Lozana had been led to believe, but in the stronghold of Peña de Martos (XLVII), near Jaén, one of the most significant castles in the region. The remarkable attention to this place in the text—it is the only location beyond Rome to receive such treatment—argues for its outsize symbolic import as a counter to the *caput mundi*. The engravings that illustrate *Lozana* reinforce the importance of Martos and the strong geographical link between character and Auctor: a bifurcated image of the Peña side by side with Córdoba (Figure 2) is repeated

¶ Comiença la historia/o Retrato Sacado del Jure ceuil natural. De la Señora Loçana: cõpueſto el año mill y quiniẽtos y veynte equatro. a treynta dias del mes de Junio: en Roma alma cibdad/ y como auia deſer partido en capitulos va por/ mamotretos/ porque en ſemejante/ obra mejor conuiene

Mamotreto primero.

LA Señora Loçana fue natural compatriota de Seneca/ y no menos en ſu intelligencia: y Reſaber. la qual deſde ſu niñez tuuo Ingenio, y memoria, y biuez grãde: y fue muy querida de ſus padres por ſer aguda en ſeruillos, e cõtentallos, e muerto ſu padre fue neçeſſario que a cõpañaſſe a ſu madre: fuera de ſu natural. Y eſta fue la cauſa que ſupo/ y vido muchas cibdades villas/ y lugares/ deſpaña, q̃ agora ſe le Recuerdan de caſſi el todo, y tiñie tanto intellecto: q̃ caſſi eſcuſaua a ſu madre procurador para ſus negocios/ ſienpre q̃ ſu madre la mãdaua yr o venir hera preſta: y como pleyteaua ſu Madre/ ella fue en Granada mirada: y tenida por ſoliçitadora perfecta: e prenoſticada futura: acabado el pleyto e no queriendo tornar a ſu propria cibdad: acordaron demorar en Xerez/ y paſar por Carmona/ aqui la madre qſo moſtrar

Figure 2. Peña de Martos and Córdoba la Llana, Delicado, *Retrato de la Loçana andaluza*, fol. A3r. From the facsimile edition of the unique copy at the Osterreichische Nationalbibliotek, Vienna, published with permission of Tipografía Moderna/Artes Gráficas Soler, Valencia. Photo by Rhonda Sharrah.

twice, appearing first before the first *mamotreto*, which gives us Lozana's origins, and again when Silvano turns to the Auctor's origins.

Silvano's classicizing paean to Martos stresses its martial and epic nature: dedicated to the Roman god of war, it is characterized by its resistance to invasion. Hercules helped build it, Alexander could not conquer it, and it has always been "honra y defensión de toda Castilla" (233) ["honor and defense of all Castile"].[24] The Peña was "sacristía y conserva cuando se perdió España" (233) ["sacristy and preserve when Spain was lost"]; at its foot were found "ataútes de plomo y marmóreos escritos de letras gódicas y egipciacas" (233) ["lead and marble coffins with Gothic and Egyptian inscriptions"]—repeated testaments to Spain's classical heritage in the face of North African invasion.[25] The idealizing construction of the Peña depends on erasing all signs of the Muslim presence that is ubiquitous in Andalucía, including making nearby Jaén (from the Arabic Yayyan) into "Mentesa" (234).[26]

At the same time, the Peña de Martos invokes a tragic history of authority questioned and denied. As Silvano observes, "Es una felice patria donde, siendo el rey, personalmente mandó despeñar los dos hermanos Carvajales, hombres animosísimos, acusados falsamente de tiranos" (235–36) ["It is a happy fatherland where, the king being present, he personally ordered that the two Carvajal brothers, most valiant men, falsely accused of tyranny, be hurled from the heights"]. The legend most consistently associated with this "felice patria" concerns two noble brothers, wrongly convicted and put to death by Fernando IV, who then predict his death. From beyond the grave, the Carvajales represent an extreme version of narrative authority, in a striking contrast to the highly compromised versions that Delicado offers in *Lozana*. Doubt in the brothers' word leads to their death, but their revenge is a prophecy so devastating and precise that it resemanticizes both the landscape and the king, both of which are renamed as a result of these events.[27] The allusion to the legend thus underscores the role of Martos as the anti-Rome: it is a place where word and deed coincide, however tragically.

Beyond the trace of the Carvajales on the landscape, the entire epic space of the Peña de Martos soon reveals itself as antithesis to the picaresque contemporary Rome: it features a chapel known as "Roma la Vieja"; the only presence of anyone remotely like a prostitute is the occasional miraculous appearance of Mary Magdalene, "la cabelluda" (235) ["the hairy one," in contrast to those who lose their hair from syphilis]; and its women are "castísimas romanas" (235) ["chastest Romans"] who content themselves with one husband. Any departure from the Peña's moral excellence, Silvano declares, is only due to the foreigners who seek it out for its riches and generosity.

Faced with this idealizing portrait, Lozana drags the discussion back to the picaresque register. When Silvano locates the Peña in relation to the nearby range of Alcaudete, Lozana irreverently transforms it to *alcahuete* [pimp], "el que hace cornudos a ojos vistas" (235) ["who makes cuckolds in plain sight"]. She also presses Silvano on the Auctor's genealogy: was his father not from Córdoba, and was he not born in that place? The Auctor's connection to the epic Peña turns out to be through his mother, a link that undoes Silvano's martial account of the place and its privileging of patriarchal values. At Lozana's challenge, Silvano further retreats into proverbial wisdom: "no donde naces, sino con quien paces" (236) ["it's not where you're born, but with whom you graze," akin to "birds of a feather flock together"]. This alternative version links the Auctor to his mother over his father, while also privileging the deracinated version of identity that Lozana represents. By this standard, surely the Auctor is a fallen, modern Roman rather than an impossible classical ideal of Spanish virtue. Or, to judge by the time he spends with his compatriot Lozana, perhaps Spanishness itself means something very different in his case from the epic synecdoche offered by Silvano.

To conclude her dismantling of the epic fantasy, Lozana invites Silvano back so he can read to her "las coplas de Fajardo y la comedia Tinalaria y a Celestina" (236). These are, of course, the extravagant *Carajicomedia* (1519), which offers a vision of Spain as a ribald space of prostitution, Torres Naharro's macaronic, cosmopolitan *Comedia Tinelaria* (1516), or "play of the mess hall," which portrays corrupt Spanish servants in a cardinal's household in Rome, and, finally, *Celestina*, the central predecessor that Delicado has been emulating all along. The Spain in this highly subversive corpus is no impermeable fortress, no Peña de Martos, but rather a leaky vessel for sexual satire, religious irreverence, and political contestation, much like Delicado's own text. Nor is Rome exempt: it represents sexual excess and debasement rather than an imperial model.

Taking up Lozana's provocation, I want to explore briefly the literary universe that she invokes, as a powerful counternarrative to the *translatio imperii* that would make of Spain a new Rome. Lozana's corpus challenges Spain's imperial presence, foregrounding instead indecorous fictions that join Spain and Rome in grotesque couplings.[28] In the ribald *Carajicomedia*, a complex set of authorial personae frames the tale of the noble Diego Fajardo, who pursues eros rather than heroic action: "Tomó tanta devoción con Venus que, dexadas las obras militares y vanidades d'este mundo, las más noches andava desatacado de puta en puta"[29] ["He became so devoted to Venus that, abandoning military feats and the vanities of this world, he spent most nights unbuttoned from whore to whore"]. Fajardo has only sexual exploits to boast of, rather than any military accomplishments. Faced with impotence, he specifies that when his penis dies he wants it taken "al Coliseo de Roma, diziendo tales palabras: 'O ingrata patria, non possidebis natura mea"[30] ["to the Roman Colisseum, saying, 'O ungrateful fatherland, you will not have my nature/sex'"]. This is *translatio imperii studiique* at its most ribald: the epitaph that Scipio Africanus, the exiled Roman conqueror of Hispania and North Africa, desired for his tomb, "Ingrata patria, ne ossa quidem habes"[31] ["Ungrateful fatherland, you do not even have my bones"], is inverted and sexualized, as the Spanish Fajardo destines his *carajo* for the Roman *culi-seo*.[32]

Scipio's complaint becomes even more frankly sexualized in Delicado's own text, when the cleric Blasón complains to Lozana about another courtesan and transforms the epitaph to suit his (erotic) purpose: "Mas mirando la ingratitud de aquella que vos sabéis, diré yo lo que dijo aquel lastimado: *Patria ingrata, non habebis osa mea*, que quiere decir: *Puta ingrata, non intrabis in corpore meo*" (179–80) ["Yet given the ingratitude of that one whom you know, I will say as that offended man said, 'O ungrateful fatherland, you shall not have my bones,' which means, 'ungrateful whore, you shall not enter my body'"]. Blasón does not so much translate between languages as switch codes, from the martial *patria* to the erotic *puta*. In the process, however, he is himself emasculated, fending off a perceived threat to his own body. His reformulation effects a double effacement of the martial, overwriting Scipio and replacing the heroic male body with one so vulnerable that it must decry penetration by a woman. Beyond the obvious anticlerical satire, the passage anticipates Lozana's wholesale dismantling of imperial pretensions and her invocation of *Carajicomedia* in the Peña de Martos episode.

The second of Lozana's touchstones, Torres Naharro's *Comedia Tinelaria*, paints a similar picture of corruption and sexual license among Spaniards in Rome. In the noble household of Cardinal Bacano, picaresque servants, primarily Spaniards, eat and drink at their employer's expense, while stealing his food and wine for the women they keep.[33] Like *Lozana* and *Carajicomedia*, *Tinelaria* foregrounds the slipperiness of authorial personae: the play opens with a metatheatrical "Introito" in which an actor-author emphasizes the multiplicity of voices with which a Roman play must speak:

Ora, pues,
si mis versos tienen pies
variis linguis tiren coces;
que vatibus hic mos est
centum his poscere voces.
  Yo's prometo
que se habrán visto, en efecto,
de aquestas comedias pocas;
digo, qu'el propio subieto
quiere cien lenguas y bocas,
  de las cuales
las que son más manuales
en los tinelos de Roma
no todas tan principales
mas cualque parte se toma.
  Veréis vos.
¡Iur'a Dio! ¡Voto a Dios!
¡Per mon arma! ¡Bay fedea!
¡Io, bi Got! y ¡Cul y cos!
¡Boa fe, naun, canada e mea! . . .
  D'esta gente
va tocando brevemente;
todo el resto es castellano
que es hablar más conveniente
para cualquier cortesano.[34]

[So then, if my verses have feet, they will kick in multiple languages, for it is the prophets' way to place the voice of hundreds. I promise you, few such plays have ever been seen; the very subject requires one hundred tongues and mouths, of which the lowliest appear in Roman mess halls; they're not all noble, but all parts must be taken. You'll see. "I swear to God!" "I vow to God!" "By my weapon!" "I swear to God!" "Yes, by God," and "Ass and body!" "Good faith, my ship, the pass is mine!" . . . It touches on all of these people briefly, and all the rest is Castilian, which is the most convenient language for any courtier.]

To represent the multiplicity of cosmopolitan Rome, *Tinelaria* speaks in multiple tongues, yet the text is not uniformly multilingual. As the prologue anticipated, most of the characters are Spanish, and the Spanish language predominates in this louche vision of corrupt servants. Once again, Spain in Rome is a far cry from Spain as Rome.

Amid the corruption of the *tinelo*, Torres Naharro underscores the venality of a recently arrived Spaniard, significantly named Manchado:[35] he is introduced as a *bisoño* (1959)—a term for newly arrived Spanish soldiers who constantly made their needs known (It. *bisogna/o*).[36] Yet this Spaniard is hardly a soldier:

Godoy: ¿Donde bueno sois, hermano?
Manchado: De Castilla.
Godoy: No sería maravilla.
Mas, ¿qué tierra es vuestra madre?
Manchado: Cuatro leguas de Sevilla,
d'allí dond'era mi padre.
Godoy: Mas codicio
que me digáis cuál indicio
vos hizo venir a Roma.
Manchado: Vengo por un beneficio
que me dé que vista y coma.
Godoy: Bien será.
Pero, ¿quién os lo dará?
Que trabajos se requieren.
Manchado: El Papa diz que los da
a todos cuantos los quieren.
Godoy: Con favor
habréis en Campo de Flor
un par de canonicatos.
Manchado: Mía fe, no vengo, señor,
a buscar canes ni gatos.[37]

Manchado, whose name evokes the increasingly racialized genealogical anxieties of an inquisitorial Spain, has origins at least as murky as Lozana's Auctor. He initially claims to be from Castile, yet his motherland is Seville, the place from which his father hails. Although Godoy takes him for a soldier, Manchado is simply on the make. Eager to benefit from the largess of the Pope himself, his ignorance is such that he transforms the *canonicatos* that Godoy imagines into a menagerie of *canes* and *gatos*. To judge from Bacano's mess hall, the corruption of those already in Rome is thus constantly supplemented by fresh new arrivals from Spain, much as in Lozana's world.

La Celestina, the third and last text in Lozana's picaresque corpus, is closest to Delicado's own experience: he explicitly invokes it as the predecessor his *Lozana* will transcend ("que contiene más cosas que la Celestina"), while in 1534 he would correct the *Tragicomedia* for publication by a Venetian printer.[38] Beyond Delicado's own role in its dissemination, the history of *Celestina* in Italy evinces the proximity and fluidity between Spanish and Italian literary cultures in the period: a 1502 dramatic performance of the text even celebrated the wedding of Lucrecia Borgia to Alfonso d'Este.[39] As scholars have long noted, the Italian version by Alfonso Ordóñez, *Tragicocomedia di Calisto e Melibea novamente traducta de spagnolo in italiano idioma* (Rome, 1506), is not only the first translation of the text, but the oldest extant version of the *Tragicomedia*, based on the lost *princeps* that solidified the transformation from the earlier *Comedia*.[40] Although the translator claims in his dedicatory letter that the text has not been disseminated in Italy, there are in fact multiple editions of the translation (Rome, Milan, Venice) as well as a number in Spanish, including the Venice edition corrected by Delicado.[41] More work must be done to reconstruct the reading public for the Spanish original, which likely included everything from Italians learning Spanish to *converso* communities across Italy. Yet the text's popularity in both languages demonstrates its transnational import: much like *Lozana*, *Celestina* cannot be fully contained within the frame of Spain or of "Spanish" literature. The reverse *translatio* of the text to Italy, and its enthusiastic reception by readers in both Spanish and Italian versions, anticipates *Lozana*'s own projection beyond the Spain that is so frequently invoked in the text and into a broader Mediterranean circulation. By invoking *Celestina*'s previous literary trajectory, Lozana recalls both her own passage to Italy and success there, and the anticipated dissemination of Delicado's text.

Lozana's corpus thus reflects not only her *imitatio* of picaresque exempla but a thorough ironization of the Spanish imperial presence in Italy. Far from extolling the Auctor's origins, the ventriloquized Peña de Martos interlude underscores how improbable a classicized, virtuous Spain appears from contemporary Rome, perhaps most of all for its skeptical citizens-at-large. Spain in Rome is emphatically not Spain as classical, imperial Rome, and the imminence of the invasion only makes the difference more glaring. The imperial *translatio* that Silvano would chart via his martial account of the Peña is effectively undone by a very different *translatio*, of picaresque Spaniards to a corrupt Rome already cosmopolitan and Hispanicized (if we recall the earlier invocation of Juvenal, classical Rome does not come off much better). In literary terms, Lozana's alternative corpus dismantles the idea of an exemplary, classicized Spain, replacing it with the most ribald of fictions.

The actual invasion will force both Lozana and the Auctor to leave the city, where Spaniards are now most unwelcome, so that the Spanish imperial triumph becomes the occasion for a second exile. Yet Lozana is allowed to plan her exit to the island of Lipari, and the first of the text's many endings comes with her resolution to retain agency in the face of the impending devastation: "Estarme he reposada. Y veré mundo nuevo, y no esperar que él me deje a mí, sino yo a él. Ansí se acabará lo pasado, y estaremos a ver lo presente" (325) ["I shall be at rest, and shall see a new world, and not wait for it to leave me, but leave it instead. So what is past shall be over, and we shall see the present"]. With Lozana and Rampín now venturing to a new world, there is nothing left for the Auctor to do but wrap up.

The concluding "Epístola" contrasts markedly with the Auctor's proprietary confidence at the start, as he first invites readers to improve his portrait: "Mas no siendo obra, sino retrato, cada día queda facultad para borrar y tornar a perfilarlo, segund lo que cada uno mejor verá" (337) ["As it is not a work but a portrait, each day there remains the ability to erase it and draft it again, according to each one's best impressions"] and ultimately begs them to do so: "Ruego a quien tomare este retrato que lo enmiende antes que vaya en público" (337) ["I beg any who take up this portrait to amend it before it becomes public"].[42] Paradoxically, the Auctor's lack of confidence and his plea to his readers stem from his excessive connection to his character, which threatens throughout to collapse the necessary distance between narrator and author. In a darker vein, the end of the text reveals connections between the Auctor and Lozana that challenge the notion that intimacy can empower a narrator.

The Empire of Disease

Lozana's concluding paratexts reveal the shared Spanishness of Lozana and the Auctor, underscored throughout, as a red herring. A more vital connection links character and narrator: like Lozana, the Auctor suffers from syphilis. In his apologia, "Cómo se excusa el autor," he belatedly explains, "Y si dijeren que por qué perdí el tiempo retrayendo a la Lozana y a sus secaces, respondo que, siendo atormentado de una grande y prolija enfermedad, parecía que me espaciaba con estas vanidades. . . . Y en el tratado que hice del leño de India, sabréis el remedio mediante el cual me fue contribuida la sanidad" (329) ["And if they should ask why I wasted my time portraying Lozana and her followers, I would answer that, tortured by a great and extended illness, these fripperies seemed to distract me. . . . And in the treatise that I wrote on the wood of the Indies, you will know the remedy that returned me to health"]. The negotiation of authority becomes ever more complex here: the Auctor shares Lozana's mark, and eventually proves more forthcoming than she is about the disease. Her entire story, he claims, is due to his illness, and provides a respite akin to the miraculous *leño* on which he is an authority.

By invoking *El modo de adoperare el legno de India Occidentale*, the Auctor offers an epistemological anchor for *Lozana*. First, an actual author is identified for the fiction. Second, and more importantly, this author claims that the *leño* described in his treatise has effectively cured him, thereby proving his authority as far afield as the flora of the New World. As medical expert, he goes beyond witnessing to claim the effectiveness of the cure in his own body. Yet the focus on syphilis—a scourge that so intimately shadowed the imperial wars in Italy—foregrounds the connection between empire and the ravages of disease, so that this moment of seeming authority over distant lands simultaneously recalls the costs of empire and the intractable damage it leaves in its wake. If the text—unreliable, slippery, impossible to pin down—provides a relief akin to the *leño,* is it because they are equally efficacious or similarly elusive? Although the shared consideration of syphilis seems to offer tantalizing epistemological certainty for the vertiginous *Lozana*, now yoked (*ayuntada*) to Delicado's treatise, it cannot ultimately provide firm ground on which to build confidence in its narrator, much less in a Spanish purview.

Delicado's multilingual treatise sounds some of the same notes of authority as *Lozana*, yet in a less playful key: whereas in *Lozana* the Auctor had claimed to offer a true portrait, here Delicado claims that he will offer a cure tested "per vera experientia," which "ni diverse persone e in se stesso longamente ha osservato"[43] ["by true experience," which "he has observed for a long time in various persons and in himself"]. For good measure, he also summons the authority of Oviedo's *Historia general y natural de las Indias* (1526), which he quotes at length, explaining to the reader that he received the book from the Venetian ambassador to Spain, Andrea Navagero, and that he included it "porque me pareció que dize mui bien en todo, máxime d'este legno santo . . . , y púselo en mi obra porque en este legno da muncha autoridad la nuestra lengua romance"[44] ["because it seemed to me that it speaks well on all things, especially this holy wood . . . , and I put it in my work because when dealing with this wood our romance tongue adds much authority"]. Moreover, Oviedo's is not just any Spanish text on New World matters, but, as Delicado reminds the reader, an epistle "a la sacra maiestà cesarea di Carolo V, el eletto imperatore catholico."[45] Beyond firsthand experience, empire and its language are thus offered as guarantors for Delicado's authority on the miraculous cure. Yet the intimate connection between empire and the disease that requires the cure undoes the force of these rhetorical warrants.

The early history of syphilis in Europe is remarkable both for its intimate correlation with the Italian wars and for the speed with which the first commentators identified that connection. It is no coincidence that Cervantes chooses a syphilitic soldier for his protagonist in the novella "El casamiento engañoso" (1613), which I discuss in Chapter 4—the illness was closely associated with the battlefield, and mercenaries returning from Italy in the 1490s seem to have first spread it across Europe. The disease was present among both sides at the siege of Naples in 1495, and soon became widespread; Charles V and Francis I would both suffer from it. Its most common names associated it with France, though the French referred to it as *mal de Naples*, recalling the site of conquest and contagion.[46]

Although experts today continue to debate whether syphilis was brought to Europe from the New World, the early treatment addressed by Delicado in his treatise firmly connects Spain's New World empire to the ravages caused by imperial conflicts in the Old. Guaiacum, a drug extracted from the guaiac tree or *leño de indias*, was used by the indigenous peoples of the Americas and imported to Europe as early as 1508, as Delicado's own treatise records. By 1519, physicians across Europe had noted the seemingly miraculous effects of the drug; the Fuggers quickly obtained a monopoly on its exploitation in return for extending further credit to Spain.[47] Syphilis is thus intimately intertwined with empire and the attendant circulation of soldiers, their illnesses and remedies, and the funds to pay for it all. Both the disease and its cure travel along imperial circuits, adumbrating not just the Spanish victories in Italy but the broader imperial project.

Delicado's treatise foregrounds the historical connection between empire and disease: "Cosi come al tempo de Tiberio Cesare, terzo imperatore d'i romani, nacque una egritudine chiamata lichene, e per avanti, al tempo de Pompeio Magno, aparve la infirmità elephantia . . . così nel anno 1488, in Rapalo de Zenova, comenzaron le broze nel'exercito del christianissimo Carlo, re di Francia"[48] ["Just as in the time of Tiberius Caesar, third emperor of the

Romans, there was born an illness named lichen, and before that, in the time of Pompey the Great, there appeared the illness elephantiasis . . . so in the year 1488, in Rapallo of Genoa, did the pustules begin, in the army of the most Christian Charles, king of France"]. Classical exemplarity is once again ironized: just as disease accompanied the Roman Empire, syphilis accompanies those with modern pretensions to emulate Rome, in this case France.

In *Lozana*, the protagonist and her friend Divicia discuss the origins of syphilis in similar terms, with even greater irony about the actions of the "most Christian" Charles and the soldiers' culpability:

> *Lozana:* Dime, Divicia, ¿dónde comenzó o fue el principio del mal francés?
> *Divicia:* En Rapalo, una villa de Génova, y es puerto de mar, porque allí mataron los pobres de San Lázaro, y dieron a saco los soldados del rey Carlo cristianísimo de Francia aquella tierra y las casas de San Lázaro, y uno que vendió un colchón por un ducado, como se lo pusieron en la mano, le salió una buba ansí redonda como el ducado. (268–69)

> [*Lozana:* "Tell me, Divicia, where did the French pox begin or have its origin?"
> *Divicia:* "In Rapallo, a town in Genoa, which is a seaport, because there they killed the poor of St. Lazarus, and the soldiers of the most Christian king Charles of France sacked that land and the houses of St. Lazarus, and one who sold a mattress for a ducat, as soon as he received it, got a pustule round as a ducat."]

The beggar Lazarus, patron saint of lepers, presides over a divine retribution of sorts: the attack on his hospital leads to the new illness. In the women's account, syphilis becomes a veritable marker of imperial shame, as killing and looting produce a fittingly coin-shaped *buba*.[49] The invasion and its excesses, as much as the circulating bed, produce disease.

The recurrence of syphilis at the close of *Lozana* sounds an ominous note about the unintended consequences of the coming invasion. Even the stability that the Auctor hopes to offer by citing the treatise on the *leño* is undercut by *Lozana*'s play with truth and power. The vexed relation between authority, empire, and disease animates one of the *pícara*'s last adventures in Rome, before we are told of the Auctor's own illness. Advising the young lover

Coridón on how to pass as a madwoman in order to gain access to his beloved, Lozana instructs him:

> *Lozana:* Coridón, esto podrás decir, que es cosa que se ve claro: "Vitoria, vitoria, el emperador y rey de las Españas habrá gran gloria."
> *Coridón:* No quería ofender a nadie.
> *Lozana:* No se ofende, porque, como ves, Dios y la fortuna les es favorable. Antiguo dicho es: "Teme a Dios y honra tu rey." Mira que prenóstico tan claro, que ya no se usan vestes ni escarpes franceses, que todo se usa a la española.
> *Coridón:* ¿Qué podría decir como ignorante?
> *Lozana:* Di que sanarás el mal francés, y te judicarán por loco del todo, que ésta es la mayor locura que uno puede decir, salvo qu'el leño salutífero. (276)
>
> [*Lozana:* "Coridón, this is what you should say, which is clear to see: 'Victory, victory, the emperor and king of the Spains shall have great glory.'"
> *Coridón:* "I would not wish to offend anyone."
> *Lozana:* "No offense is given, for, as you can see, God and fortune favor them. It is an old saying: 'Fear God and honor your king.' See what a clear prediction, for no one wears French clothes or shoes anymore, but only Spanish styles."
> *Coridón:* "What could I say as a fool?"
> *Lozana:* "Say that you shall cure the French disease, and they will judge you completely mad, for that is the greatest madness one might utter, except for the healing wood."]

Lozana would make of Coridón a wise fool, speaking the truth of the imminent invasion, which all can see in the changing Roman fashions though none wish to acknowledge. Prudently, Coridón would rather appear a foolish fool, for which Lozana recommends the preposterous claim that he can cure syphilis. Planted here is a moment of devastating irony: the Auctor's own subsequent claim to a name and an incontrovertible authority hinges on the fragile exceptionality of "salvo que" in this passage—either he, too, is a madman who claims he can cure the disease, or he channels the miraculous, exceptional cure.

The conflation of Spain's imperial triumph with the recollection of syphilis in Lozana's equivocal advice to Coridón, moreover, recalls how the *mal francés* follows hard upon the imperial expansion: the routes of empire are also the roots of disease. Yet empire functions as a pharmakon of sorts, embodying both cause and cure. As Delicado's treatise explains, the Spaniards are quickly healed once they are instructed by the "insulari indiani" in the use of the miraculous guaiacum. Although this information must be relayed back to the Old World, it is treated as an experiential, immediate truth, and leads to stringent regulations to procure the wood: "La qual cosa, ricontata poi alla sacra Maiestà di Spagna . . . e vista la mirabile experientia in alquanti, comandarono che niuno naviglio da le preditte isole ritornasseno senza una certa quantità di legno guaiaco"[50] ["This, recounted later to Spain's sacred Majesty . . . and as the miraculous experience among some was seen, they ordered that no ship sailing from said islands should return without a certain quantity of guaiacum wood"]. Both disease and cure have oceans to cross, however, so that the imperial cure cannot immediately undo the effects of empire. That temporal gap—the time of illness—becomes, as the Auctor claims in *Lozana*, the space of fiction, in which he writes the text. While he fills the time, he also offers the reader a way to experience Rome from a safe distance, through his prophylactic text: "Por tanto, ruego al prudente letor, juntamente con quien este retrato viere, no me culpe, máxime que, sin venir a Roma, verá lo que el vicio de ella causa" (329) ["And thus I beg the prudent reader, as well as anyone who views this portrait, not to blame me, especially as, without coming to Rome, he will see what its vice causes"]. Knowing and ironic, pocked and imperfect, Delicado's *Retrato de la Lozana andaluza* becomes the debased and modest alternative to the march on Rome.

In Delicado's treatise, only the end of war offers any chance that the plague may abate: "Pregamo Dio optimo massimo che cessi Marte e cessarà Saturno e la piaga incurabile"[51] ["Let us pray to the great good God that Mars may cease and so may Saturn and the incurable plague cease"]. This reference to Mars provides a clue to one of the most perplexing aspects of the text: it concludes with the same engraving of Martos and Córdoba included twice in *Lozana*, with the addition in this case of Roman epitaphs, newly provided by Navagero from his visit to Martos (Figure 3).[52] A signature of sorts, the engraving functions as the reciprocal equivalent of the Auctor's admission, late in the text of *Lozana*, that he wrote the treatise on the *leño* (329). In this case, the engraving encapsulates the contradictions that the text has embodied, simultaneously invoking empire as cure, guarantor of authority, and harbinger of war. The god Mars, halfway down the mountain, is *in medias res*—or rather, *in mediis bellis*—and has not ceased, despite the fact that his epitaph—Summo

del legno santo 15

alos quales pueblos Tholomeo llama Tuci. Estos epitaphios lo prueuan. Por tāto escriui aqui tres el primero que esta escritto en la misma peña/ouero Monte lapideo ala fuēte santa Martha El otro en la yglesia de santa Martha. Que antiguamente era el tē plo del fortissimo planeta Marte. Como parece en esta efigie aq figurada: El tercero en el foro ala fuēte d la republica Tucitana.

Epitaphio puesto en la misma peña.

Summo, Marte, Superno. Maximo.
S. M. S. M.

Quintus Quinti filius, Titi, Nepos, Sergius,
Q. IVLIVS. Q. F. T. N. SER. CAELSVS.
aedilis, Duum.
AED. .II. VIR. BIS. DE. SVO. DEDIT.
In foro publico.
HERCVLI. INVICTO.

Figure 3. Peña de Martos and Córdoba la Llana, Delicado, *El modo de adoperare el legno de India Occidentale* (Venice, 1529), unpaginated. Photo by Barbara Fuchs.

Marte Superno Maximo—lies below the image. The diminished, marginal "Lozano" that appears below a house in the Cordoban side of the image—a healed Delicado, or perhaps one before the syphilis that made him analogous to his Lozana—remains wishful thinking, with a name as perverse as that which graces his protagonist.[53] At the same time, the supplemental epitaphs recall the passing of classical Rome, now reduced to the ruins and curiosities that Navagero bestows on Delicado. As a shared signature, the reworked engraving undoes the purported imperial authority of the treatise relative to the fiction, recalling instead their joint authorship, and their vulnerability to an unending time of Mars. The Peña de Martos is no stronghold: just as in the episode within *Lozana* it proved vulnerable to her irony, it here crumbles in the face of the enduring connection between empire and syphilis.

In a treatise written shortly before—and published shortly after—the Spanish invasion of Rome, the image profoundly ironizes Delicado's hopefulness.[54] Not only has war not abated, allowing syphilis to recede, but it impedes the very circulation of Delicado's prescribed cure. The section tantalizingly entitled "Recipe" instead gives us his excuse: "No puse en esta segunda estampa la composición del lectuario, no por auaricia más por la excellentia de la cosa en la tercera estampa lo diré, Deo dante et diuo Jacobo, cuyo peregrino so al presente por la gratia recebida en Roma"[55] ["I did not include in this second printing the composition of the electuary, not from avarice but for its excellence {as} I will tell in the third printing, God and the divine Jacob willing, whose pilgrim I am at present for the grace received in Rome"]. He then obliquely notes his "dispersion" to Venice.[56] War produces a void at the heart of Delicado's treatise, as the cure becomes inexpressible, infinitely postponed until some future edition that is not to be.[57] The treatise that promises to ground the Auctor, and solidify the narrative authority of *Lozana,* is thus revealed to be just as susceptible to the vicissitudes of empire. Despite its invocation of the newly emboldened imperial language and its texts, it provides hollow claims rather than a solid purchase.

La Lozana andaluza limns a complex relation between geographic and narrative limits, and, in turn, the limits of authority. The tension between Auctor and character cannot be resolved by shared origins, which fail to make Lozana any more pliable or available to the narrator whom she challenges as often as she praises him. Lozana's skeptical distance from Spain, and particularly its synecdochal representation in the Peña de Martos, allows her to construct a picaresque alternative to any heroic sense of national identity, sending up epic ideals and offering instead a deterritorialized canon. Meanwhile, in the face of the devastation wrought on Rome by the Spanish invasion and the subsequent epidemics, the narrator loses the bravura of his opening salvos, turning instead to a series of apologies and pleas for readerly benevolence. This more modest stance reflects also the gradual acknowledgment of the most powerful connection between Auctor and character, not in a shared Spanishness, but in their syphilis. The intertwining of syphilis with imperial expansion, in Italy as in the New World, further complicates the relation between this imperfectly authorized text and the vision of Spain as a new Rome. For all its seeming focus on the picaresque world of Roman prostitution, *Retrato de la Lozana andaluza* paints a much larger canvas, as it draws and redraws the boundaries of Spanish identity and the lineaments of empire, all while interrogating the authority required to render them in written form. Delicado's construction of a picaresque Hispano-Italian canon for and around *Lozana* performs a powerful literary *translatio* while profoundly challenging the imperial *translatio* with which it coincides.

Chapter 2

Picaresque Captivity

The *Viaje de Turquía* and Its Cervantine Iterations

> He querido pintar al bibo en este comentario a manera de diálogo a Vuestra Magestad el poder, vida, orígen y costumbres de su enemigo, y la vida que los tristes cautibos pasan, para que conforme a ellos siga su buen propósito.
>
> —("Dedicatoria," in *Viaje de Turquía*)
>
> [I have tried to paint from life for Your Majesty, in this commentary in the form of a dialogue, the power, life, origin, and customs of your enemy, and the life of the poor captives, so that you may follow your good purpose accordingly.]

Beyond the flows of exiles and soldiers depicted in *La Lozana andaluza*, the early modern Mediterranean was marked by a remarkable circulation of captives and their stories. If, as Fernand Braudel noted, Mediterranean piracy served as a "secondary form of war" between Christianity and Islam in the sixteenth century,[1] arguably its main goal was to take captives: one recent study estimates over one million Christian captives in Morocco and the Ottoman Maghrib between 1530 and 1780, with a matching number of enslaved Muslims in Christian Europe.[2] Mediterranean captivity was not experienced in isolation, nor did it represent social death for the captive—captives taken by corsairs on either side of the Mediterranean could and did remain in touch with their society of origin, and a whole network of institutions existed to negotiate their ransoms.[3]

Given that they might spend years in captivity, with more or less mobility within a city, captives often became expert in the societies and places that held them. During captivity, they could serve as the source of continuous intelligence, while their longer accounts might resemble early ethnographies, full of information of the highest interest, including, from the European side, accounts of the Ottomans and their protectorates in North Africa. At the same time, first-person accounts of Christian captives often recorded individual trials and suffering, including the captive's resistance to assimilation and forced conversion. There is a fine balance between expertise and reliability in these narratives: to renege, whether or not of one's own volition, was to become both more authoritative about the world one joined, and less trustworthy to the world left behind. If the cultural work of the captivity narrative, as Lisa Voigt has noted, is "to reinforce a Catholic identity while demonizing a powerful religious enemy and imperial rival," then that work is paradoxically enabled by the captive's immersion in the society that holds him captive.[4]

By the late sixteenth century, a number of procedures and institutions had developed to try to pin down the authenticity of captives, particularly renegades, as they communicated with their societies of origin, and to safely reincorporate them on their return home. While captives served as informants to the Crown, it was crucial to assess the quality of the information they provided, especially when they offered military intelligence.[5] When they wished to return to Spain, letters from other captives might testify to their probity; the Inquisition would assess these letters and also examine captives upon reentry.[6] Despite this apparatus, the captivity narrative, as the testimonial narration of one who has survived all efforts at incorporation and forced conversion, fundamentally depends on the authority of its witness-narrator. Even as it becomes a key source of knowledge about other cultures, as a specific type of travel literature or espionage,[7] the narrative banks on its own reliability: it is a testament to the captive's enduring loyalty to his original identity, and to the permanence of his faith.

Yet because so much rides on the authority and authenticity of the narrative voice, the captive also becomes a figure ripe for picaresque ironization. The structural similarities between picaresque and captivity narrative are significant: both are often told in the first person, and both describe a peripatetic existence that requires of the protagonist a great deal of flexibility and forbearance. Both follow the protagonist as he (generally, these protagonists are male) serves a number of different masters, all of whom treat him ill, or attempts to survive by practicing a variety of more or less debased trades, until he finds some kind of accommodation with his condition or breaks definitively with it. The main distinction between these two kinds of stories thus has to do with their authenticity: while the unreliable *pícaro* must be taken with a grain of salt, the captive presents himself as an authentic figure, a suffering, much-abused subjectivity that nonetheless clings to his essential identity and, particularly for the Mediterranean context, his Christianity. The structural analogies between captivity narrative and picaresque highlight the inevitable partiality of each genre and, indeed, suggest a certain contamination of the former by the latter. If the picaresque presents us with an interested, partial, and unreliable narrator who attempts retrospectively to explain and exculpate his younger self, to what extent does the captive also tell a convenient story, one that makes sense of his time among the enemy while emphasizing his moral *entereza* (wholeness) as he returns home?

In light of the homology between picaresque and captivity narrative, this chapter explores the captive as both an authoritative and a profoundly unreliable source, a destabilizing reminder of the limits of first-person authority. Yet does such a reading do violence to the captivity genre, ignoring its basic assumptions of reliable self-sameness? Is it not willfully perverse to find analogies between genres that position themselves very differently vis-à-vis political, social, and religious orthodoxies, and to deploy the assumptions of a seemingly extraneous genre? The payoff for this critical perversity is considerable, as it affords a far richer sense of the work that a text does in a particular ideological context, foregrounding its intentionality and conditions for telling. This chapter explores the homologies between picaresque and captivity narrative in the anonymous *Viaje de Turquía* (1557/58), a richly heterogeneous text that features a contradictory narrator both privileged to know and venally instrumentalized by his audience. I then turn to the false captives of Cervantes's *Los trabajos de Persiles y Segismunda* (1616), and the knowing, unreliable figures in his plays of captivity (1615), whose intimate acquaintance with religious others, whether through eros, food, or violence, threatens to incorporate them into the world where they are held captive.

Caveat Lector: The Odyssean *Viaje*

The *Viaje de Turquía*, subtitled *Diálogo entre Pedro de Hurdimalas y Juan de Voto a Dios y Mátalas Callando que trata de las miserias de los cautivos de turcos y de las costumbres y secta de los mismos haciendo la descripción de Turquía*, is a bewildering combination of Renaissance dialogue, captivity narrative, travel account, and, I will argue, picaresque.[8] Like Delicado's *retrato* in Chapter 1, it touts a faithful portrayal of its subject by a witness-narrator ("pintar al bibo," 160), yet it is also similarly slippery. Since its publication in 1905, editors and critics have attributed the highly anomalous, anonymous text to a variety of different Erasmian humanists working within the increasingly repressive climate of Spain in the 1550s, including Cristóbal de Villalón and Andrés Laguna, but no satisfying identification of its author has emerged.[9] Much of the critical debate has centered on the extent to which the text conveys historically precise information, and, more specifically, corresponds to its first-person narrator's actual experience. Arguments about the *Viaje*'s authorship are often closely tied to narratorial fidelity: if the experiences depicted are accurate, the assumption goes, they must point to one historical author or another.

Yet this approach tends to underestimate the rhetorical complexity of the text. For, unlike most of the contemporary treatises on the topic in Latin, Italian, Spanish, or French, the *Viaje* offers a remarkably sophisticated and self-conscious engagement with the representation of "the Turk." Contemporary Spanish humanist accounts of the Ottomans such as Vasco Díaz Tanco's *Palinodia de los Turcos* (Orense, 1547) or Pedro Mexía's *Silva de varia lección* (Seville, 1540) emphasize distance, whether in order to maintain their strong anti-Ottoman tone, or to remove any subjective traces of the author in favor of established sources.[10] Conversely, the *Viaje* actually foregrounds its embeddedness, in an account whose knowingness transcends the referential or the citational and repeatedly alerts us to its own unreliability.

In formal terms, the *Viaje* is a dialogue between three characters over two days, followed by a description of Constantinople and an account of the origins of the Ottoman Empire, also in dialogue form. As the subtitle anticipates, the three interlocutors bear names out of Spanish folklore, and two of them are barely more individuated than their names would suggest.[11] These two serve primarily as audience and sounding posts for the bulk of the narration, while consistently betraying the venality of the Spanish church. The third character, who bears the name of the trickster figure Pedro de Hurdimalas (generally rendered as Urdemalas, as in Cervantes's play of the same title), is a former captive who has arduously made his way back to Spain. Encountering his former acquaintances, he agrees to share his experiences with them: on the first day, he relates his captivity among the Ottomans, and on the second he describes the threatening "Turks" and their society. Interspersed with Pedro's account of his experiences elsewhere is a sharp Erasmian critique of the debased state of Christian charity and institutionalized religion in Spain, as well as pointed advice to the king on how his army should be run and compensated.

Critical reception of the *Viaje* has noted the importance of witnessing and its potential unreliability. From the Odyssean frame invoked in its dedication, the text touts direct experience as its warrant, while simultaneously recalling its literary and rhetorical manipulation. Beyond dubbing Pedro "l'Ulysse espagnol" for his errancy and wiliness, Marcel Bataillon notes, "Dire que le narrateur se proclame à tout propos témoin oculaire, c'est trop peu dire. Veracité et imposture sont, par leur antagonisme, l'âme de ce livre dialogué"[12] ["To say that the narrator proclaims himself for all purposes an eyewitness is to say too little. Veracity and imposture are, by their opposition, the very soul of this dialogic book"]. Albert Mas gestures toward the *Viaje*'s slipperiness and its picaresque flavor, noting how it ventures from the documentary "dans le domaine de la fiction littéraire par son récit autobiographique qui rappelle le climat des romans picaresques, par son style familier ou cru, par les anecdotes populaires ou savantes dont Pedro de Urdemalas prétend être le héros"[13] ["to the realm of literary fiction through an autobiographical account that recalls the atmosphere of picaresque novels with its familiar or crude style and the popular or learned anecdotes of which Pedro de Urdemalas pretends to be the hero"]. Florencio Sevilla Arroyo analyzes the tension between dialogue and novel in the text, given its privileging of first-person narrative and the pressures on that voice as it constantly negotiates dialogue. Sevilla Arroyo understates the narrative's complexity, however, noting only in passing its "resbaladiza ambigüedad intencional"[14] ["slippery intentional ambiguity"].

The *Viaje*'s extensive use of earlier texts repackaged as first-person experience, its considerable irony, and its thematization of the utility of first-person authority all invite a picaresque reading. Where readers might seek the authentic experience of a traveler or a captive, key sections of the *Viaje* provide instead the iteration and often silent citation of previous texts. In the dedication and the account of the Ottomans, a purely textual authority both supplements and disguises the lack of authorial experience as a guarantor for the text. Citation destabilizes the authority of the *Viaje*'s "I"—fashioned out of a tissue of previous discourses—and also of the earlier texts that are so easily recirculated and divorced from their own immediacy.[15] In the captivity narrative itself, the narrator's experience is not mediated by previous texts, but framed instead by a calculus of profit and utility, as direct witnessing is instrumentalized for the successful impersonation of experience. Thus the *Viaje* insistently poses the question of how reliable we should consider first-person narrators, especially when they loudly signal their unreliability, and casts a skeptical eye on the supposed authority that captivity affords.

When the *Viaje* was first edited and published by Manuel Serrano y Sanz in 1905, he singled out the dedication as proof that it was an autobiographical narrative.[16] The extensive address to Philip II certainly lays out the stakes of witnessing and authority, yet it is far from transparent. As Bataillon noted long ago, the dedication—a paratext that generally purports to offer more direct access to the author—becomes in the *Viaje* a tissue of recycled and translated accounts of the "Turks," primarily Giovanni Antonio Menavino's *Trattato de costumi et vita de Turchi* (Florence, 1548), with Giorgievits's appended commentary, and the prologue by Lodovico Domenichi to Theodoro Cantacusino Spandugino's *Della casa regale de Cantacusini, delle historie et origine de principi de turchi.*[17] From its very start, with and beyond the silent citations, the dedication of this paradoxical portrait-cum-commentary-cum-dialogue constantly foregrounds the question of textual authority and of the utility of texts. The opening lines translate and recombine Domenichi, invoking both direct witnessing and its literary elaboration:

> Aquel insaçiable y desenfrenado deseo de saber y conoscer que natura puso en todos los hombres, Çésar invictíssimo, subjetándonos de tal manera que nos fuerza a leer sin fructo ninguno las fábulas y fictiones, no puede mejor executarse que con la peregrinaçión y ver de tierras estrañas, considerando en quánta angustia se enzierra el ánimo y entendimiento que está siempre en un lugar sin poder extenderse a especular la infinita grandeza d'este mundo. Y por esto Homero, único padre y autor de todos los buenos estudios, habiendo de proponer a su Ulixes por perfecto dechado de virtud y sabiduría, no sabe de qué manera se entonar más alto que con estas palabras:
>
> > "'Ἄνδρα μοι ἔν[ν]επε, Μοῦσα, πολύτροπον, ὃζ μάλα πολλὰ πλάγχ[θ]η . . ."
>
> Ayúdame a cantar o musa un varón que vio muchas tierras y diversas costumbres de hombres. (158–59)
>
> [That insatiable and unrestrained desire to know and become acquainted that nature placed in all men, most unvanquished Caesar, subjecting us so that it forces us to read fruitlessly fables and fictions,

> cannot be better accomplished than by pilgrimage/travel and seeing strange/foreign lands, given the great anguish that confines a spirit and mind that is always in one place without the ability to extend itself to speculate on/observe the infinite greatness of this world. And thus Homer, only father and author of all worthy studies, who would propose his Ulysses as the paragon of virtue and wisdom, knows not what words to sing loudly but these:
>
> "'Ἄνδρα μοι ἔν[ν]επε, Μοῦσα, πολύτροπον, ὃς μάλα πολλὰ πλάγχ[θ]η . . ."
>
> Help me, oh muse, to sing a man who saw many lands and diverse customs of men.]

The *Viaje* stands in for the actual voyaging of a confined mind, affording it a different status than "fábulas y fictiones." Yet it discusses exploration in terms that reintroduce the referential instability that it would transcend, highlighting a tension between the pilgrim, who confirms the sacred status of an established landmark, and the seeker of rarities.[18] The "peregrinaçión" in the passage above stems from secular curiosity rather than religious feeling. "Especular," for its part, means here primarily "to observe," yet it also suggests more open-ended ruminations.

The invocation of Homer to recommend voyaging is not exclusive to the *Viaje*—Bataillon finds it in Domenichi's prologue, and also in Laguna's *Dioscórides*[19]—yet it takes on a special ironic force after the critique of the fruitless reading of "fábulas y fictiones." Homeric texts enjoyed an exemplary status in the period, with Ulysses even imagined as a paragon of prudence and discretion, a suitable model for a king.[20] Yet he did not entirely shed his fame as a trickster, in the long medieval tradition that considered him wily above all things. Note the irony, for example, in Peter Giles's letter to Jérôme de Busleyden about *Utopia*, in which the witness-narrator Raphael Hythloday—etymologically, from the Greek, the "peddler of nonsense"—is described as "a man with more knowledge of nations, peoples, and business than even the most famous Ulysses."[21]

In the *Viaje*, the dedication's early reference to the Homeric version of Ulysses reframes not only the text to follow but also, retrospectively, the classics themselves. The subsequent invocation of Dido, dangerously susceptible to Aeneas's pleas as she recognizes her own suffering in him (161), clarifies the stakes. Ulysses—like Aeneas after him—tells the stories he needs to tell, and his relationship to the world he experiences is supremely utilitarian, born of the need to survive and return home rather than of detached curiosity. As the trickster-hero, master of storytelling, is recast as representative traveler, paragon of virtue and wisdom, the authority of both travel writing and classical exemplarity are cast into doubt. Instead of dignifying the *Viaje*, the dedication's references underscore how all travelers tailor their relations to the exigencies of their situations. *Caveat lector*.

The playfulness of the dedication's opening quickly takes a more serious turn, as the author compares Philip himself to Ulysses, for his desire to know and his extensive travels through Europe. The *Viaje* addresses the king's prudent desire to understand the "Turk," while reminding him of the suffering of captives. Here the text appears to align itself with the much more orthodox purpose of a work such as Díaz Tanco's *Palinodia*, whose dedication is unwavering in its suspicion of the Ottomans, unleavened by the curiosity that animates the *Viaje*.[22] Unlike those whose authority comes "del diz que y que oyeron dezir a uno que venía de allá" (161) ["from hearsay and what they heard someone say who came from there"], the *Viaje*'s narrator will write from memory, "como fiel intérprete, y que todo quanto escribo vi" (162) ["as a faithful interpreter, having seen all that I write"]. Yet the very claim of direct witnessing is recycled from a series of prologues to earlier texts on the Turks, as Bataillon notes and Ortola traces in her edition.[23] From the dedication, then, the *Viaje* foregrounds the slipperiness of a narrative "I" that claims reliable firsthand experience, all while aligning himself with trickster-figures and relying on preexisting texts. If iterability and citationality are hallmarks of travel literature, the *Viaje* exposes the partiality and artificiality of one who claims a witness's perspective.

Moreover, the Ottoman world that the *Viaje* promises is not just food for a traveler's curiosity or an urgent assignment for a Habsburg ruler. It also embodies the threat of captivity and attempts on the Christian faith, thus problematizing the authenticity of religious identity warranted by a confessional "I." In a context of Mediterranean exchanges and religious fluidity, captivity provides both the occasion for knowledge and the reason to take that knowledge under advisement, producing a witness simultaneously enabled and compromised by his location among the Ottomans. The *Viaje* also appears in a context of increased suspicion about Protestantism in Spain—hence, in part, its anonymity—and its bewildering combination of travel authority and clerical corruption constantly foregrounds the problem of what version of an authentic Christian identity a captive who manages to resist the inducements of conversion to Islam might in fact espouse.

The *Viaje*'s dedication invokes the apostolic authority of John and Peter to undergird the authority of this version among so many potential stories of captivity:

> Ni es de maravillar si entre todos quantos cautibos los turcos an tenido después que son nombrados me atreba a dezir que yo solo vi todo lo que escribo, porque puedo con gran rrazón dezir lo que Sant Juan por Sant Pedro en el 18 capítulo de su escritura: "Discipulus autem ille erat notus pontifici et introiuit cum iesu in atrium pontificis, Petrus autem stabat ad hostium foris." Dos años enteros después de las prisiones estube en Constantinopla, en los quales entraba como es costumbre de los médicos en todas las partes donde a ninguno otro es líçito entrar, y con saver las lenguas todas que en aquellas partes se hablan y ser mi avitaçión en las cámaras de los mayores prínçipes de aquella tierra ninguna cosa se me ascondía de quanto pasaba. (163–64)
>
> [Nor should one wonder if, among all those captives held by the Turk whom I will name, I should dare to say that only I saw all that I write, because I can justly say what Saint John said about Saint Peter in the eighteenth chapter of his scripture: "That disciple was known unto the high priest and went in with Jesus into the palace of the high priest. But Peter stood at the door without."[24] I was in Constantinople for two whole years after the imprisonment, during which, as is the custom for physicians, I went into all those places where no one else is allowed to enter, and as I knew all the languages spoken in those parts and lived in the rooms of the greatest princes in that land, nothing of what went on was hidden from me.]

The narrative negotiates the reportorial and the metonymic: to achieve its full effect, the immediacy of the eyewitness report must be generalizable to the fate of the many captives for whom he speaks. The cited passage from John in the New Testament comes just before Peter's first denial of Christ, an oblique reminder of the excruciating circumstances in which the captive must have found himself, and of what must have been the constant trials of his faith during captivity. Yet what is the relationship between that Peter and the eponymous narrator, whose own faith will be sorely tested? Beyond this reminder of the fragility of faith under duress lies the larger problem of how to guarantee that his text is representative. As the author offers the king "sola la voluntad de mi baxo estilo con que muestro las fatigas de los pobres cautivos" (169) ["only the intent of my low style in which I show the travails of the poor captives"]—he claims an experience paradoxically both singular and representative.

Within the text itself, Mata compares Pedro to Daedalus or Ulysses for his inventiveness. Pedro refuses the comparison, insisting instead on his witnessing: "Lo de [Ulises] dízelo Homero, que era ciego y no lo vio, y también era poeta; mas yo vi todo lo que pasé y vosotros lo oiréis de quien lo vio y lo pasó" (253) ["All that about {Ulysses} is related by Homer, who was blind and did not see it, and who was, moreover, a poet. But I saw everything that happened to me and you will hear it from the one who saw it and experienced it"]. Unlike the blind poet, Pedro is a proximate eyewitness, intimately familiar with what he has seen and ready to relate it. Although the narrator's authority overgoes Homer's, the sustained comparisons of him with the wily Ulysses beg the question of what purpose his narrative will serve.

Sailing to Jerusalem: Venality and Utility

The obverse of the useful, situated knowledge promised in the *Viaje*'s dedication is Pedro's surprising willingness to instrumentalize his tale for venal ends. As a prelude to his actual account, he and his two interlocutors discuss the various perversions of Christian good works in Spain. In a frankly Erasmian satire, Juan de Voto a Dios and Mátalas Callando display all their bad faith: skimming generously off the top, they care more about the quality of their own dinners and the magnificence of the hospital they are ever so slowly building than about actually helping the poor. The discussion of poverty leads to pilgrims—how are they to be succored when there is so little charity? Pedro is definitive on this count: if they have no resources, would-be pilgrims should stay home. Pilgrimage signals incredulity, Pedro argues, for faith should suffice to confirm the experience of Christ's crucifixion: "Luego si ubiese tantas Hierusalenes, y tantas cruzes, y lanzas y rreliquias, como estrellas en el cielo y arena en la mar, todas ellas no valdrían tanto como una mínima parte de la hostia consagrada, en la cual se enzierra el que hizo los çielos, y la tierra, y a Hierusalem y sus rreliquias" (232) ["If there were as many Jerusalems, and as many crosses, and lances, and relics, as there are stars in the sky and grains of sand in the sea, all of them would not be worth an iota of the consecrated host, in which is contained he who made the heavens and the earth, and Jerusalem and its relics"]. The concentrated experience of communion contrasts with the dispersal of believers and belief in the act of pilgrimage. At the same time, Pedro's cutting dismissal of others' pilgrimage, paradoxically based on "lo que . . . he visto por la luenga experiencia" (233) ["what I have seen from long experience"] promises a distinction between his own travels and a frivolous pilgrimage born of incredulity.

Pedro's corrupt interlocutors ignore his critique and instead ask for his story. When he first reveals that he was a captive, they are both skeptical: Mátalas Callando assumes he must be trying to get a rise out of them "con esta ficción" (236) ["with this fiction"], while Juan begins to pepper him with questions. Mata explains that Pedro is being tested by one who "no haze sino ir y venir de aquí a Hierusalem" (237) ["does nothing but come and go between here and Jerusalem"]. The tables are soon turned, however, as Pedro begins to interrogate Juan on his experience of Jerusalem—what languages did he speak there, what countries did he traverse on his way, did he perchance approach by sea? Juan recognizes too late that he has fallen into a trap, his supposed authority undone. He claims that his own memory has failed him, and as for Pedro, he appears so wise, and so changed, that Juan cannot be sure he is the same man: "venís tan trocado que dubdo si sois vos" (238) ["you are so changed that I doubt whether it's you"]. Juan's justifiable suspicion—Pedro is protean, unverifiable, unlike his former self—cannot quite cover his own confusion, especially once he has indicted his own memory.

Pedro's exposure of the false pilgrim Juan and his mess of relics, whose only point is to make money ("El aforro de la volsa" ["stuffing our bags"], 240), is of a piece with the text's broader Erasmian critique. Yet the dialogue then takes an unexpected turn, as the two friars convince Pedro to participate in their deception. Juan complains that he has previously been exposed as a fraud when describing his pilgrimage—particularly his remarkable arrival in Jerusalem by sea—for his reliance on a book that has led him astray: "Un libro que hizo un fraire del camino de Hierusalen, y las cosas que vio, me ha engañado, que con su peregrinaje ganaba como con cabeza de lobo" (244) ["A book that a friar wrote of the way to Jerusalem, and the things he saw, has tricked me, and he profited from his pilgrimage as though he had brought in a wolf's head"]. Ortola identifies a likely source in the Franciscan Antonio de Aranda's *Verdadera información de la tierra sancta* (Toledo: Juan Ferrer, 1550),[25] and notes the delicious origin of Juan's confusion: Aranda writes "después que últimamente se desembarca en Jafo no ay tierra, sino doze leguas pequeñas hasta Hierusalem" ["after one finally disembarks in Jaffa, there is no land save for twelve short leagues to Jerusalem"]. The precision of the source—Jerusalem is in fact twelve leagues from Jaffa—introduces a whole set of new problems into the *Viaje*: a witness may be truthful and yet misunderstood by a reader who lacks context or sophistication. This may not bode well for the reception of Pedro's own narrative, except that Juan has every incentive to get it right this time. At the same time, while the captivity narrative proper makes little use of previous texts, the *Viaje* as a whole relies heavily on them, just as Juan did on his friar's account of travel to Jerusalem.

Beyond the condemnation of a specific source-text, Pedro scathingly dismisses all those "que hablan de lo que no saben" (245) ["who speak of what they do not know"]. Yet he also resists the notion that faith requires any referential certainty: "De manera que en aver dos pulgadas de distançia de más a menos de la una a la otra parte está el creer o no en Dios. ¿Y qué se me da a mí para ser christiano que sean más dos leguas que tres, ni que Pilato y Caiphás viban en una mesma calle?" (245) ["So that belief in God depends on whether there are two inches more or less from one place to another. What does it matter to my being a Christian if it's two leagues rather than three, or if Pilatus and Caiaphas lived on the same street?"]. Pedro's position on narrative authority is complex: where faith is concerned, he bespeaks a kind of Erasmian skepticism that transcends referential punctiliousness. At the same time, he condemns other books because their authors lack knowledge and insists on his own authority, born of direct experience.

Mata offers the perfect solution to the problem of Juan's ignorance about Jerusalem: borrowed authority. If Pedro relates what he knows, he will provide a much more trustworthy source than the dubious travel narrative on which Juan has relied to this point, "de lo cual Juan de Voto a Dios podrá quedar tan docto que pueda hablar donde quiera que le pregunten como testigo de vista" (247) ["and from this Juan de Voto a Dios will be so learned that he will be able to speak as an eyewitness whenever they ask him about anything"]. Bewilderingly, Pedro agrees to have his own tale serve as corrective—better material that will allow Juan to lie more effectively as he only pretends to have been an eyewitness. Pedro swears on his beloved freedom to tell the truth, warranted by his knowledge of and familiarity with Ottomans and Greeks: "las condiçiones y costumbres de turcos y griegos os contaré con apresçibimiento, que después que los turcos rreinan en el mundo jamás ubo hombre que mejor lo supiese ni que allá más privase" (248–49) ["I will carefully relate to you the conditions and customs of Turks and Greeks, for since the Turks rule there never was a man in the world who knew it better nor was more favored/had more access"]. This devastatingly ironic moment undoes the relationship between place and faith—there is nothing holy or transformative about pilgrimage, or about an intimate knowledge of holy places that may in fact be borrowed or transferred, to become a valuable commodity. Beyond the immediate implications for religious practice, moreover, this framing scene troubles the fundamental relationship between travel or witnessing and moral authority, with much larger implications for Spain's imperial project in the period.

To what extent can we read this moment as a hermeneutic prod, or even a mise-en-abîme for the narrative that follows? How are we to reconcile Pedro's sharp critique of venality with his own participation in it, and his insistence that his own authority escapes the broader condemnation of travel-knowledge mobilized for the sake of a corrupt utility? At a minimum, the passage presents a tension between Pedro's informed, savvy account of the Ottomans and their sphere of influence, and the radical relativization of that account as part of a humanist critique of church corruption. More broadly, the preamble impugns not only Pedro's own narrative but the genres of captivity narrative and travel account, demonstrating how even the most authentic of voices can be enlisted in utilitarian and corrupt projects. This is the central ironic insight that Cervantes picks up in the famous episode of the false captives in his *Persiles*, which I discuss below: when witnesses lend their voices to impersonators, authenticity becomes that much more elusive.[26]

The problematization of narrative truth is less explicit during the rest of the *Viaje*, although there is plenty of evidence to complicate the authenticity of the narrator. Yet, lest the reader forget the complex and paradoxical terms under which the narrative is offered, Pedro's interlocutors periodically inquire whether the cities he describes are located on the coast, in a virtual refrain that recalls the venal purpose to which his narrative is being put. If Juan was once caught out because he claimed to sail into Jerusalem, he will not repeat his mistake for any other city: "MATA.—Antes que se nos olvide, no sea el mal de Gerusalem, ¿llega allí la mar?" (569, with multiple examples passim) ["MATA: 'Before we forget, to avoid that Jerusalem problem, is it on the sea?'"]. Occasionally, Pedro taunts his interlocutors, as when he encourages them to pay careful attention to his account of the monasteries of Monte Sancto, "para que no vais tropezando en ello" (489) ["so that you not trip up on it"]. At other points they insist on more information: though Pedro attempts to wind up his first-day narrative when he reaches freedom in Italy, his interlocutors will not hear of his skipping the details about the various cities through which he then traveled (567). As captivity narrative shades into travelogue, the utilitarian motive is again foregrounded: the more objective information Pedro brings to the table, the more useful his narrative becomes.

Beyond the leading questions, moreover, the dialogic interventions themselves recall the intradiegetic audience and its less-than-noble purposes. When Mata or Juan question Pedro, their skepticism works on two levels: even as Pedro reassures them with his unassailable authority about seemingly incredible experiences, we are reminded that his narrative needs to sound convincing because of its utilitarian purpose, as Juan will not be able to contextualize or explain as Pedro himself does. With the exhausted Pedro finally off to bed, Juan and Mata congratulate themselves not just on what they have learned, but on how they could now effectively impersonate the traveler: "JUAN.—Agora me paresçe que le haría en creer, si quisiese, que he andado todo lo que él, quanto más a otro" (619) ["JUAN: 'Now I think I could make even him believe that I have traveled all that he did, let alone any other'"]. Yet as they attempt to convince themselves of the effectiveness of Pedro's narrative, they invoke a much broader context of narrators about whom they are skeptical: "MATA.—Si lo que diçe es verdad, él dará rrazón d'ello como ha hecho siempre; si no, no queremos oír mentiras, que hartas nos quentan todos esos soldados que vienen del campo de su Magestad y los indianos" (619) ["MATA: 'If what he says is true, he'll account for it as he's always done; if not, we have no wish to hear lies, for the soldiers who come from his Majesty's battlefields, and those back from the New World tell us enough of those'"]. Mata's devastating irony skewers the channels of reporting on which the empire must depend: if soldiers and travelers to the New World lie, on whom can it rely?

The *Viaje* also betrays a certain skepticism about the power of the eyewitness account to change received opinion. Mata argues that incorrect texts and false captives shape beliefs so powerfully as to be unshakeable:

> *MATA:* . . . porque no hai ombre en toda esta corte de tomo, letrado ni no letrado, que no piense que sin haber andado ni visto nada de lo que vos, porque leyó aquel libro que hizo el fraire del camino de Hierusalem y habló con uno de aquellos vellacos que deçíais que fingen haberse escapado de poder de moros, que les atestó las cabezas de mentiras, no les harán entender otra cosa aunque vaxase Sant Pablo a predicársela. . . .

PEDRO: Pocos trançes d'esos pensaréis que he pasado con muchos señores que ansí me preguntan de allá cosas, y como no les diga lo que ellos saben, luego os salen con un vos más de media vara de largo: "Engañaisos, señor, que no sabéis lo que deçís, porque pasa d'esta y d'esta manera." Preguntado que cómo lo saben, si han estado allá por dicha, ni aun en su vida vieron soltar una escopeta. Y por esto yo estoi deliberado a no contar cosa ninguna jamás si no es a quien ha estado allá y lo sabe. (444, 446)

[*MATA:* "For there isn't a man in all this court, lettered or unlettered, who, without having traveled or seen any of what you have, because he read the book that friar wrote about the way to Jerusalem and spoke to one of those scoundrels whom you spoke of, who pretend to have escaped from the Moors, who filled their heads with lies, would agree to change his mind even if Saint Paul himself were to come down to preach to him."

PEDRO: "Do you think I have been through few such straits with the many lords who ask me about things over there? If I do not tell them what they know, they come out with a long riposte: 'You are fooling yourself, for you don't know what you're saying, for it happens thus and thus.' Asked how they know, and if by chance they've been there, it turns out they've never seen a gun fired in their lives. And for this reason I am determined never to relate anything except to one who has been there and knows it."]

Pedro capitulates in the face of obstinacy. Yet if he can share his experience only with those who have also been there, knowledge becomes solipsistic, a closed circuit of reference. Where does that leave the *Viaje*, which is explicitly presented as a transfer of knowledge from one who knows to those who do not, albeit for suspect ends? If the witness can share his account with none but those who already share his experience, he can only mutually confirm information, rather than proving or expanding knowledge.

Whatever the doubts expressed here about the ability of a witness-narrator to change a reader's mind, the entire *Viaje* proceeds under the aegis of the trick. We learn as Juan learns, even though surely we read for a very different purpose than his venal focus on profit. Or do we? The implication of the reader herself in the trick is one of the most powerfully destabilizing moves in the text. I turn now to the broader question of how closeness can prove far more problematic than distance in texts of captivity, despite our tendency to privilege the authority of the first-person account.

Knowing the Ottoman

Beyond the utilitarian preamble to Pedro's narrative, and the many moments when the venal utility of the narrative compromises its reliability, there is much in Pedro's actual experience as a captive that complicates the value of the first-person report. The more access Pedro has to the Ottoman centers of power, the more successfully he manipulates them; the more fully he knows them, the less reliable he appears. To put it another way, the more adept he becomes as an intermediary, a conduit for knowledge, a protean source, the harder it becomes to exempt his narrative of captivity from his standard rhetorical legerdemain.

Pedro's experience as a captive among the Ottomans and during his long voyage home through the eastern Mediterranean includes many moments of dissembling and dissimulation. On board the galley that captures him and also in Constantinople, Pedro pretends to be a doctor and to know medical Greek texts; as he makes his escape, he passes for months as a Greek Orthodox priest. Indeed, it is as much for this dissembling as for his long voyage home that Pedro recalls Ulysses. Nonetheless, throughout his travels he remains a Christian despite all the pressure that his masters bring to bear on him to convert. His trickery is presumably justifiable for the goal of living freely as a Christian—the underlying authenticity of Pedro's purpose trumps any necessary dissimulation along the way.[27]

The medical interlude, which takes up a good portion of the captivity narrative, has at times been read as a source on early modern medicine. Yet it is far from straightforward: although it includes several discussions on method and empiricism, it is just as rhetorically complex and slippery as the rest of the text. In an extended test of his authority, Pedro must establish his preeminence over the Sultan's Jewish doctors. Deeply imbued with anti-Semitism, the episode is hence largely about convincing an internal audience of something—the captive's medical expertise—that the reader knows to be untrue. Pedro argues for his own authority, born of observation, over that of the learned Jews and their books, as when he forages a fresh curative herb that he had noticed on his walks to replace the dried—and presumably less effective—versions offered by the Jewish doctors (390). Yet his is not quite an empiricist position: he never refuses books entirely, and instead argues for the value of certain books over others, vaulting over the Semitic heritage of medieval Spain to the Greeks. At the same time, he recognizes that he must make his best guess and hope for a lucky outcome: observation only gets him so far, and his hastily self-taught practice is often a stab in the dark. He may be better than the Sultan's Jewish physicians, but that is not saying much. Even Pedro's most powerful criticism of the Jews—when he mocks them for their claim that their children might inherit their medical wisdom ("los llaman liçenciaditos" ["they call them the little masters"], 402)—obliquely critiques anti-Semitism itself, indicting the *limpieza de sangre* statutes that assume a similar continuity between Jewish forebears and their *converso* children. If it is ridiculous to assume that the child of a Jewish doctor will inherit his medical knowledge, that is, it is no less ridiculous to believe that the Christian child of a convert from Judaism will inherit Jewishness. Ultimately, the medical interlude, although it proffers empiricism as a solid anchor for the narrative, cannot deliver on its promise, for it is too deeply ensconced within Pedro's deception. As such, it recalls the allusions to Delicado's treatise on syphilis in *La Lozana andaluza*, which I discussed in Chapter 1: though empiricism might offer the promise of epistemological certainty, it is as susceptible to rhetorical manipulation as the broader narrative that surrounds it.

The central moment in Pedro's narrative, which ostensibly cancels out every other deception, is his master's attempt to convert him through intimidation. Mata has already anticipated the crux, noting that he has been waiting to ask Pedro about forced conversions, given how many renegades claim to have been forced, and misogynistically comparing the converts to women who claim to have been raped but actually enjoyed themselves (322–23). At the most heightened moment of threat to Pedro, the text emphasizes that the proceedings are secret, as his master spirits him away to the woods with only an interpreter for company (327). Unlike much of what Pedro relates elsewhere, this cannot be corroborated, but is accessible only through his version of the story. Two renegades jump out of the bushes and threaten to have Pedro's head cut off immediately if he refuses to convert. When he refuses, they entreat him, reminding him that the conversion need not be authentic: "Di de sí aunque guardes en tu corazón lo que quisieres, que nosotros aunque nos ves en este hábito tan christianos somos como tú" (327) ["Say yes even if you keep what you wish in your heart, for we, although you see us in this dress, are as

Christian as you"]. Instead of accepting the accommodation of passing—as the young Miles Philips arguably does in a similar crux on the other side of the world—Pedro accuses the renegades of wanting to damn his soul as well as their own. Recalling Christ's words in Matthew 10:33—"But whosoever shall deny me before men, him will I also deny before my Father which is in heaven"[28]—he insists that they cannot serve two masters. Despite his righteous vehemence, the moment recalls the shadowy double identification of the narrator with the John who has special access, but also the Peter who denies Christ, in the *Viaje*'s dedication (163–64). Thus, even at this moment, clearly meant as a touchstone of Pedro's steadfastness in contrast to the renegades and dissemblers who surround him, the text recalls the complex negotiation of access and knowledge that faith demands.

Other troubling instances of dissembling exceed the carefully considered content of Pedro's narrative to contaminate its frame. Perhaps most strikingly, Pedro does not fully shed his identity as a Greek Orthodox priest, even upon his return to Spain. When he happens upon Juan and Mata, he greets them in Greek. They fail to recognize him in his Orthodox religious habit, and he becomes legible to them as the man they knew only when he chooses to reveal his identity (204–11). *El hábito no hace al monje* [the habit does not make the monk], one might say. Yet the prolongation of Pedro's disguise troubles the identification of home and Spain with Christianity on which a captivity narrative would seem to depend. In fact, there is Christianity across the Mediterranean, even within Ottoman domains, where it exists in a fragile equilibrium of tribute and toleration. Eastern Christianity is used to underscore the arbitrariness of religious ceremony and outward forms, as well as the failings of Spanish institutionalized religion.[29] Mata cannot believe that the Greek priests are as poor as they appear to Pedro, and claims they must be faking poverty for the benefit of visitors, as they would do in Spain:

> *MATA:* Que son mañas de fraires quando hai huéspedes forasteros, por comprobar la pobreza que tienen predicada, mas entre sí y'os prometo que lo pasan bien, y tienen alguna rrazón, porque luego les acortarían las limosnas por la fama que los huéspedes les darían.
>
> *PEDRO:* De los de acá yo bien creo lo que vos deçís, mas de aquellos no, porque lo sé muy bien que hazen la mayor abstinençia del mundo siguiendo siempre ellos y los clérigos griegos la orden evangélica. (480)

> [*MATA:* "These are friars' tricks for when there are foreign guests, to prove the poverty that they preach, but when they're among themselves I warrant that they have a good time. And that's reasonable, or their alms would dry up when the guests talked."
>
> *PEDRO:* "I can well believe that of the ones over here, but not of those, for I know full well that they practice the greatest abstinence in the world, as they and the Greek clerics always follow the evangelical mandate."]

The irony is intense: Mata assumes the Greek friars must be dissembling, because that is what he would do, while Pedro, the false friar, sets him straight on the authenticity of the Greeks. Although the immediate point is the Erasmian satire of religious venality in Spain, in contrast to the humble Greek monks, Pedro's own disguise limits his critique of Mata's skepticism.

Within the captivity narrative, Pedro's insight about the relationship between the Ottomans and their religious minorities often challenges Spanish orthodoxy. His success as conduit and intermediary serves to voice pointed criticisms. After many postponed promises of freedom and frustrating reversals, Pedro finally manages to evade his captors and leave Constantinople. When he relates how he takes refuge with a Greek, Juan immediately zeroes in on that person's status, asking: "—Pues ¿qué griego hera aquél? ¿Hera libre? ¿Hera christiano? ¿A quién estaba subjeto?" (451) ["What Greek was that? Was he free? Was he a Christian? Whom was he subject to?"]. Pedro responds with a knowing account of the Ottoman polity: just because it is called Turkey, he explains, does not mean that all who live there are Turks. Instead, there are even more Christians than Turks, although they are subject not to the Pope or the Latin church, but to their own patriarch. Yet as long as they pay their tribute, what is it to the Sultan? Pedro's concluding comparison is deeply ironic: were there not once, he asks, Moors and Jews in Spain (452)?

Pedro eventually finds a spy to spirit him away, and reaches the island of Sciathos. Although the townspeople there are Christian, they are loath to help him. Back in Spain, Pedro's audience cannot believe that Christians would behave this way. Religious affiliation is far less important than political accommodation in the Ottoman sphere: if escaped captives are recognized, Pedro explains, they will be returned to their masters, because even if the Christians are their own men ["están por sí," 529], they are subject to the Turk and pay him yearly tribute. Pedro's clear-eyed account of the Orthodox Christians' loyalty to their Ottoman master challenges any Spanish sense of religious solidarity as political capital. Whatever the perceived threat of religious minorities within Spain, the opposite was not true in the eastern Mediterranean, where political allegiance to the empire trumped any sense of religious solidarity, and where Orthodox Christians were reluctant to upset in any way the careful equilibrium of tolerance under which they existed in in the empire's sphere of influence.[30]

Thus the situated knowledge of the captive, who has experienced the lack of solidarity between Eastern and Western churches firsthand, and barely survived it, undoes the abstract and ideological assumptions of the universalizing Christian expansionism that Spain championed.[31] At close range, the idealizing abstractions that motivated crusader fantasies well into the sixteenth century dissolve into the reality of complex political arrangements based on accommodation, tribute, and tolerance. Ironically, the venal lie of the supposed pilgrims—I reached Jerusalem by sea!—voices a similar wish-fulfillment to the Christian expansionist and crusader rhetoric that assumes solidarity from Eastern Christians: if Jerusalem were actually on the sea, then its conquest would be more feasible. While the *Viaje* reminds us of how the report from enemy lands functions at multiple levels—authentic account or instrumentalized, constructed authority—it also exposes the wishful thinking of Christian expansionism.

Pedro's account of his captivity is threaded throughout with reminders of his rhetorical dexterity and ability to manipulate the truth to suit his purposes. The more he is tested, the better he becomes at both reading the Ottomans and dissembling before them. To aid the Christians who come to negotiate with the Ottomans ("negoçios de christianos," 537), he serves as a highly creative interpreter of their letters. Attuned to Ottoman codes of honor and address, Pedro silently corrects the Christians' faults and supplements their lack: "Léyla a mi propósito supliendo, como yo sabía tan bien sus costumbres" (537) ["I read it to my purposes supplementing as necessary, for I knew their customs so well"]. Once again, a narrative is adapted to suit its audience and extract from it a desired end. More blatantly, at the very end of Pedro's captivity narrative, Mata reminds us that he and Juan have learned from it how to avoid precision when they do not know and have not witnessed anything: "Aunque os pregunten cosas que no hayáis visto, podéis dar rrespuestas comunes: Pasé de noche. No salí de las galeras. Como la çibdad es grande no bi eso. Esto vi y estotro vi, que era lo que más había que mirar. Y con eso os ebadiréis" (619)

["If they should ask you about things that you have not seen, you can give general answers: I passed through at night. I never left the galleys. I never saw that, for the city is large. I saw this and I saw that, which is what there was most to look at. And with that you shall get out of it"]. This moment is more corrosive than the recurring refrain about cities on the coast: it underscores the instrumentalization of Pedro's relation even as it envisions a rhetorical ability shared with any who might mimic him.

Well into Pedro's narrative, and in exchange for his account of Venice, Juan regales him with a third-hand parable. Mata nudges him to offer "aquel quento que os contó el duque de Medinaçeli del pintor que tubo su padre" (587) ["that story that the duke of Medinaçeli told you about the painter his father had"]. The painter had spent a long time on a supposed pilgrimage to Italy, yet never seen Venice. Upon his return the duke required him to describe a city in detail at every meal. When he asked for Venice, the painter promptly left on pilgrimage again, and did not return until he could give an account of it, picking up where he had left off months earlier and leaving the duke dumbfounded at his absence and return (587–88). This parable about authority challenges the political and social hierarchy—the painter, whatever his gifts, must paradoxically refuse the duke's interpellation if he is to answer truthfully. Moreover, the story calls attention to the power of narrative over any other form of description: why else would a painter not paint, but rather narrate, what he had seen?

At such moments, the *Viaje de Turquía* exposes a new anxiety about narrative authority, born of the huge expansion of Europe's horizons in the period and the particular weight that eyewitness accounts acquired as guarantors of new worlds. As the assumption of authenticity that undergirds the travel narrative, the formal *relación*, or the captivity tale disappears, to be replaced by a corrupt utility, the various forms ostensibly warranted by the narrator's authentic experience come to resemble the partial, interested, and unreliable narration that is the picaresque. Original and authentic narrations are replaced by verisimilar imitations, such as the much-improved story of his travels that Juan will tell after Pedro bequeaths to him his better story, even as the original narrative is tainted by this shady transactionality. As Daniel Hershenzon notes, there was considerable anxiety in the period about the reliability of historical captives' accounts, from their petitions for ransom, which required supporting evidence, to the even less verifiable claims of would-be informants and spies.[32] Solving this problem required moving beyond the single account, to external corroboration: "Authority was distributed, on the one hand, among captives, friars, spouses, and fleet officers and, on the other hand, among textual artifacts."[33] The *Viaje* shows how even distributed authority might not offer any guarantees: even if an original is true, those who copy it learn to lie better.

More than fifty years after the *Viaje*, Cervantes, himself famously a former captive, gives us in his *Persiles* a related episode of false captives that sharpens our sense of what is at stake in first-person accounts of captivity and the mimetic appropriation of original experience.[34] Two itinerant young students pretend to be former captives in order to extract alms from the townspeople they address, representing their supposed knowledge of Algiers on a painted *lienzo* [canvas]. As Marie-Blanche Requejo Carrió notes, the episode takes on a picaresque character, particularly given the analogies between the false captives and the false beggars that so exercised moralists in the period.[35] The suspicious mayor of the town, a former captive himself, soon exposes the students' ruse by quizzing them on Algiers, of which they actually know very little. In a resolution that closely recalls the *Viaje*, the mayor decides not to punish them but instead to furnish them with the necessary information so that they will not be caught again. Once again, intimate knowledge gained through a Mediterranean ordeal augments the false captives' bag of tricks. Unlike the *Viaje*, however, the *Persiles* has an omniscient narrator to contain the instability introduced by such brief moments, and we are never actually told what the mayor teaches them.

The *Viaje* speaks with a forked tongue. Even as it announces itself as a way to impersonate the authority of a witness, it enables many observations about Spain's place in the world and its socio-political organization that could not be stated more directly. The persecution of religious minorities, the corruption of the Spanish church, the deliriousness of crusading fantasies—these are just some of the delicate topics that the text can touch on after it has established itself as a venal, utilitarian aide-mémoire. Picaresque affinities fundamentally transform the text beyond the formal register, as the moral and narrative authority of Pedro's tale is profoundly ironized by both its putative utility and the intradiegetic fiction of his sustained dissimulations. More broadly, by promising military intelligence only to then dismantle the rhetorical apparatus of authority on which power relies, the *Viaje* shows how the literary, and more precisely the picaresque, undermines the certainties of identitarian and imperial oppositions. As the captive reveals his picaresque side, he challenges the structures of belief and difference that undergird early modern imperial power, offering instead a heady dose of skepticism.

Urdemalas Redux

Cervantes's own *Comedia famosa de Pedro de Urdemalas* shares an eponymous protagonist with the *Viaje de Turquía*, yet it is set in Spain, and more concerned with the protean, folk aspects of the character than with the *Viaje*'s experience of the Ottoman world.[36] Elsewhere in Cervantes's oeuvre, however, there are intriguing traces of a richer, more oblique engagement with the *Viaje*. (Although we have no evidence that Cervantes actually read the unpublished *Viaje*, it circulated widely in manuscript.) Perhaps the most striking echo is the episode of the false captives in the *Persiles*, which I referred to above: neither the first nor the last opportunistic impersonators wandering around Spain, they are adept at repurposing another's authority, including its material supports. Much like the famous discussion of Ginés de Pasamonte's picaresque in *Don Quijote* 1.22, the *Persiles* interlude underscores Cervantes's knowingness about the malleability and appeal of first-person accounts, and his recognition that the stakes are particularly high when those accounts supposedly represent the fidelity of a Christian subject among Spain's religious others.

Cervantes's *Los baños de Argel* and *La Gran Sultana,* two plays of captivity in the Muslim world, problematize the notion of authority born of experience at greater length. Though they offer vivid, proximate detail about captivity, the plays are sophisticated fictions that negotiate the Iberian imaginary of North Africa as well as Spain's own cultural complexities. Even their most dismissive and satiric representations evoke points of contact among the cultures of the Mediterranean, revealing via humor what may otherwise be unspeakable about the proximity between supposed enemies. Erotic entanglements and outsize appetites undo the distance between the captives and the worlds that surround them and, crucially, complicate the stories that they tell about themselves. As in *La Lozana andaluza*, intimacy undoes authority as much as it enhances it.

The ludic figures who provide comic relief in these texts inherit the knowingness and slipperiness of the *Viaje*, combining the first-person authority of the traveler Pedro with the corruption and prejudice of his interlocutors back home. These unreliable *pícaros* manipulate the story to their advantage, all while betraying their own close engagements across confessional lines. While they vociferously mock and torment Jews and Muslims, they nonetheless betray an intimate knowledge of confessional others. Their frequent recourse to cultural ventriloquism, moreover, constantly qualifies the force of their own experiences, on which the authority of the captive as narrator necessarily depends.

Especially when juxtaposed with actual scenes of martyrdom within the text, the *pícaros'* opportunistic invocation of religion reveals them as fundamentally unreliable. Like Pedro, they have firsthand knowledge of the world of Islam and survive to tell the story, when others choose death over conversion.

Both *Baños* and *La Gran Sultana* feature a figure of misrule who voices the most explicit anti-Semitic and anti-Islamic prejudice in the text. Critics have struggled to characterize these figures: in ethical terms, their humor emphatically fails to translate for modern sensibilities and produces instead a profound discomfort. In formal terms, they do not match the characteristics of the Lopean *gracioso*, who serves as the hero or heroine's aide and counsel and is generally a sympathetic figure.[37] In fact, Cervantes's ludic figures are not servants but instead function independently;[38] they paradoxically enjoy far greater latitude in their actions, despite their status as captives. Theirs are not the familiar transgressions of *graciosos*, which involve primarily breaching class decorum in their relations with their masters. Instead, they systematically undo the very religious and civic hierarchies that they invoke. Reading these ludic figures as *pícaros* sheds new light on the plays, foregrounding the basic unreliability of the witness/narrator and challenging the force of the captivity narrative. The mutability of the captive *pícaros*, based on their circumstance and situatedness, reprises the unreliability of the captive's authorial positionality in the *Viaje*. The plays portray the messiness of captivity as it occurs, further ironizing the version that the captive will recollect after the fact. The inherently perspectival nature of drama, moreover, underscores the partiality of the *pícaro*'s version of events, underscoring the limitations of his narrative authority.[39]

Most striking is the picaresque figures' negotiation of cultural difference while in captivity. Strong prejudice coexists with an enduring fascination with both Muslims and Jews, whom the *pícaros* cannot seem to leave alone, whether in North Africa or in Constantinople. In both *Baños* and *La Gran Sultana*, they betray an intimate understanding of such matters as Jewish dietary law and the restrictions of the Sabbath, which they use to torture the miserable Jews on stage. In both plays, too, they voice an erotic fascination with Muslim women. Via their engagement with the abject and the forbidden, these Cervantine figures embody a cultural lability that the texts must paradoxically discount in their efforts to sustain Christian exceptionality. The *pícaros'* erotic attachments, moreover, further destabilize any effective othering of the Semitic. Although the characters transgress as they entertain, they also voice a cultural and erotic proximity that is often unspeakable in more serious registers.

In the main plot of *Baños*, the fascination with a veiled and forbidden Muslim femininity is explored through the figure of Zara, with whom Don Lope falls in love after she gives him money to rescue himself, and who, the logic of the plot demands, must prove to be a secret Christian (a plot that Cervantes revisits in the much better known "Captive's Tale" in the first part of *Don Quijote*). Zara's ultimate conversion neutralizes the exogamous fascination, reinscribing Christian dominance: whatever erotic entanglement develops between her and Lope is ultimately (and teleologically) in the service of the Christian religion. At the level of the humorous subplots, however, there is no saving grace—no secret identity redeems the fascination. Thus the erotic thrall to the other remains far more disruptive, as humor reveals what cannot otherwise be spoken.

The picaresque *gracioso* in *Baños* is an irreverent sexton named Tristán, introducing an echo of the anticlerical satire that animates the *Viaje*. (Is this what Mátalas Callando or Juan de Voto a Dios would be like as captives?) Pervasively identified with his role, Tristán is referred to as "Sacristán" from the *dramatis personae* on, even though he performs no such function in Algiers, where no church requires his services. Instead, he is characterized by his appetites and his irreverence, even as he insistently—and lewdly—underscores his role in ringing the bells to broadcast his religion and congregate the faithful. When corsairs attack his town to take captives, he laments: "Como persona aplicada a la Iglesia, y no al trabajo, / mejor meneo el badajo / que desenvaino la espada"[40] ["As a person dedicated to the Church rather than to work, I can ring a clapper better than I unsheathe a sword"]. Interrogated by his captors on his profession, he explains: "Como yo soy sacristán/ toco el din, el don y el dan / a cualquiera hora del día" (739–41) ["I'm a sexton, so I play *ding, dong* at any time of day"]. And when he contemplates his return to Spain, it is once again with reference to his bells:

¡Oh campanas de España!
¿Cuándo entre aquestas manos
tendré vuestros badajos?
¿Cuándo haré el tic y toc o el grave empino?
¿Cuándo de los bodigos
que por los pobres muertos
ofrecen ricas viudas
veré mi arcaz colmado? (2860–67)

[O bells of Spain! When shall I hold your clappers in these hands? When shall I make the ding and dong or the solemn ascent? When will I see my coffer filled with the rolls that rich widows give in remembrance of the poor departed ones?]

Beyond the ribaldry of Tristán's obsession with bells and clappers, these passages underscore the strong synecdochal association between the sexton and the Catholic church, much like the synecdoche of *campana* for *iglesia* that Covarrubias notes in his *Tesoro*.[41] Thus his symbolic association with the church is both emphasized and satirized, even as he transgresses in Algiers.

The Sacristán is also the only character to emphasize his Old Christian origins: "Es mi tierra Mollorido, / un lugar muy escondido, / allá en Castilla la Vieja" (83) ["My homeland is Mollorido, a very remote village in Old Castile"].[42] Yet in his encounters with the more earnest Christians in the bagnio, he pragmatically insists that he will eat meat whenever his master gives him any, and not only on the permitted days, proclaiming, "Que no hay aquí teologías" ("There are no theologies here," 1160–66). Hunger undoes any conviction or morality, in the best picaresque tradition. The Sacristán's interlocutor, whose young son will become a martyr by the end of the play, warns Tristán about the slippery slope of apostasy. His counterexample to the Sacristán's moral relativism is none other than the story of the martyred Maccabees:

VIEJO: ¿No te recuerdas, por ventura,
de aquellos niños hebreos
que nos cuenta la Escritura?
SACRISTAN: ¿Dirás por los Macabeos,
que, por no comer grosura,
se dejaron hacer piezas? (1167–72)

[*OLD MAN:* "Don't you remember, by chance, those Hebrew children in Scripture?"
SEXTON: "You must mean the Maccabees, who let themselves be sliced to pieces rather than eat pork."]

The story in Maccabees 7:1–42 features *Jewish* martyrs gladly embracing death rather than breaking dietary law—a highly ironic tale for two Christian captives to recall, insofar as it invokes the contemporary Spanish persecution of *conversos* and underscores the continuities between Judaism and Christianity.[43]

Moreover, the reference to the "Hebrew" Maccabees anticipates the portrayal of the Jew as the one who sticks to his law, and the Sacristán's testing of that resolve as he encounters the Jews of Algiers.

From dietary temptations, the Viejo turns to the erotic threat of Islamic women to Tristán's Christian identity: "Yo recelo / que si una mora os da el pie/deis vos de mano a ese celo" (1179–81) ["I fear that if something's afoot with a Moorish woman, you'll hand over such zeal"]. The Sacristán claims he has already received such offers, although he has not yet acted upon them: "Luego no me han dado ya / más de dos lo que quizá / otro no lo desechara?" (1182–84) ["Now, haven't two already given me what another might not reject?"].

The Sacristán's most extensive reflection on the lure of the *mora* is spoken in jest, to discomfit the corsair captain Caurali, who is actually in love with a Christian. When the Christians are allowed to present a play in the bagnio, Tristán derails it by launching into an extended praise of his (imaginary) Moorish beloved, presumably in the voice of the Moor. The clue lies in the stage direction: "*Todo cuanto dice agora el Sacristán, lo diga mirando al soslayo a Caurali*" ["*Everything that the Sexton says now, he says looking sideways at Caurali*"]. Tristán simultaneously ventriloquizes and satirizes desire for the Moor, rehearsing a poem that Cervantes uses also in the novella "El amante liberal," where two Spanish poets fall for a beautiful blonde *mora* in a more earnest moment.[44] The Sacristán's humorous evocation of exogamous desire undercuts the ideological certainties of the main plot, in which Moors automatically fall for Christians, but Christians only love Moors if they turn out to be Christians in the end. Although voiced in jest, the poem nonetheless bespeaks an erotic intimacy that the play, with its strong warnings against apostasy, would otherwise belie. As in *Lozana*, the erotic register features unexpected *ayuntamientos* that simultaneously bolster and compromise narrative authority.

The intimation of Christian desire for a Moor deflected in *Baños* returns more forcefully in *La Gran Sultana*. Its main plot centers on the love of an Ottoman emperor for the Christian Spanish captive Catalina, who so enchants him that he agrees to let her retain her faith, even at the heart of the Muslim world. Yet a humorous subplot presents exogamous desire in a more complicated light. The *pícaro* in *La Gran Sultana* is the captive Madrigal, whose name evokes both Madrid and *madrigado* (experienced, practiced).[45] Like the Sacristán, he is granted a kind of official status as the Spanish voice of the text. Whereas the Sacristán refers constantly to his ringing of the bells, Madrigal tells his captors that he is a *pregonero*, or town crier (2162).[46] The play insistently links him both to ventriloquism and to privileged speech, as he invents a series of linguistic hoaxes to prolong his life, from promising the Cadí that he will teach an elephant how to speak, to claiming that he can interpret prophecies offered by birds. Despite these perversions of his role as mouthpiece, Madrigal becomes by the end a veritable author figure, who announces he will carry the story that the audience has just witnessed safely back to Madrid.

Yet this conclusion is by no means evident as the play begins. Madrigal has been seduced by an "alárabe," a dalliance that makes him reluctant to escape captivity. In his first encounter with the spy Andrea, who offers to help him get away, the captive demurs, explaining, "Son las leyes / del gusto poderosas sobretodo" (502–3) ["The laws of taste are powerful over all"]. This is not the spy's first attempt to get him out, he reminds Madrigal, as he questions the captive's partial and interested recollection:

ANDREA: La memoria
tenéis dada a adobar, a lo que entiendo,
o reducida a voluntad no buena.
¿No os acordáis que os vi y hablé la noche
que recogí a los cinco y vos quisistes
quedaros por no más de vuestro gusto,
poniendo por excusa que os tenía
amor rendida el alma, y que una alárabe,
con nuevo cautiverio y nuevas leyes,
os la tenía encadenada y presa?
MADRIGAL: Verdad; y aun todavía tengo el yugo
al cuello, todavía estoy cautivo,
todavía la fuerza poderosa
de amor tiene sujeto a mi albedrío. (484–97)

[*ANDREA:* "Your memory's gone to rot, as far as I can tell, or been reduced to no good purposes. Don't you remember that I saw you and spoke to you the night I picked up those five, and you wanted to stay solely for your pleasure, with the excuse that your soul had surrendered to love, and that an Arab woman had imprisoned and chained it in a new captivity and new laws?"

MADRIGAL: "True; and I still have the yoke around my neck, I'm still captive, the great power of love still rules over me."]

Madrigal's *cautiverio*, it turns out, is more Petrarchan metaphor than actual hardship, and his willing service sends up the earnest suffering on which a captivity plot would seem to depend. In a striking contravention of the captivity narrative's assumptions, Madrigal languishes in Constantinople because that is what he desires, and he conveniently forgets what he prefers not to remember.

In the face of Madrigal's erotic thralldom, and his reluctance to fight his *gusto*, Andrea taunts him: "¿No sois vos español?" (506) ["Are you not a Spaniard?"]. Madrigal's lengthy and blustery bravado in response is clearly compensatory, as he protests all too much about his wish to be gone:

MADRIGAL: ¿Por qué? ¿Por esto?
Pues por las once mil de malla juro
y por el alto, dulce, omnipotente
deseo que se encierra bajo el hopo
de cuatro acomodados porcionistas,
que he de romper por montes de diamantes,
y por dificultades indecibles
y he de llevar mi libertad en peso
sobre los propios hombros de mi gusto,
y entrar triunfando en Nápoles la bella
con dos o tres galeras levantadas
por mi industria o valor, y Dios delante,
y dando a la Anunciada los dos bucos,
quedaré con el uno rico y próspero,
y no ponerme ahora a andar por trena,
cargado de temor y de miseria.
ANDREA: ¡Español sois, sin duda! (507–22)

[*MADRIGAL:* "Why? Because of this? Well, by the eleven thousand coats of mail, and by the high, sweet, potent desire under the collar of four rich boarders, I swear that I will break through mountains of diamonds and unspeakable obstacles, and I shall hoist my liberty on the very shoulders of my pleasure, and enter triumphant into the beautiful Naples with two or three galleys that will have rebelled because of my cleverness and valor, and God willing, after giving two ships to the Annunziata, I'll live rich and prosperous with the other one, instead

of wandering through the bagnios weighed down with misery
and dread."
ANDREA: "You're a Spaniard, there's no question!"]

Despite the outsize oath that supposedly identifies Madrigal as a Spaniard, not even his own fantasy can see him back to Spain. It instead leaves him in a Mediterranean limbo, plying the sea on a galley, as elusive and ambiguous as ever. Given the prevalent stereotype of the Spaniard as *miles gloriosus*, moreover, Andrea's conclusion reads as an ironic indictment.

Although the *pícaro* finally manages to tear himself away, presumably taking the story to Madrid, his tangential love plot is never resolved. Madrigal's *gusto* does not align itself neatly with the large-scale ideological maneuvers of the text or its categorizations; instead, it remains personal, unpredictable, and irrepressible.[47] If the permeability of race and religion is especially pronounced for abject characters, as it was in Rome's Pozo Blanco, *pícaros* and captives share a particular susceptibility. The more desperate their situation, the greater their need or appetite, the more unlikely these characters are to sustain identitarian difference, however much they proclaim it or anathemize it in others.

While eros establishes a paradoxical intimacy between Spaniards and their ostracized others in *Baños* and *La Gran Sultana*, food quickly becomes similarly charged, as anticipated by the reference to the Maccabees noted above. In comic subplots that have not aged well, to say the least, Tristán and Madrigal continuously taunt and torture the Jews of Algiers and Constantinople, respectively, who often appear even more abject than the captives. As Ruth Fine puts it, the plays exhibit "un notorio conocimiento de . . . las leyes de *kashrut*" (442) ["a striking knowledge of the laws of *kashrut*"], suggesting the store of cultural knowledge that underlies the *pícaros'* highly effective attacks. While *La Gran Sultana* features trite jokes about spoiling Jewish food with bacon, the negotiation of dietary law in *Baños* is more detailed and extensive. In a powerful catachresis, food becomes a stand-in for the captives themselves. Much as the famous episode of the *paraíso panal* (breadly paradise) in *Lazarillo* ironizes not just the lack of charity from one master but Catholic theology more broadly,[48] these episodes go beyond anti-Semitism to problematize the moral force of captivity.

In Act II of *Baños*, the Sacristán enters with a dish he has stolen from a Jew. He flaunts his power over his victim, which depends on the religious prohibitions ("mi ley," 1681) that circumscribe the Jew's actions and render him even more helpless than the Spanish captive who baits him. Offering the dish up for ransom ("Rescátame esta cazuela" ["Ransom this stew from me"], 1682), Tristán interrogates the inanimate *cazuela* on its own worth and voices its responses: "Di, cazuela: ¿cuánto vales? / 'Paréceme a mí que valgo / cinco reales, y no más.' / ¡Mentís, a fe de hidalgo!" (1701–4) ["Tell me, pot: what are you worth? 'I think I'm worth five *reales*, and no more.' You lie, by my faith as a gentleman!"]. Tristán's ventriloquizing reminds the audience of the incommensurability between the mock *fe de hidalgo* and the Jew's all too earnest *mi ley*. Tristán is emphatically not an *hidalgo*, and has previously made it clear just how flexible his own hunger renders him where *teologías* are concerned. His ability to speak in different voices here, as in the episode where he ventriloquizes love for a Moorish woman, challenges the notion of any self-identical core to the captive's voice, and relativizes his attachment to orthodoxy, especially by contrast to the Jew, who will not allow circumstances to get in the way of his observance.

The injuries mount when the Jew must ask the Sacristán to take the money from his shirt to ransom the *cazuela*. Tristán takes three times as much as he had claimed, vowing to give the Jew credit for the *cazuelas* he has yet to steal from him. Before turning over the dish, he further taunts the Jew, tasting it and detailing all the *tref* (non-kosher) elements it does not contain: "¿Que hay tan gustoso guisado? / No es carne de landrecillas / ni de la que a las costillas / se pega el bayo que es trefe" (1716–19) ["Is there any such delicious dish? It's not nerve meat, nor meat that sticks to the ribs of the bay horse, which is *tref*"]. As Fine notes, the detailed account here of what meat can and cannot be eaten, and the use of the Hebrew *trefe*, or *tref*, bespeaks an intimate familiarity with Jewish dietary law.[49] In his mockery, the Sacristán speaks as a Jew. As in his faux plaint for a Moorish beloved, or his comical voicing of the *cazuela*'s worth, the *pícaro* endows the captive with a range of voices. To do captivity in different voices, as T. S. Eliot might say, is to underscore the opportunistic ventriloquism of the captive instead of his probity.

Perhaps the most extreme example of ventriloquism in *Baños* is when Tristán embodies anti-Semitic stereotypes in order to attack the Jew. After demanding ransom for the Jew's *cazuela*, Tristán next vows to take the Jew's child: "¡Vive Dios, / que os tengo de hurtar un niño / antes de los meses dos: / y aun si las uñas aliño . . . !/¡Dios me entiende!" (1722–26) ["By God, I shall rob a child from you before two months are up; and if I season its feet . . . ! God knows what I mean!"]. Between the two invocations of his God, the Sacristán terrifyingly threatens to steal the child and eat him, once he has improved the flavor. The threat is partially carried out in Act III, when he appears before the Cadí carrying the Jew's baby son (2514 and following). As Or Hasson notes, the episode inverts the anti-Semitic chestnut that Jews steal

Christian children.[50] The stage direction, which specifies that no real child be subjected to this treatment, betrays the violence of the scene: "(*Entra el SACRISTAN con un niño en las mantillas, fingido, y tras él el JUDIO de la cazuela*)" ["Enter the *SEXTON with a baby in blankets, make-believe, and behind him the JEW of the casserole*"]. The more savage appetites insinuated earlier to scare the Jew are rendered here as the baby's delectability, though the Sacristán simultaneously claims that he wants the child for ransom, and will bring it up as a Christian if the Jew does not pay up:

> *CADI:* ¿Para qué quiere el niño?
> *SACRISTAN:* ¿No está bueno?
> Para que le rescaten, si no quieren
> que le críe y le enseñe el Padrenuestro. (2517–21)

> [*CADÍ:* "What does he want the child for?"
> *SEXTON:* "Isn't he a good/tasty one? So that they ransom him, if they don't want me to raise him and teach him the Our Father."]

If he does not physically consume the child, that is, he will incorporate him into the body of Christianity. The irony in forcibly converting a captive child, albeit to Christianity, is patent here, as the play anticipates in a comic key its most tragic dimension.[51] Before this can happen, the Cadí quickly resolves the issue of the kidnapped Jewish baby, demanding his return while agreeing to make the Jew pay Tristán for the time he took to steal him. Despite the redoubled joke on the Jewish scapegoat and the oblivious Muslim judge, the cruelty of the moment is never fully resolved, especially as that resolution would depend on Tristán's probity. For the Jews decide to redeem Tristán themselves in order to free themselves of his torments, yet the *pícaro* reserves the right to break his word: "Yo he dado mi palabra / de no hurtarles cosa / mientras me fuere a España / y por Dios que no sé si he de cumplirla" (2836–39) ["I've given my word not to rob anything from them while I make my way to Spain, and by God, I don't know if I'll keep it"]. The contradictory counter-oath—"por Dios que no sé si he de cumplirla"—makes Tristán an ever more equivocal figure, particularly in the context of negotiations for ransom such as Christian captives would depend on.[52]

Both Tristán's dubious approach to his faith and his menace to a Jewish child hang in the air in the key scene that occurs between the ransoming of the Jewish baby and that of Tristán himself. The cruel humor of the baby's kidnapping anticipates the most tragic and melodramatic of *Baños'* many plots: the martyrdom of young Francisquito, who refuses to convert to Islam. Immediately following the courtroom burlesque above, the Viejo witnesses on stage his son's martyrdom and, anguished, welcomes it as an *imitatio Christi*. This extraordinarily heightened moment cannot but color what comes immediately before it. Even if farce here precedes tragedy, the analogies between the two episodes are unavoidable: while Tristán jokingly threatens to raise his Jewish captive into forced Christianity, the young Francisquito's resistance to forced conversion to Islam leads to his bloody death.[53]

Yet what significance can we ultimately ascribe to characters whom even the most sophisticated critics would marginalize as "limited to the sphere of the ridiculous and grotesque"?[54] Cervantes clearly underscores their emblematic potential: the Sacristán as synecdoche of the church; Madrigal as the mouthpiece of Spanishness. At the same time, their pleasure and appetite complicate any sense of distinction, as they actively consume Jews and their food, and sleep with Muslim women. Their sensual engagement, however qualified by humor, challenges the notion that identitarian difference—much less any kind of Christian exceptionalism—underlies captivity.

As these irredeemable Christians engage the other in visceral detail, in a resolutely anti-idealizing vision of Mediterranean connectedness, they embody a version of captivity that is fallen, interested, fully implicated. Moreover, the venality of the captive *pícaros'* voices—their justifications, facile ventriloquizing, and questionable oaths—undoes any authority that their experience of captivity might grant them. Especially when juxtaposed with an actual martyr, a *pícaro* who lives to tell his tale renders that story dubious. As they enact on stage the complexities of what it means to be a knowing captive, Cervantes's Madrigal and Tristán bring home what the *Viaje de Turquía* had already made clear: the negotiation of authority and interestedness, witnessing and appetite, problematizes the distinction between captive and *pícaro*.

Chapter 3

"O te digo verdades o mentiras"

Crediting the *Pícaro* in *Guzmán de Alfarache*

> Aun aquellos à quien jusgamos ánjeles entre nosotros, tengo por sin duda, que si un poco los manoseásemos, los hallaríamos umanos, i vestidos de nuestra misma carne, sin escaparse alguno, que no la tenga ribeteada de inorancias, descuidos, pasiones i flaquezas. (Mateo Alemán, *Ortografía castellana*, 113)
>
> [Even those whom we judge as angels among us, I am certain, were we to handle them a bit, we would find human and clothed in our same flesh, for none can escape its marbling with ignorance, carelessness, passions and weaknesses.]

Unlike the sui generis, motley texts that I have considered in earlier chapters, Mateo Alemán's two-part *Vida del pícaro Guzmán de Alfarache* (1599, 1604) is often considered the echt-picaresque.[1] Perhaps more clearly than *Lozana* or the *Viaje de Turquía*, *Guzmán* reveals how the picaresque ironizes the force of the narrative "I" as guarantor of truth. Fully implicated in the story he tells, Guzmán famously alternates between moralizing retrospectively in the voice of a reformed *pícaro* and minutely relating the adventures that eventually necessitated his reformation. The text thus serves as an examination, in a consummately unreliable voice, of the kinds of narrative that might stand in for an unavailable or even indeterminable truth. Unlike *Lozana* or even *Don Quijote*, in which the contest for narrative authority becomes an explicit part of the text and its form, the *Guzmán* internalizes the struggle, giving us a single narrator and his imperfect attempts to convince the reader, whom he repeatedly addresses.

Critics have long debated how convincing Guzmán proves, noting how late his reformation comes within an extensive diegesis of picaresque mayhem. Much of the renewed interest in the text from the 1980s on has been the product of this critical skepticism.[2] At the same time, the most recent generation of critics to take the text at its word, arguing for the moral force of Guzmán's narrative voice, underscores its commitment to reform and to the social nature of morality.[3] My interest is less in the intentionality of *Guzmán de Alfarache* than in the way it complicates the supposed referentiality and reliability of the first-person voice. Relentlessly ironizing the truth of narratives, the *Guzmán* highlights how much of its own context is discursively produced, in a constant negotiation among often contradictory texts.[4] This chapter revisits the critical suspicion of Guzmán in relation to the texts and institutions that the narrator ironizes, especially the inquisitions into virtue and origins that so dominated the period, to argue for the skeptical force of the picaresque. Beyond the text's concerns with intimate genealogies, its geographic capaciousness, including the *pícaro*'s extensive adventures in Italy, further problematizes its negotiation of authority and truth. Perhaps most corrosively, the *pícaro*'s perverse manipulation of credit—as both ethical reliability and economic trust—upends the mechanisms of interpersonal and commercial exchange on which early modern mercantile circuits increasingly relied.

An Inquisition into Origins

Although Guzmán relates many different kinds of deception, he is particularly fixated on questions of origins, genealogy, and class. From Américo Castro on, critics have read this sort of textual preoccupation as evidence for authors' *converso* origins.[5] Beyond the uncertain evidence for Alemán himself, I am less concerned with the autobiographical register than with the broader intersection of literary fiction and social anxiety, as expressed in the epistemological questions that the first-person narrator obsessively revisits. In a series of preliminary paratexts variously addressed to different classes of readers, from a nobleman to the *vulgo* to the *discreto lector*, Alemán's narrator appears just as preoccupied with origins as his protagonist. The dedications attempt to fix hierarchies, yet much like the text itself they ultimately reflect the fragility and opacity of social categories. As Guzmán's own first-person narrative demonstrates, perceptions of identity and lineage are highly susceptible to inflation, despite the careful mechanisms set in place to verify origins. The *pícaro*'s account provides alternative versions of the self, underscoring the partiality and interestedness of any such narrative.

In an early modern Spanish context of profound anxiety about genealogy, a whole range of bureaucratic and judicial procedures existed to try to place subjects within a social hierarchy, in an increasingly racialized religious landscape. Legal and bureaucratic procedures, of which *probanzas* are the best known, examined subjects and their associates for their legitimacy and *limpieza de sangre* (absence of Semitic origins), and more generally for the status and lineage of their families. Procedures for granting university positions, for example, included complex investigations *de vita et moribus*.[6] As Baltasar Cuart Moner notes, everyone knew how much was at stake in such processes and how likely it was that witnesses would be swayed by their own sympathies or antipathies, or by the influence of those investigated; similarly, all involved recognized that memory itself, as well as the process of relating what they remembered to investigators, was fully manipulable.[7] The investigations *de vita et moribus* were only one genre of inquiry into origins and identity: *averiguaciones de limpieza, relaciones de méritos y servicios,* and so forth were all similarly susceptible to the manipulations that Cuart Moner records.[8]

The *pícaro*'s amoral, interested narrative picks up on this profoundly flawed system of identitarian certification, flouting legalities and social constraints to offer a different version of how identity is constructed. Guzmán's pointed satire of prestige for sale or identities easily fabricated on the move is fictional, to be sure, yet it slyly signals the extent to which every identity was also susceptible to fictionalization. The restlessness of the *pícaro* and the resulting episodic narrative increasingly removes him from his origins, making them more difficult to trace. As the 1551 testimony cited by Cuart Moner states, "siempre los advenedizos traen sospecha con su benida"[9] ["those who have just arrived are always suspect for their coming here"]. Thus even the episodic form and constant displacements of the picaresque refract the suspicion attendant upon those who move between geographic or social spaces.

Alemán's prefatory paratexts, which occupy the liminal zone between the text and the world, return obsessively to the problem of status and reputation. Their narrator appears exquisitely sensitive to how writing the picaresque exposes him to calumny. His address to Francisco de Rojas, Marquess of Poza, imagines the act of dedication, rather than anything in the book itself, as the greatest transgression, from which only the nobleman's ample clemency will shelter him. Beyond the conventionality of *captatio benevolentiae*, Alemán imagines the marquess's favor trumping all social distinctions: his protection will transform the protagonist, making "de un desechado pícaro un admitido cortesano"[10] ["of a shunned *pícaro* an admitted courtier"]. The conventional wishful fantasy from a struggling author addressing an exalted reader nonetheless anticipates the stakes of a narrative centrally concerned with what the *pícaro* can be and how far he can be transformed.

Conversely, the pugnacious prefatory letter to the uneducated ("Al vulgo") condemns not only the ignorance of that potential audience, but their predilection for calumny and dishonor: "qué presto en disfamar, qué tardo en honrar" (1:108) ["how quick to defame, how slow to honor"]. A long list of rhetorical questions charts the malice of this vulgar reader (or listener), who is not only ready to find fault where there is none, but unwilling to dissimulate what faults do exist: "¿Cuáles defetos cubre tu capa? ¿Cuál atriaca miran tus ojos, que como basilisco no emponzoñes? ¿Cuál flor tan cordial entró por tus oídos, que en el enjambre de tu corazón dejases de convertir en veneno? ¿Qué santidad no calumnias? ¿Qué inocencia no persigues?" (1:108) ["What defects does your cape cover? What antidote do you look upon without poisoning it like a basilisk? What cordial flower enters your ears without becoming venom in the hive that is your heart? What sanctity do you not slander? What innocence do you not persecute?"]. Alemán plays a game of dare with his reader that is reminiscent of Cervantes's *Retablo de las maravillas*—if he or she participates in the calumny, he or she belongs in the category of the uneducated.[11]

The next preface turns to the wise reader ("Al discreto lector") for refuge and consolation, while also admitting that the book has been misrepresented: "Empeñeme con la promesa deste libro; hame sido forzoso seguir el envite que hice de falso" (1:110) ["I pledged myself with the promise of this book; now I've been forced to follow through on my bluff"]. The doubleness of *empeñar*—to pursue something, and to pawn or leave as security—further complicates the claim here: the author's determination to go forward involves borrowed credit as well as the card sharp's trickery. As credit itself becomes a loaded term within the *Guzmán*, setting trust into mercantile circulation and mobilizing it for chicanery, the metaphorics of this preface become ever more resonant.

Unlike the dedication to the Marquess, which imagined the *pícaro* ennobled by the nobleman's favor, the preface to the *discreto* envisions a very different kind of transformation. Whatever the learned reader might find in the text that is neither "grave ni compuesto" (1:112) ["serious or composed"], the author warns, is simply due to "el ser de un pícaro el sujeto de este libro" (1:112) ["this book having a *pícaro* as its subject"]. Yet he then encourages the reader to slum as he or she reads, becoming in effect a *pícaro*: "Las tales cosas, aunque sean muy pocas, picardea con ellas" (1:112) ["with those things, although they be very few, make like a *pícaro*"]. Although the entire text is ostensibly offered for its moral value as a counterexample ("no te rías de la conseja y se te pase el consejo" ["do not laugh at the tale and miss the moral"], 1:111), the author here imagines readers who might treat picaresque episodes as exempla. In an echo of the instrumentalized *Viaje de Turquía*, the suggestion that a knowing fiction might serve as an example for its readers threatens to radically shift its purpose and ironize its significance.

Alemán's paratexts work within the conventions of the dedication—self-deprecation, *captatio benevolentiae*, praise for the patron and the educated reader. Yet they also enact a hierarchy of readers only to recall its fragility: the *pícaro* ennobled, or conversely the slumming reader. Moreover, as the invitation to *picardear* suggests, the transformations of identity within the *Guzmán* extend beyond class to morals. How then to reconcile the *pícaro* whose adventures we trace in its pages with the first-person narrator who claims repentance as he relates them? His moralizing offers the illusion of access to a reformed self, but only foregrounds the question of that self's opacity.[12] If what the narrative offers is a series of tricks, what is to say that the revelations themselves are any more reliable?

In the prefatory "Declaración para el entendimiento de este libro" ["Declaration for the Understanding of this Book"], Alemán takes on the problems caused by the publication of only half the *pícaro*'s story. (This moment anticipates the problem of Ginés de Pasamonte's narrative in *Don Quijote* 1.22, which I discuss in Chapter 4.) Only the entirety of Guzmán's story, which Alemán had not written by the time he published the first volume in 1599, but which he nonetheless announces as done, will reveal the moral arc that leads to the narrator's reformation. Much depends on the claim that Alemán uses to justify the first person's moralizing tone:

> Él mismo escribe su vida desde las galeras, donde queda forzado al remo por delitos que cometió, habiendo sido ladrón famosísimo, como largamente lo verás en la segunda parte. Y no es impropiedad ni fuera de propósito si en esta primera escribiere alguna dotrina; que antes parece muy llegado a razón darla un hombre de claro entendimiento, ayudado de letras y castigado del tiempo, aprovechándose del ocioso de la galera. (1:113)

> [He himself writes his life from the galleys, where he is forced to row for the crimes he committed, having been a most famous thief, as you shall see at length in the second part. And it is not an impropriety or impertinent if in this first part he should write some doctrine; rather it seems most reasonable for a man of clear understanding to offer it, aided by learning and chastised by time, making good use of idle moments on the galley.]

The uncertainty about origins that will haunt the *Guzmán* is thus matched by an uncertainty about ends: how exactly does the *pícaro* get from immorality to morality, and what kind of trust in the narrator can sustain the reader in the temporal gap before the second part? What does it mean to publish an entire text that does not include the rationale for its narrative voice, except in the extraneous paratext designed for that purpose, and which can only claim a retrospective logic? In a sense, Alemán's insistence that the end of *Guzmán* is the key to believing or understanding the eponymous narrator may be read as a corrective to the overdetermined inquisition into origins in early modern Spain: what matters is not beginnings but endings. However much Guzmán ponders his own genealogy, however problematic his many adventures, all that this extensive narration achieves is to postpone the supposed reformation that both authorizes him and makes him an author.

Guzmán's opening salvo to his readers invokes the context of scholastic inquiry, such as the *de vita et moribus* investigations, that could quickly shade into very personal inquisitions. In a first chapter, significantly entitled "En que cuenta quién fue su padre"[13] (1:125) ["In Which He Relates Who Was His Father"], Guzmán claims to have been in such a hurry to tell his story that he neglected his origins: "Me olvidaba de cerrar un portillo por donde me pudiera entrar acusando cualquier terminista de mal latín, redarguyéndome de pecado, porque no procedí de la difinición a lo difinido, y antes de contarla no dejé dicho quiénes y cuáles fueron mis padres" (1:125–26) ["I was forgetting to close the loophole through which any scholastic with bad Latin could get in {to me}, accusing me, arguing that I had sinned because I did not proceed from the definition to the thing defined, and did not establish who and which my parents were before telling it"]. Beyond the striking sexualization of the probing second-rate scholastic, Guzmán's defensiveness in this passage highlights precisely that which he would avoid. Although he admits there is no way to bypass his lineage, his extensive preamble sets up a supremely self-conscious and deliberate version of the story. Still Guzmán demurs—he wants neither to be like the hyena, who digs up dead bodies, nor to break the commandment to honor his parents. Ultimately, he decides to proceed only because relating the "puro y verdadero texto" (1:127) ["pure and true text"] of their story might undo the glosses that have adorned it. His detailed account of how susceptible the story is to perspective and interest stands as a warning to the reader:

> Pues cada vez que alguno algo dello cuenta, lo multiplica con los ceros de su antojo, una vez más y nunca menos, como acude la vena y se le pone en capricho; que hay hombre [que], si se le ofrece propósito para cuadrar su cuento, deshará las pirámidas de Egipto, haciendo de la pulga gigante, de la presunción evidencia, de lo oído visto y ciencia de la opinión, sólo por florear su elocuencia y acreditar su discreción. (1:127)
>
> [For any time that someone tells of it, he multiplies it with as many zeroes as he pleases, making more of it but never less, as the whim takes him. For there are those who, in order to square their story, will tear down the pyramids of Egypt, making a giant of a flea, evidence of surmises, something seen of what was merely heard, and science of opinion, only to show off their eloquence and credit their intelligence.]

As in the *Viaje*, the knowing fiction sounds its warning: *caveat lector*. The mercantile overtones of the multiplying zero anticipate the problem of Guzmán's merchant and Semitic origins, while the reference to the pyramids places him even further beyond a Spanish context. Perspective is everything as the story is squared. The central concern becomes how truth is constructed, and for what purpose: once presumption becomes evidence, hearsay witnessing, or opinion science, all to bring credit to the teller, it becomes very difficult to rely on any particular version of the story.

When Guzmán finally gives us the story of his parents, it becomes clear why it required such extensive prefacing. As Anne Cruz notes, "His is . . . an overdetermined status, one that encompasses all the dubious circumstances of the 'other.'"[14] Famously, the narrator identifies a certain *levantisco* (man of the Levant/man from the east, 1:130) merchant as his father, while his mother, mistress to a "caballero viejo de hábito militar" (1:144) ["old gentleman in military garb"], could not really have said whose son he was. The boy's name will reflect the uncertainty: once all possible fathers are dead, Guzmán abandons his mother, his house, and his name, taking her fanciful, aggrandizing last name as his first, and a place name—Alfarache—as his last.[15]

Guzmán notes the possibilities of deception about rank and lineage as part of his general moralizing, but also experiences them firsthand. His moralizing commentary about such deception, far more pronounced in Part 2, is offered in part to ensure that it will not succeed again:

> El mal nacido y por tal conocido quiere con hinchazón y soberbia ganar nombre de poderoso, porque bien mal tiene cuatro maravedís, dando con su mal proceder causa que hagan burla dellos, diciendo quién son, qué principio tuvo su linaje, de dónde comenzó su caballería, cuánto le costó la nobleza y el oficio en que trataron sus padres y quiénes fueron sus madres. Piensan estos engañar y engáñanse. . . . Otros engañan con fieros, para hacerse valientes, como si no supiésemos que sólo aquellos lo son que callan. Otros con el mucho hablar y mucha librería quieren ser estimados por sabios y no consideran cuánta mayor la tienen los libreros y no por eso lo son. (2:75)
>
> [One who is of low birth and known as such wishes with haughtiness and arrogance to achieve renown as a powerful man, while he scarcely has four cents to his name, and his ill behavior gives others occasion to mock him, asking who he is, of what origin was his lineage, where his nobility came from, and how much the title cost him, what his father's trade was and who was his mother. These set out to deceive and deceive themselves. . . . Others deceive with their fierce looks, trying to appear brave, as though we did not know that the truly brave keep quiet about it. Others with their talking too much and their many books want to be taken for learned men, and they do not consider how many more books the booksellers have, and they are no wiser for it.]

Unlike the accusatory dedication to the *vulgo* in Part 1, Guzmán's satiric account here involves the reader ("como si no supiésemos") in a general ability to see through deceptions, even as the narrator obliquely pokes fun at his own bookish authority. It also underscores the central role of testimony in the construction of identity: false witnesses are a dime a dozen, easily persuaded to claim "ochenta años de conocimiento" ["eighty years' knowledge"] of a family's history or, alternatively, to destroy "seiscientas mil honras" ["the honor of six hundred thousand"] (2:265).[16] At the same time, the *pícaro* notes the power of wealth to undo all obstacles, making truth relative: "¿Qué alturas no allanó? ¿Cuáles dificultades no venció? ¿Qué imposibles no facilitó?" (2:334) ["What great heights did it not bring low? What difficulties did it not conquer? What impossibles did it not ease?"]. In a perfect circuit, riches undo their own negative effects: "siendo como es un tan ponzoñoso veneno . . . es justamente con esto atriaca de sus mismos daños: en ella está su contraveneno" (2:334) ["although it is a most poisonous venom, it is the antidote to its own harm: in it lies the countervenom"]. As Guzmán's experiences in Italy will confirm, riches can effectively construct an identity no longer bound by the inconvenient facts of one's origins, especially in conjunction with physical distance from the circumstances of birth. Thus, however clear-eyed the moralizing Guzmán might be on the construction of identity, his own experiences exploit the difficulty of ascertaining the truth behind a convincing narrative.

Italian Imposture

Like Lozana in Chapter 1, Guzmán travels from Spain to Italy, although he sets out in search of origins rather than to escape them. As soon as he leaves home, Guzmán announces his desire to "ir a reconocer en Italia mi noble parentela" (1:163) ["go recognize/acknowledge in Italy my noble kin"], even if it is by no means clear that it will be up to him to acknowledge them. In Alemán's text, Italy functions as a mercantile space, a rich terrain for beggars, and a fount of culture. It transforms the *pícaro* so that he ceases to seek his actual origins and instead learns to fake them effectively as he performs a range of identities, enabled by the distance between Spain and Italy. Whether living as a beggar or impersonating wealth, Guzmán experiences the dizzying instability of truth as he tries on different selves.

At the beginning of Part 1 the *pícaro* states vaguely that his father was a "levantisco" who came to reside in Genoa, of a family "agregados a la nobleza; y aunque de allí no naturales, aquí los habré de nombrar como tales" (1:130–31) ["adjoined to the nobility, and although they were not naturals of that place, I will describe them as such here"]. Adjacent to the nobility, and not quite of Genoa, Guzmán's extended family appears almost as ambiguous as the *pícaro* himself. More proximately, Guzmán's *mercader* father introduces a cosmopolitan commercial world into the text, albeit a morally suspect one: his business was "el ordinario de aquella tierra, y lo es ya por nuestros pecados en la nuestra: cambios y recambios por todo el mundo" (1:131) ["the usual one in that country, as it is now for our sins in ours: change and exchange the world over"]. Caught in Italy's financial thrall, Spain unwillingly participates in its economic legerdemain.[17]

Any ambiguity regarding his progenitor's status or ethics is brushed aside as Guzmán decides to seek out his father's family and with it his own advancement. His welcome in Genoa as he tries to claim noble parentage despite his abject appearance is hardly encouraging: "Hecho un espantajo de higuera, quise hacerme de los godos, emparentando con la nobleza de aquella ciudad, publicándome por quien era; y preguntando por la de mi padre, causó en ellos tanto enfado, que me aborrecieron de muerte" (1:378) ["Despite looking like a scarecrow in a fig tree, I pretended to be descended from the Goths, and related to the nobility of that city, announcing who I was, and asking after my father's [family], which made them so angry that they abhorred me to death"].[18] Beyond the general outrage, the response tars the Spaniard as a Jew and further stigmatizes him: "El que menos mal me hizo fue, escupiéndome a la cara, decirme: '¡Bellaco, marrano ¿Sois vos ginovés? ¡Hijo seréis de alguna gran mala mujer, que bien se os echa de ver!' Y como si mi padre fuera hijo de la tierra, o si hubiera de doscientos años atrás fallecido, no hallé rastro de amigo ni pariente suyo" (1:378–79) ["The least offensive was one who spit in my face crying, 'Rogue, *marrano*! You, a Genoese? You must be the son of some great whore, by your appearance!' And as though my father had been born of the earth, or died two hundred years earlier, I could find no trace of any friend or relative of his"].[19] Guzmán's proverbial language as he relates his rejection mocks the ideal of genealogical certainty: he claims an ancient lineage ("hacerme de los godos"), only to find that it is as if his father had disappeared into the depths of history. As an "hijo de la tierra," moreover, his father lacks any patrilinear legitimacy to link him not just to Genoa but to any place in particular.

The only exception to the general rejection of Guzmán's claims comes from an old man, possibly his uncle, who cruelly tricks the young *pícaro*. Offering to host him and to tell him of his noble parentage, the old man instead has him spooked and tossed in a blanket in the middle of the night, so that Guzmán soils himself and hurriedly quits the city. Leaving aside the attacks on his genealogy and ethnicity, the *pícaro* attributes his shaming to his destitution—"con qué pesada burla quisieron desterrarme, porque no los deshonrara mi pobreza" (1:383) ["with what a cruel jest they set out to banish me, so that my poverty would not shame them"]—and vows to take revenge. The implications are significant: if the shame of poverty is the problem, presenting himself as a rich man, whether he actually is one or not, will afford him the affiliation and respect that he so desires. In fact, Guzmán's extensive time in Italy provides the opportunity for his most sustained transformation, if not in moral terms, then at least as far as his education and self-presentation are concerned.

Guzmán then spends an extended time as a beggar, learning the elaborate codes that organize that "nation." Poverty and any attempt to regulate its exploitation are heavily ironized in this section of the text: in Italy, poverty is but a simulacrum, though remarkably effective and productive. By setting this extensive account of poverty outside Spain, Alemán breaks the ready association of the *pícaro* with Spanish poverty that *Lazarillo* promotes so effectively. At the same time, his representation of beggars abroad strikes many of the same notes as were sounded in contemporary Spain: suspicion of poverty as a performance, anxiety about how to identify authentic need, and a fear of those who had very little to lose.

Beyond the actual crises of the late sixteenth century, poverty was conceived in Spain as a problem of representation, and hence susceptible to imposture. Like the false captives of the *Persiles*, analyzed in Chapter 2, fake beggars could simply learn the ropes. Examining and licensing worthy beggars was widely perceived as the only solution to control false ones, and was recommended by the Council of Trent as well as a series of Spanish reformers.[20] From its very title, the influential treatise on poverty by Cristóbal Pérez de Herrera, *Discursos del amparo de los legítimos pobres y reducción de los fingidos* (1598), focuses obsessively on the performance of poverty and the need to distinguish between the authentic poor and those who just pretend neediness.[21] Yet the reiteration of proposed solutions for the problem of *fingidos* over the course of decades suggests how difficult it was to fully control the self-representation of the poor.[22] Beyond the practical problems posed by the false beggars, they represent a challenge to social mores, as in the case of the former university student who claims that in begging, "estoy quitado de cuidados de honra y de estudios"[23] ["I am free of worrying about honor and studies"]. As Cavillac notes, even efforts to license the poor could go awry, as the authorities were often generous in determining the markers of authenticity that allowed beggars to beg.[24] Well beyond the pages of Alemán's text, the examination of the poor only underscored how every system of licensing confronted the possibility of imposture.

Although Alemán was scathing about the fake poor, he was intensely concerned about poverty, as demonstrated by his correspondence with reformers such as Pérez de Herrera, and his report on the abysmal conditions of the *galeotes* in the mercury mines of Almadén.[25] The Almadén experience is a kind of ground zero of first-person narration: in his role as *juez visitador*, Alemán interrogates the forced laborers directly; they relate their experiences, as Germán Bleiberg notes, "en un repertorio documental que supera con creces la dramática ficción de cualquier novela picaresca"[26] ["in a documentary repertoire that goes well beyond the dramatic fiction of any picaresque novel"]. But the truth proves elusive: perhaps to protect themselves, the *galeotes* give partial answers, rely on indirection, or, quite simply, prove unable to muster a coherent narrative, affected as they are by mercury (*azogados*). The immediacy of their trembling, ravaged bodies must relay their story, yet even that fails to secure reform.

Alemán's novel echoes much of this contemporary discussion about poverty. As he is inducted into the beggars' society, the *pícaro* is questioned by one of its (mock) officials: "Como si fuera protopobre, examinó mi vida, sabiendo de dónde era, cómo me llamaba, cuándo y a qué había venido" (1:388) ["As though he were a licenser of the poor, he examined my life, asking where I was from, what my name was, when and for what I had come"].[27] Alemán's neologism, *protopobre*, puns on *protomédico*, the official in charge of licensing medical professionals since the time of Philip II. Yet even the body can lie, as when the *pícaro* is taught how to feign illness to beg more effectively: "Enseñóme a fingir lepra, hacer llagas, hinchar una pierna, tullir un brazo, teñir el color del rostro, alterar todo el cuerpo" (1:398) ["He taught me how to fake leprosy, make ulcers, swell up a leg, cripple an arm, change the color of my face, and alter my whole body"]. Despite the misery that Alemán had witnessed in Almadén, in his novel the self-presentation of the poor constitutes a fully interested account—a perverse mise-en-abîme for the text as a whole.

The relation between the two texts—*informe* and novel—echoes Delicado's hopeful treatise on syphilis versus his skepticism about a cure within *Lozana* itself, which I discussed in Chapter 1. In both cases, the picaresque not only subverts narrative authority *tout court* but, more specifically, challenges a referential, extrafictional text by the same author, in a kind of picaresque contagion. By the turn of the seventeenth century, in a context of far more elaborate institutions to safeguard authenticity, the cynicism of the *Guzmán* suggests that all systems of documentation are susceptible to imposture, particularly when the source of information is an interested first-person narrator. The precision of the artifice mounted by the fake beggars suggests how any system that attempts to codify distinctions between the authentic and the inauthentic also furnished the materials for a convincing simulacrum.

The distancing of these scenes, via the Italian setting for what was a pressing Spanish problem, only underscores how difficult it was to advocate for reform when poverty could be simulated by a convincing narrative, aided as necessary by bodily performance.

Moreover, in the *Guzmán* it is not just the poor who are caught up in the theatricality and imposture of poverty: as Cavillac notes in his suspicious reading of Guzmán in Rome, the performance of poverty extends also to its relief. When the Cardinal gives aid to the malingering *pícaro*, instructing his servants to put the beggar in his own bed, two "expertos cirujanos" (1:425) ["expert surgeons"] abet Guzmán in his deception. This is the logical corollary of Alemán's earlier pun on *protomédico/protopobre*: neither the beggar nor the medical professionals are to be trusted. Meanwhile, the most spectacular instance of charity in the novel, when Guzmán is showered with coins by a Roman gentleman, is itself a considered representation, an extravagant gesture that the donor performs in order to credit himself with generosity.[28]

The experience of sustained imposture as a beggar frees Guzmán to abandon all pretense of respectability, despite what might be considered cautionary exempla. Cured of his false beggar's ailment and in the employment of the Cardinal, he is furnished with an education, and eventually goes to serve the French ambassador. There Guzmán is presented with a mirror image of himself, which he experiences as an affront and a challenge. A Spanish soldier forces himself into the ambassador's house, claiming noble origins: "Dijo ser un soldado natural de Córdoba, caballero principal della y que tenía necesidad, y así le suplicaba se la favoreciese haciéndole merced" (1:467) ["He claimed to be a soldier from Córdoba, and a principal gentleman of that city, who was now in great need and thus requested the favor of his mercy"].[29] His countrymen, hot on his heels, soon unmask him. When Guzmán inquires whether they know the gentleman in question, they correct him in no uncertain terms:

> —Conocemos a aquel bodegonero. Su padre no se hartó de calzarme borceguíes en Córdoba, donde tiene su ejecutoria en el techo de la Iglesia Mayor. Esta es la desventura nuestra, que si pasamos veinte caballeros a Italia, vienen cien infames cual éste a quererse igualar, haciéndose de los godos. Como entienden que no los conocen, piensan que en engomándose el bigote y arrojando cuatro plumas han alcanzado la nobleza y valentía, siendo unos infames gallinas, pues no pelean plumas ni bigotes, sino corazones y hombres. (1:467–68)

> ["We know that tavernkeeper. His father never tired of fitting me for boots in Córdoba, where his name is posted on top of the main church. This is our misfortune: if twenty gentlemen come to Italy, one hundred lowlifes such as this come too, trying to equate themselves with us, and to pretend they descend from the Goths. Since they are well aware that no one knows them, they think that as long as they wax their mustaches and sprout four feathers they have achieved nobility and bravery, even though they are but infamous chickens. For it's neither feathers nor mustaches that fight, but hearts and men."]

The gallant soldier in Italy is but a tavernkeeper at home, son of a cobbler and a crypto-Jew, at least in the eyes of his enemies. Distance emboldens his imposture, even if it not entirely successful, and more broadly that of the hundreds who come to Italy from Spain. His detractors accuse him of exactly the same move that Guzmán attempts, in his goal to "hacerme de los godos" (1:378) ["make myself of the Goths"], highlighting the generalized use of the *pícaro*'s Italian strategy.

Guzmán resents the Spaniards' accusations, yet also objects to the presumptuous soldier: he comes a little too close for comfort. Ignoring Guzmán's snubs, the soldier eloquently defends his position, claiming his privilege: "Lo primero, la calidad de mi persona y noble linaje merece toda merced y cortesía. Lo segundo, ser soldado me hace digno de cualquier tabla de príncipe, por haberlo conquistado mis obras y profesión. Lo último, que se junta con lo dicho mi mucha necesidad a quien todo es común" (1:468) ["First, the quality of my person and noble lineage deserves all mercies and courtesies. Second, my being a soldier gives me the right to sit at any prince's table, for my feats and profession have won me as much. Finally, add to all I have said my great necessity, which holds everything in common"]. Beyond the vexed question of birth versus works, which might authorize the soldier's claims to gentility, necessity has the last word, annulling all possible objections. Undaunted by the servants' slights, the soldier just helps himself to what he wants and leaves on his own terms, after which the ambassador mockingly compares him to Guzmán: "Se parece a ti y a tu tierra, donde todo se lleva con fieros y poca vergüenza" (1:469) ["He's like you and your country, where it's all about bravado and shamelessness"].

Guzmán chooses a different way forward, betting instead on the appearance of wealth as his entrée. His decision is partly born of his own version of necessity: scorned in Rome for his attempts to arrange an affair for the

French ambassador, he is forced to go. The scene of shaming is almost painfully apt: Guzmán is knocked over by a pig who runs through the streets with the unfortunate *pícaro* on his back, covered in mud and excrement, in a very public rehearsal of the enduring insult to Spaniards in Italy, and especially those of dubious origins: *marrano*. Although the insult had dogged him since his arrival in Genoa, this public instantiation is insurmountable, and Guzmán decides to leave the ambassador's employment to visit the great cities of Italy. He is soon fleeced of his savings by a fellow Spaniard, Sayavedra, who deceives him despite Guzmán's supposed experience with deceptions born of distance. Though Sayavedra, too, claims to be a noble gentleman of Seville, he is actually a *pícaro* from Valencia, whose wily self-fashioning deceives Guzmán regardless of his own previous experiences. Guzmán befriends Sayavedra nonetheless, and Sayavedra repays the favor by helping him trick and steal his way back into solvency, as I discuss below.

Thus it is that Guzmán finally returns to Genoa with the funds to impress his father's family. Once rejected in his frank poverty, he is embraced when he returns as an apparently wealthy man, even as he sets out to swindle those who had disowned him. Money is not enough, however: he also sports a different name. Dubbing Sayavedra "Guzmán de Alfarache," he calls himself "don Juan de Guzmán" (2:259), despite recognizing that the multiplication of "dones" exposes the Spaniards to mocking incredulity in Italy. (The locals wonder, with so many Spanish nobles, who takes care of the pigs [2:258]). Interestingly, Guzmán presents his new name as "el mío propio que de mis padres heredé" (2:258) ["my very own, inherited from my parents"], although Part 1 made it clear that the adopted name was on the mother's side, and deliberately chosen for its aristocratic overtones.

Guzmán has finally understood that appearances are everything: "Cuando fueres alquimia, eso que reluciere de ti, eso será venerado. Ya no se juzgan almas ni más de aquello que ven los ojos. Ninguno se pone a considerar lo que sabes, sino lo que tienes, no tu virtud, sino la de tu bolsa; y de tu bolsa no lo que tienes, sino lo que gastas" (2:271) ["Even if you are made by alchemy, whatever shines in you shall be venerated. No one judges souls any more, nor anything beyond what the eyes can see. No one stops to consider what you know, but only what you have; not your virtue, but that of your purse; and from your purse not what you have, but what you spend"]. His ploy works: now that he seems well off and spends freely, the Genoese fall all over themselves to welcome him, "y a pocos días creció mi nombre y crédito tanto, que con él pudiera hallar en la ciudad cualquiera cortesía" (2:274) ["and in a few days my name and my credit were so enhanced that with them I could find all favor in the city"]. So successful is Guzmán's imposture that he now finds relatives everywhere, as they consider the advantage that might come from being related to him. Once again, proverbial language brings out the interestedness of the Genoese. Guzmán tells us: "A pocas vueltas hallé padre y madre, y conocí todo mi linaje" (2:275) ["In short order I found father and mother, and found out my entire lineage"]. "Hallé padre y madre" is a proverbial expression for finding protectors, yet here it recalls the key problem of origins: the only reason Guzmán finds these metaphorical parents is that he appears rich, whatever his actual lineage, so that he can end up "con más deudos que deudas" (2:275) ["with more relatives than debts"] and everyone claiming an ancestral connection to him.

Ironically, the old man who once had Guzmán tossed in a blanket does turn out to be his father's brother, now intent on pursuing a relationship with the apparently wealthy nephew, whom he does not connect to the earlier incident. He relates to Guzmán with great relish how a young *pícaro* tried to pass himself off as part of the family, and how, affronted, he ran him out of town. Despite all that has transpired, Guzmán experiences the moment as a wound reopened, and defends the *pícaro* interloper as honoring the family by choosing to seek a place in it. Unmollified, the uncle insists that no honor can come to the lineage from one so poor: "Pues que no trujo vestido de bodas, llévese lo que le dieron" (2:279) ["Since he did not bring wedding attire, he deserves what he got"]. Given that Guzmán's newly extensive family will attempt to marry him off, the better to capture his supposed wealth, the anticipatory reference to the parable of the wedding feast in Matthew 22 can only prove ironic. As I discuss below, Guzmán's revenge will use everything that Italy has taught him about successful imposture, as he mobilizes the workings of credit to punish those who once refused to believe him.

Thus the *Guzmán* explores the vexed connections between place, identity, and belonging. The Italian setting of much of the two-part text complicates our sense of the picaresque even as it interrogates what it means to be Spanish. Italy is presented as a paradigmatic land of beggars and thieves, diluting the *pícaro*'s identification with Spain. At the same time, the Italian perspective dismantles Spanish pretension, as both Spaniards and Italians recognize how geographical distance makes it easy to construct the genealogies on which the former places such importance. When the Italians ask who is left at home to mind the pigs, given the multitude of Spanish nobles in Italy, they expose the interlinked anxieties about *limpieza* and status that motivate Guzmán's own travels and his search. If Italy provides a vexed origin for Guzmán himself, it more broadly represents the possibility of imposture, as Spaniards remake themselves at will.

Credit and *Cambio*

Ya todo es mohatra.
—*Guzmán de Alfarache*, 2:229

Throughout the two parts of the novel, Guzmán plays a multitude of tricks on his victims, subjecting them to ridicule and swindling them of their property. So many schemes are described that the *Guzmán* at times feels closer to the contemporary coney-catching pamphlets of the English tradition, which claim to expose rogues and warn their victims even as they entertain readers, than to the compromised innocence of *Lazarillo*. The crucial difference between *Lazarillo* or *Guzmán* and the coney-catching pamphlets, however, is surely the narrative voice: how to trust a knowing first-person narrator who evinces his rhetorical slipperiness even as he purports to confess?

Among Guzmán's plethora of strategies, many stemming from a long folkloric tradition, are a number of episodes that invoke and pervert mercantile procedures. These feature the narrator as a canny manipulator of credit, leveraging his reputation and his carefully calculated actions to dupe his unwitting partners. Hence the broader threat of the *pícaro*: his untrustworthy, implicated "I" is not merely a literary puzzle, but a challenge to the emerging economic institutions that depend on the gradual development of credit. Certainly, the *pícaro* is unproductive and focused on aping his (aristocratic) betters, as Guzmán, like Lázaro before him, does when he buys a sword and cloak with his money rather than investing or saving the capital. Guzmán's relation to the world of money is complex: as the son of a *levantisco*, he understands the mechanisms of commercial exchange and manipulates them to his advantage, disrupting the structures of credit, broadly understood, on which mercantile activity depends. If, as Laurence Fontaine has argued, credit is a complex structure linking various social milieus in a negotiation of power, the *pícaro*'s impostures and his corrupt schemes expose the dangers of such exchanges.[30] As Guzmán moves easily between the worlds of aristocrats and merchants, he upends any distinctions between them with his ploys.

Covarrubias's definition of *crédito* succinctly gathers the overlapping meanings of the term in the period: "La credulidad que damos a lo que se nos dize. Crédito, buena opinión y reputación. Crédito, entre mercaderes, abono de caudal y correspondencia con los demás. Acreditar a uno, abonarle. Acreditarse, cobrar crédito"[31] ["The belief we grant what is said to us. Credit, good standing and repute. Credit, among merchants, payment of funds and correspondence with others. To credit someone, to pay him. To credit oneself, to gain credit"]. Early on, Guzmán considers the possibility of a narrator who manipulates the story in order to "acreditar su discreción" (1:127) ["credit his intelligence"]. Yet his own adventures with credit go well beyond rhetoric, so that the problematization of narrative authority expands onto broader realms of representation that are also ostensibly warranted by an "I" who claims probity.

Michel Cavillac's influential account of the *Guzmán* finds in the text a sustained bourgeois critique of the financial credit industry, dominated by the Genoese, which threatened to annihilate the commercial bourgeoisie of Castile.[32] Cavillac's reading, based on the pioneering research of economic historian Felipe Ruiz Martín, situates the text in relation to pressing economic debates of the period, as a series of reformers attempted to alert the Spanish monarchs to the true costs of Genoese credit. While Italo-Hispanic credit circuits may well be Alemán's immediate target, however, the *Guzmán* offers a much broader reflection on the rhetorical dimensions of credit. Crucially, rhetoric serves to mask the tortuous development of alternatives to moneylending, nominally forbidden to Christians. Thus the *mohatra* (from the Arabic *muḫāṭarah*, to take a risk), a term that recurs frequently in the *Guzmán*. In lieu of lending money at interest, the *mohatra* involved selling something at an inflated price to a person who actually wanted to borrow money, to then buy it back at a much lower price once the period of the loan was over. Covarrubias notes, "Los que se veen en necessidad para cumplir alguna deuda, hazen estas mohatras"[33] ["Those who are in need to pay back a loan, make these *mohatras*"]. Although technically they involved no loan and no interest, *mohatras*, which existed across the continent, were forbidden in the *Nueva instrucción* of 1543 and condemned by the Vatican.[34] Cervantes's use of the term in the second *Quijote* charts how the meaning of *mohatra* gradually exceeded the purely financial to designate any impersonation or subterfuge: Don Quijote worries that if Sancho behaves boorishly the Dukes will think him a "caballero de mohatra."[35] Already in the *Guzmán* there is a sense that the financial *mohatra* contaminates other spheres, posing a significant threat to social interactions and probity more generally. As the novel explores the intersections between financial, rhetorical, and moral misrepresentation, the *pícaro*'s malfeasance not only participates in but reveals the broader disorder of the credit economy.

One of Guzmán's signal strategies is precisely to *acreditarse*, or gain the trust of his future victims, by first investing his own resources in the schemes that will serve to fleece them. His key alliance with the captain who will spirit him away from Genoa after he exacts his revenge on his father's family, for example, comes about when Guzmán, perceiving the other's need, gives him part of his winnings at cards: "Tiempos hay que un real vale ciento y hace provecho de mil" (2:273) ["There are times when one *real* is worth a hundred and does as much good as a thousand"]. The move becomes, in proverbial terms, "aguja de que había de sacar una reja" (2:273)—literally, the needle from which you get a wrought-iron gate.[36] Beyond ensuring the captain's loyalty, Guzmán's handouts buy him credit all around: "viéndome afable, franco y dadivoso, me acredité de manera que les compré los corazones, ganándoles los ánimos" (2:273) ["upon their seeing that I was affable, generous and open-handed, I gained credit with them so that I bought their hearts and gained their goodwill"]. He even invokes the biblical parable to shore up his point: his largesse is as the seed that falls on good earth and leads to a good harvest (2:273). Hence the greatest irony of Guzmán's strategies: they reliably produce increase even though they are based on deception.

In order to take revenge on the Genoese who had once denied him but embrace him when he appears rich, Guzmán plans carefully, mobilizing the lessons learned during his time in Italy, and deciding on a lasting financial wound over any physical vengeance. First, he convinces the captain whom he had previously cultivated that he has only come to Italy to seek revenge, and needs his assistance to escape back to Spain. Then he systematically inflames the greed of his newfound Genoese relatives by displaying his wealth, entertaining them, and gambling conspicuously. As his plan matures, he asks his uncle to guard his heavy chests, supposedly full of plate and jewelry. In an elaborate plot that again evokes the parable from Matthew, he claims to have promised to provide the jewels for the wedding of two Spanish nobles and announces that he will pawn his own great chain in order to secure them. The seed falls on fertile ground: Guzmán's uncle, convinced that his rich long-lost nephew merely has a short-term cash-flow problem, assures him that there will be jewels enough from his many family members to fulfill his obligations. And so the jewels pour in, while Guzmán pawns a fake chain for extra cash. Having taken the utmost advantage of his relations far and wide, Guzmán skips town with the loot and sails for Spain, emphasizing the break of distance where he had so assiduously sought connection.

Where does the money that Guzmán so liberally distributes in Genoa come from? It results from an elaborate earlier scheme by which different *pícaros* invest in deception and effectively manipulate commercial norms. In Milan, Guzmán notices his associate Sayavedra deep in conversation with Aguilera, a "fino español" (2:233) ["fine Spaniard"] and a "gran escribano y contador" (2:234) ["a great notary and accountant"], who has invested a year of his time in working as a cashier for a merchant in the city, himself in the business of *logros* and *mohatras*.[37] Sayavedra shares the tip that Aguilera needs an accomplice, then slyly allows Guzmán to insist on participating. Guzmán carefully considers risk and investment in this "negocio de consideración" (2:236) ["significant business"], as a good businessman might: "Que meter costa en lo que ha de hacer poco provecho es locura. Los empleos han de hacerse conforme a las ganancias" (2:236) ["For to sink resources in what will be of little advantage is madness. One must employ oneself according to the profits to be made"]. Ironically, Aguilera's "tan buena relación" (2:239) ["such a good narrative"] of duplicity toward his master convinces Guzmán to trust him as his partner. Embroiled in his scams, the *pícaro* is as susceptible to rhetoric as his eventual victims.

Guzmán comes up with an elaborate plan to ask the merchant to hold his supposed cash and then demand it back, without ever having deposited it—the ultimate *mohatra*. Guzmán's purported need is that of any actor in a primitive credit system: the supposed cash with which he needs to pay for wedding jewels leaves him vulnerable to theft, and the merchant is the closest thing to a bank. The swindle replicates the forms of credit negotiation in the period, mobilizing the rich resonances between mercantile accounting (*cuentas*) and Guzmán's account (*cuento*).[38] Aguilera extracts the merchant's *borrador*, which serves as his *libro de memoria* (2:245), and Guzmán adds a fake entry, which acknowledges the cash received from Guzmán, in the exact currency that Aguilera knows the merchant keeps locked up, and then, in a different hand, a statement that it has been returned. The better to pull off the swindle, and as part of his investment, Guzmán has Aguilera *add* money to the merchant's stash, planting specific denominations as evidence. As the everyday, most informal of account books, the *borrador* both preserves information for memory and offers the possibility of erasure and rewriting. It contrasts with the *libro manual* and the *libro mayor*, in which all important transactions would eventually be recorded, and echoes the selective rewriting of the *pícaro*'s own life in the book that we are reading.[39]

Guzmán then goes back to the merchant and asks him to return the money when his servant comes for it. The merchant agrees, assuming Guzmán speaks of a future conditional, or at least a future perfect: once Guzmán has actually left the money with the merchant, he will send his servant to retrieve it from him. But Guzmán changes the notional terms of deposit, requesting his money then and there. Now the merchant must explain to witnesses why he has just said he would return Guzmán's money, when he claims he has none of it. To add drama to his performance, Guzmán first calls for the *libro mayor*, then the *libro manual*, before finally insisting on the *borrador*, which reveals the false transaction planted there (2:249). The canceled entry in the *borrador* that serves as *libro de memoria*, the exact denominations planted earlier, and even the location of the cash within the merchant's office all match Guzmán's claims perfectly, and convince the law that the merchant owes the money: "Eran en mi favor la voz común, las evidencias y experiencias vistas y su mala fama" (2:253) ["All spoke with one voice in my favor, as did the evidence and the events seen, and the merchant's ill repute"]. Guzmán's successful swindle thus depends on mirroring mercantile practices, even as he mobilizes a personalized form of credit that lies outside any institutional structure. Beyond the deliberate subornation that was so often the case in *averiguaciones de limpieza* or other legal processes, moreover, Guzmán's swindle stages "evidencias y experiencias" that effectively manipulate even the most honest of witnesses.

Perhaps the most elaborate scheme in the novel features Guzmán back in Spain and in cahoots with his *mohatrero* father-in-law, who advises him, "También habéis de hacer como con vuestro buen crédito paséis adelante. Y, si habéis de ser mercader, seáis mercader, poniendo aparte todo aquello que no fuere llaneza, pues no se negocia ya sino con ella y con dinero: cambiar y recambiar" (2:369) ["You must also use your good credit to get ahead. And if you are to be a merchant, be one, setting aside anything that is not plain dealing, for none trades in anything but that and money: changes and exchanges"]. Echoing Guzmán's earlier account of his own Genoese relatives, his father-in-law urges him to join him as a *mohatrero*. Setting Guzmán up in business involves creating capital where there is none, by manipulating the institutions of credit, from written documents to personal testimony. As the father-in-law explains, in what is a baroque account of a baroque operation:

> Otorgaránse luego dos escrituras y dos contraescrituras. La una sea *confesando* que me debéis cuatro mil ducados, que os presté, de la cual os daré luego carta de pago como la quisierdes pintar. Y ambas las guardaremos para si fueren menester, aunque mucho mejor sería

que tal tiempo nunca llegase... La otra será: yo haré que os venda mi hermano quinientos ducados que tiene de *juro* en cada un año y haráse desta manera. No faltará un amigo cajero, que por amistad haga muestra del dinero, para que pueda el escribano *dar fe* de la paga, o ahí lo tomaremos y nos lo prestarán en el banco a trueco de cincuenta reales. Y cuando se haya otorgado la escritura de venta, vos le volveréis a dar a él poder en causa propia, *confesando* que aquello fue fingido; mas que real y verdaderamente siempre los quinientos ducados fueron y son suyos. (2:372, my italics)

[Then there shall be issued two deeds and two counterdeeds. One will confess that you owe me four thousand ducats, which I have loaned you, and to cancel this I shall then give you a receipt in any form you like. And we'll save them both in case we ever need them, though it would be best if such a time never came. . . . The other will be that I shall have my brother sell you five hundred ducats that he has per year in a bond, and it shall be done in this way: we'll find a cashier willing to make a show of the money for friendship's sake, so that a notary may avow that it was paid, or else we'll take it there and they'll lend it to us in a bank for fifty *reales*, and once this bond is made over to you with a deed of sale, you will return it to him, confessing that it was all feigned, and that really and truly the five hundred ducats were and still are his.]

Confieso, juro, doy fe: all these supposed attestations of truth underlie debased financial transactions, as *reales* disguise what is *real y verdaderamente* the case. The (in)famous *juros*—performative guarantees transformed into credit mechanisms—make the irony patent: once discounted, instruments of credit undo the force of testimony more broadly.[40] Thus part of the discomfort of Guzmán's strategies is how they evoke or mirror the financial maneuvers to which even the Crown turned when necessary. As I. A. A. Thompson reminds us, the systematic defalcation of unsuspecting creditors was not simply practiced by *pícaros* and *mohatreros* in the period: "The ability of the Spanish Crown to replace creditors worn out by its own defalcations with a succession of fresh opportunistic lenders, and thus to draw on the capital generated and then released by the progressive stages through which the world economy was passing in the sixteenth and seventeenth centuries, was the benefit it derived from heading a world empire and the secret of its survival."[41] Thus the problem of credit complicates the larger question of the narrator's reliability, and the broader implications of the

Guzmán: even as the *pícaro* reveals to us the mechanisms of his transgression, he reminds us that his doings are not specific to him or to picaresque spaces, but permeate the economic system. Moreover, the text's constant reflection on credit and trustworthiness reminds the reader that she, too, participates in the dynamic that Guzmán delineates if she places any credit in his confession.

Beyond the specifics of any particular swindle, Guzmán treats his own reputation—his good credit—as an investment, giving alms in order to be considered virtuous and exacting his enhanced reputation as payment: "Todos aquellos pasos eran enderezados a cobrar buena fama" (2:476) ["All of my steps were aimed at acquiring a good reputation"]. His credit with the public is an essential part of the business model:

> ¡Oh cuántas veces, tratando de mis negocios, concertando mis mercaderías, dando mis logros, fabricando mis marañas por subir los precios, vendiendo con exceso, más al fiado que al contado, el rosario en la mano, el rostro igual y con un "en mi verdad" en la boca—por donde nunca salía—, robaba públicamente de vieja costumbre! Y descubriólo el tiempo. Quién y cuántas veces me oyeron y dije: "Prometo a Vuestra Merced que me tiene más de costo y no gano un real en toda la partida y, si la doy barato, es porque tengo de dar unos dineros para . . . ." Y daba otras causas, no habiéndolas para ello más de querer ganar a ciento por ciento de su mano a la mía. ¡Cuántas veces también, cuando tuve prosperidad y trataba de mi acrecentamiento—por solo acreditarme, por sola vanagloria, no por Dios, que no me acordaba ni en otra cosa pensaba que solamente parecer bien al mundo y llevarlo tras de mí. (2:475)

> [How many times, when dealing with my business, arranging for my merchandise, charging my interest, fabricating my ruses to raise prices, selling overmuch, more on credit than on the spot, with a rosary in my hand and an expression on my face to match and an "Upon my word!" in my mouth—which never spoke true—I stole openly as was my old custom. And time revealed all. How many times and how many heard me say, "I promise your lordship that it costs me more and I will not make a penny in the whole business, and if I charge so little, it's because I need to raise some monies for. . . ." And I would give other causes, when the only real one was the desire to make one hundred per cent on what passed from his hand to mine. How many times, too, when I was well off and intent

upon my climbing, simply to credit myself, and for vainglory, rather than for God, did I forget everything but looking good to the world so that I could bring it along with me.]

Guzmán's narration participates in this economy—what is the extended confessional text, if not an attempt to display the narrator's newfound virtue and secure credit from the reader? If it is impossible to escape the unease that comes from the repeated account of how those who have placed their credit in Guzmán in the past have been fleeced, a cautious skepticism may be in order.

The text thus offers an extended meditation on the double sense of *cambio* as ongoing mercantile exchange—which had been the business of Guzmán's father (1:131)—or reformation, which animates the narrative of his son. Covarrubias is again helpful here, with a double definition: "Cambiar vale solamente trocar y permutar una cosa por otra. . . . Cambio, en sinificación más ceñida, vale la persona pública, que con autoridad del príncipe o de la república, pone el dinero de un lugar a otro con sus interesses"[42] ["To change is to transform and permutate one thing for another. . . . Change, in a more narrow sense, is the public person, charged by the prince or the republic, who moves money from one place to another with its interest"]. Strikingly, the second, economic definition stresses movement across places, which, as Guzmán's peripatetic Mediterranean relation, or Lozana's, or Pedro's, repeatedly shows, opens up the space for deception. *Cambios* attempt to stabilize the relationship of distance to credit, enabling international financial transactions and, more generally, mercantile activity, as in Cervantes's fantastically detailed account of how the queen of England manages a payment to her Spanish protégé during the Anglo-Spanish war, in "La española inglesa."[43] Yet in the hands of the *pícaro,* distance destabilizes truth, so that *cambio* becomes instead the duplicitous exchange of one thing for another. Whether in legitimate or illegitimate exchange, moreover, the economic meanings of *cambio* function very differently from the moral economy of reformation. The final conversion, which ostensibly warrants the *pícaro*'s account and takes him out of circulation as a corrupt economic actor, replaces his own circulation with that of the more reliable text—or at least so would Guzmán have us believe.

Guzmán's transformation aboard the galleys (where, we recall, he writes the entire text [1:113]) also explores the limits and possibilities of change, in both moral and identitarian terms. Convicted and condemned to forced labor, he seems to be undergoing a gradual process of reform, only to find that he has no more credit. Paradoxically, now that Guzmán serves loyally and attempts to redeem himself, he is more vulnerable to the depravity of others.

In an episode that reprises the tricks Guzmán has so often played on others, he is effectively framed as a thief by his archenemy, the slippery Soto. Soto finds an accomplice to steal silver from the captain's table, plants the evidence to incriminate Guzmán, and then proceeds to confirm what people already think they know about him. Tale and teller find themselves at a rhetorical impasse: now the proof of Guzmán's sincerity, vis-à-vis the reader, is the generalized lack of belief in him. Yet unless he can convince his masters of his reformation, he will not live to tell the tale.

In a narrative departure that effectively externalizes what has been the *pícaro*'s intimate conflict throughout, Guzmán is saved only by Soto's attempted mutiny and plot to flee to North Africa. The other's perfidy, and the supposed starkness of the divide between Christianity and Islam, Europe and Africa, Spain and its historical enemies, provides the perfect occasion for Guzmán to prove his good intentions:[44]

> Soto, mi camarada, no vino a las galeras porque daba limosnas ni porque predicaba la fe de Cristo a los infieles; trujéronlo a ellas sus culpas y haber sido el mayor ladrón que se había hallado en su tiempo en toda Italia ni España. Una temporada fue soldado. Sabía toda la tierra, como quien había paseádola muchas veces. Viendo que las galeras navegaban por el mar Mediterráneo y se encostaban otras veces a la costa de Berbería buscando presas, imaginó de tratar, con algunos moros y forzados de su bando, de alzarse con la galera. (2:520)

> [My friend Soto did not end up on the galleys for giving alms or for preaching the faith of Christ to the infidels; he was brought there for his faults and for having been the greatest thief of his time in all of Italy and Spain. He was for some time a soldier. He knew the land well, as one who had traversed it many times. When he saw that the galleys sailed on the Mediterranean and that they at times drew close to the coast of Barbary in search of prizes, he thought of attempting to take the galley with some Moors and convicts from his band.]

The cutting irony here about Soto's presence on the galleys reminds the reader that Guzmán, too, is sentenced for a reason. With its geographic and cultural range, the passage addresses the impasse of Guzmán's fate by expanding the diegetic universe. Infidels to be converted, thieves and soldiers operating in Italy and Spain, Mediterranean itineraries that bring North Africa into the picture—all of these telescope out from the intimate problem of Guzmán's inner conviction to a series of stages on which allegiance to Spain and to Catholicism might be proved. In this sense, the final test of Guzmán's reformation echoes the problematic conversion of Ozmín and Daraxa in the interpolated novel in Part 1, in which intimate conviction must negotiate *realpolitik*.[45]

Although Guzmán never specifies Soto's willingness to renege, claiming only that the proximity of North Africa encourages him to mutiny, the specter of that irredeemable change haunts Guzmán's own supposed conversion, and the reversal of his fate. Ever wily, Guzmán pretends to join the conspiracy, but instead reveals it to the captain, who "casi no me daba crédito" (2:521) ["could barely credit me"]. Thus the *pícaro* must return to his lying ways, if only to unmask the conspiracy. Yet his fate hinges on whether the captain can lend him the necessary credence, which, in his eyes at least, Guzmán has not earned. Ultimately, it is the enormity of Soto's proposed treason, which would deliver the galley to North Africa and to Spain's enemies, that underwrites Guzmán's legitimacy, despite his duplicity until the end. Credit and *cambio* remain intricately intertwined, and it is by no means clear that the final change in the *pícaro* merits our crediting the moralizing portions of his narrative. The ambivalence is underscored by the narrative's lack of resolution: Guzmán narrates his life during that indefinitely postponed wait for the king to resolve whether or not he will be pardoned, and although the narrative eventually brings us to his present moment, his future is never decided.[46]

Yet Guzmán's extended narrative is devastating whether or not the reader accepts the sincerity of his conversion. Over and over again, whether in the theory of his moralizing or the practice of his own adventures, he demonstrates how fictionality, hardly ensconced within the literary, permeates society in deceptions large and small, many of them arguably inescapable if that society is to function. From the shared genealogical constructs on which Spanish hierarchies depend, to the successful impersonation of wealth, to the fragility of mercantile credit, Guzmán presents a world permeated by doubt despite constant inquisitions. As the *pícaro* manipulates and exploits the structures of identity and authentication that surround him, certainty remains elusive, while fictions appear both endemic and necessary. In telling the *pícaro*'s story, *Guzmán de Alfarache* thus constructs a knowing reader for whom skepticism seems like the most reasonable response.

Chapter 4

Cervantes's Skeptical Picaresques and the Pact of Fictionality

—¿Tan bueno es?—dijo Don Quijote.
—Es tan bueno—respondió Ginés—que mal año para *Lazarillo de Tormes* y para todos cuantos de aquel género se han escrito o escribieren. Lo que le sé decir a voacé es que trata verdades, y que son verdades tan lindas y tan donosas, que no puede haber mentiras que se le igualen.
—¿Y cómo se intitula el libro?—preguntó Don Quijote.
—*La vida de Ginés de Pasamonte*—respondió el mismo.
—¿Y está acabado?— preguntó Don Quijote.
—¿Cómo puede estar acabado—respondió él—, si aún no está acabada mi vida?

—Cervantes, *Don Quijote de la Mancha*

["Is it that good?" said Don Quijote.
"It is so good," answered Ginés, "that it'll be a bad year for *Lazarillo de Tormes* and for all of its kind, whether written or yet to be written. What I can tell you is that it deals with truths, and such beautiful and such agreeable truths that no lies can equal them."
"And what is the book's title?" asked Don Quijote.
"*The Life of Ginés de Pasamonte*," replied the same.
"And is it done?" asked Don Quijote.
"How can it be done," answered he, "when my life is not yet done?"]

With his penchant for ironizing narrative authority, playfulness with genre, and constant exploration of perspectivism, Cervantes occupies a central role in any reconsideration of the picaresque. His ruminations on the genre in *Don Quijote* through the recurring figure of the convict Ginés de Pasamonte, who claims to be writing the history of his own life in Part I and returns as the dubious puppet master Maese Pedro in Part II, are well known. Though Ginés boasts that his story of his own life will surpass *Lazarillo*, announcing his filiation with the picaresque, he also touts the beautiful *verdades* of a text that outdoes any *mentiras* in its predecessors or competitors. Thus, no sooner is the genre conjured than it is riven by the distinction between two possible versions—truth versus lies. Moreover, Ginés's *Vida* is inescapably and insistently partial: both unfinished and evidently biased in favor of its grandstanding narrator. Although the picaresque may proffer tantalizing possibilities of resolution and redemption, the protagonist's story exceeds the text, complicating a tidy ending. Any conclusion is provisional, good only until the next conviction. Once the pugnacious Ginés throws down his gauntlet, can the picaresque even cohere as a genre? Certainly the ragtag assortment I have stitched together in this book seems to strain at the seams. What characterizes the form, I suggest, is its probing questioning of *verdades*. In its constant exploration of what can be known and relayed by an unreliable narrative "I," the picaresque unsettles the givenness of any particular version, and instead offers the fictional as the locus for a particularly productive skepticism, leading not to the nihilistic questioning of the possibility of knowledge overall, but rather to critical reading.

Beyond *Don Quijote*, Cervantes probes picaresque knowing and knowingness in both drama (discussed in Chapter 2) and prose. As experiments in narrative reliability, his texts examine the often-vexed negotiations that underlie uncomfortable truths. In his picaresque novellas as in his plays of captivity, Cervantes foregrounds speakers whose interested versions underscore the partiality of even—or especially—the most proximate sources. From the captive's authoritative claims to Mediterranean knowledge in the *comedias* to the domestic *pícaro*'s passionate defense of improbable wonders in the novellas, Cervantes's picaresque figures probe the limits of credulity even as they ironize the stakes of the story.

The picaresque enables Cervantes to go beyond irony to the epistemological questions of the truth of narratives and how they might be assessed. My argument here expands upon the foundational work that explored how legal and inquisitorial confessional contexts impacted the development of fiction, and particularly of the first-person picaresque, in Spain.[1] While critics have usefully foregrounded the structural resemblances between the fictional *Lazarillo* and inquisitional confessions that attempted to placate their respective interrogators, I want to explore the affordances of those strategies as literature. In this alternative realm, we value the irony and contradiction of the picaresque in a manner that would be no less than obscene for an inquisitional confession. As knowing fictions, moreover, picaresques suggest a broader skepticism, gesturing to the larger apparatus that produces ostensibly trustworthy narratives. Fiction's interested, partial responses render the literary a site of contestation from which to challenge the mechanisms of interpellation and subjectification. Whether by privileging pleasure over necessity or foregrounding less than fully forthcoming characters and narrators, the picaresque encourages a productive skepticism about the stories told, while simultaneously presenting fiction as a protected space for ambiguity.[2]

My exploration of literary skepticism is aligned with ongoing interdisciplinary investigations by Mercedes García-Arenal, Stefania Pastore, Felipe Pereda, and others that identify the development of skepticism in early modern Spain as a response to mass conversions and other challenges to confessional verities.[3] The larger contention of this recent work is that we have not found skepticism in early modern Spain in the wake of the profound upheavals that transformed religious practice only because we have not looked for it. Though my own focus is on literary explorations of skepticism in relation to narrative authority, I see these as responses to a much larger ideological context of doubt in response to confessional pressures. Well before the Enlightenment, and even before the development of scientific skepticism, Cervantes offered a sustained interrogation of what we can know and how we know it. Indeed, one might say that doubt produces in his texts the category of fiction itself.

While the playful perspectivism and skepticism of the *Quijote* have been abundantly noted, the skepticism of the picaresque *Novelas ejemplares* (1613) is equally striking.[4] Cervantes's intent to have us read advisedly is evident from the prologue to the collection, which provides the famous hermeneutic prod to read them for "el sabroso y honesto fruto que se podría sacar, así de todas juntas, como de cada una de por sí"[5] ["the tasty and honest fruit that one might take from them all together, as from each one on its own"]. He describes the project of the *Novelas* as "poner en la plaza de nuestra república una mesa de trucos" (1:52) ["to place in the square of our commonwealth a billiards table"], tipping his hat to the waywardness and fortuitous connections that complicate any promised exemplarity. In recent years, critics have increasingly emphasized the ironic slant of the *Novelas*, particularly their skeptical account of what moderns would term class.[6] Beyond the general ironic stance that these critics identify, and with which I fully concur, I am interested in how the novellas more explicitly aligned with the picaresque negotiate exemplarity and skepticism—the former offering models for behavior that presume belief, the latter encouraging instead doubt and critical distance.[7] Beyond the emptiness of baroque *desengaño*, Cervantes's picaresque skepticism offers as an alternative to exemplarity a fruitful and fully engaged fictionality.

The range of picaresque narrations and narrators across the *Novelas* demands of readers a nuanced form of skepticism—a suspension of belief that complements what Coleridge much later termed "suspension of disbelief" and that resonates with particular strength in a Counter-Reformation context.[8] By highlighting how the picaresque frames narratives—in both the judicial and the literary, generic sense—Cervantes underscores the negotiated nature of any narrated truth, and the impossibility of certainty. At the same time, his paradoxical *Novelas ejemplares* make evident that by the early seventeenth century, and particularly in the wake of the expulsion of the Moriscos, all of whom should have been abundantly catechized, the kind of moral certainty and mimetic modeling involved in exemplarity are neither available nor particularly desirable.[9]

By the time Cervantes turned to the picaresque, its ironic force was well established, as the humorous references to the self-serving nature of first-person narratives in the Pasamonte episode recall. Cervantes's own version in the *Novelas* further develops the picaresque's skeptical bent. In "La ilustre fregona," "Rinconete y Cortadillo," and especially the dyadic "El casamiento engañoso/El coloquio de los perros," the metaliterary reflection on the picaresque exposes and challenges the complex interplay between narrative authority and belief.

Itineraries of the Self

Despite announcing themselves as exemplary, the *Novelas* offer remarkable representations of choice and *gusto*. Plots often depend on characters who abandon the straight and narrow for the pleasures of waywardness. Romance errancy is thus miniaturized into the space of the novella—or the aforementioned *mesa de trucos*—as one young man after another chooses to eschew his obligations and explore instead a picaresque version of experience. These itineraries of the (male) self determined by pleasure and whim rather than necessity or a given social position, problematize the idea that readers can know these figures from any external or preexisting hierarchy. Far from exemplary, their itineraries take the protagonists on a series of highly personal, whimsical detours and ill-advised wanderings across and beyond Spain. Beyond the four novellas that explicitly reference the picaresque lie others whose far from exemplary characters espouse itinerancy, debauchery, or the avoidance of obligation: "La gitanilla," "El licenciado vidriera," "La fuerza de la sangre," "El celoso extremeño," "Las dos doncellas," "La señora Cornelia." (The astute reader will notice that this is most of the novellas, with the exception of "El amante liberal" and "La española inglesa." Those bear a closer relationship to the captivity narrative, which the picaresque challenges in a different key, as I discuss in Chapter 2.)

As critics have noted, in the *Novelas* the picaresque is often a choice for protagonists, in a version of aristocratic slumming. The straitened circumstances that Lázaro famously offers to exculpate his younger self—"Consideren los que heredaron nobles estados cuán poco se les debe, pues Fortuna fue con ellos parcial, y cuánto más hicieron los que, siéndoles contraria, con fuerza y maña remando salieron a buen puerto"[10] ["Those who inherited a noble estate should consider how little is owed to them, for Fortune was partial to them, and how much more was accomplished by those whom it opposed, and who got somewhere through their own strength and skill"]—do not apply here. Most strikingly, young men evade the call to arms to pursue instead their own penchant for another place, another self, another version of experience. Much like those of Delicado's Lozana and her narrator in Chapter 1, their perverse itineraries sidestep the martial or heroic to question Spain's place within Europe and the vexed pursuit of European empire. Soldiering—a prime rationale for displacement in the world of the *Novelas*—becomes more often than not a mere excuse to skip town. The characters' meandering journeys allow us to register the contingency of subjectivity, and to consider the implications for how these stories are told. With protagonists not simply displaced, but often AWOL, any account of their activities implicitly justifies them.

To take perhaps the signal example, the two protagonists of "La ilustre fregona," Carriazo and Avendaño, renounce both arms and letters to become *pícaros*. Their perverse itinerary, set entirely within Spain, repatriates the subversive detours to Italy of so many other *Novelas*, and reiterates the picaresque as a Spanish avocation. Carriazo is the first to run away, "llevado de una inclinación picaresca, sin forzarle a ello algún mal tratamiento que sus padres le hiciesen, sólo por su gusto y antojo, se desgarró, como dicen los muchachos, de casa de sus padres, y se fue por ese mundo adelante" (2:139) ["led by a picaresque inclination, and not forced to it by any mistreatment at his parents' hand, but simply for his own pleasure and whim, took off, as the lads say, from his parents' house, and went off into the world"]. The narrator shares in Carriazo's predilections, noting appreciatively "que pudiera leer cátedra en la facultad al famoso de Alfarache" (2:139) ["he might lecture at university the famous Alfarache"].[11] He waxes most enthusiastic when evoking the epitome of picaresque life in the *almadrabas* (tuna fisheries) of Zahara (2:140) and the *pícaros* from across Spain who must pass through them if they are to deserve the name:

> ¡Oh pícaros de cocina, sucios, gordos y lucios, pobres fingidos, tullidos falsos, cicateruelos de Zodocover y de la plaza de Madrid, vistosos oracioneros, esportilleros de Sevilla, mandilejos de la hampa, con toda la caterva innumerable que se encierra debajo deste nombre *pícaro*! Bajad el toldo, amainad el brío, no os llaméis pícaros si no habéis cursado dos cursos en la academia de la pesca de los atunes. . . . Aquí se canta, allí se reniega, acullá se riñe, acá se juega, y por todo se hurta. Allí campea la libertad y luce el trabajo; allí van, o envían, muchos padres principales a buscar a sus hijos, y los hallan; y tanto sienten sacarlos de aquella vida como si los llevaran a dar la muerte. (2:141)

> [O kitchen boys, dirty, fat, and greasy, fake paupers, false cripples, pickpockets of the Zodocover and the plaza in Madrid, reciters of prayers who pretend to be blind, porters of Seville, pimps' assistants from the underworld, and all the innumerable hordes that fall under the name of *pícaro*! Close up shop, hold your horses, and do not call yourselves *pícaros* unless you've taken two courses at the academy of the tuna fisheries! . . . Here they sing, there they renege, over there they quarrel, over here they gamble, and everywhere they steal. There freedom takes the field and work shines; there do many noble parents go for their children, or send for them, and find them, and {the children} are as sorry to be taken from that life as if they were being taken to their deaths.]

In describing the exemplarily picaresque existence of the *almadrabas*, the narrator also makes Carriazo simply one instance of a generalized condition, by which the children of the upper class must be hauled back to their obligations like so many recalcitrant tunas.[12] As is often the case for Cervantine narrators, this one appears fully complicit with his characters' enthusiasms: although not in the first person, the narration is clearly sympathetic to the *pícaro* and involves the reader in the pleasures of his slumming.

Although idyllic as a site where responsibility is relinquished, the *almadrabas* also function as a dangerously liminal space, vulnerable to attacks from sea: "Pero toda esta dulzura que he pintado tiene un amargo acíbar que la amarga, y es no poder dormir sueño seguro sin el temor de que en un instante los trasladen de Zahara a Berbería" (2:141–42) ["But all this sweetness I have depicted is made bitter by a bitter draught, and that is the inability to sleep safely without fearing that in one instant they will be transported from Zahara to Barbary"]. In a picaresque narrative otherwise entirely domestic, the *almadrabas* thus open up to a larger Mediterranean geography of corsairs and captivity—compelled transformations of the self that serve as dark doubles for the entirely willed slumming by Carriazo, and remind us of the vexed narratives produced retrospectively by a compelled subjectivity, as in the cases of Lozana, Pedro, and Guzmán in my earlier chapters.

In order to return home to Burgos after three years away, the prodigal Carriazo must slough off his new self via a prudent preliminary stop in Valladolid: "Estúvose allí quince días para reformar la color del rostro, sacándola de mulata a flamenca, y para trastejarse y sacarse del borrador de pícaro y ponerse en limpio de caballero" (2:142) ["He spent fifteen days there to reform the color of his face, and bring it from mulatto to Flemish, and to take himself from the rough draft of a *pícaro* into the clean copy of a gentleman"]. Even Carriazo's physicality is reformed as he fashions himself into a gentleman once again. Skin color—so central to essentialized, genealogical categories of race—appears susceptible to change, while the social and moral qualities of a gentleman are nothing more than a careful copy of the draft that is the *pícaro*. (The properly pale gentleman is Flemish, as though the category of pale noble Spaniard were somehow less available.) Not only does Carriazo choose to live as a *pícaro*, and succeed at it for three years, he effectively reverses the transformation in just a short time out of the sun. Although this protean privilege may pertain primarily to male aristocratic characters (such as the young men who spend time as gypsies in "La gitanilla"), their transformations imply a contingent idea of selfhood and suggest at least the possibility of an upward social mobility to match the slumming. If nobles can be *pícaros*, cannot *pícaros* be noble? This is of course the question explored in a more pessimistic or repressive vein by the *Guzmán* and by Quevedo's *Buscón*, which both envision the possibility only to reassure readers of its necessary failure and violent repression.

Perhaps unsurprisingly, so protean a character as Carriazo is a very effective liar: "Contó Carriazo a sus padres y a todos mil magníficas y luengas mentiras de cosas que le habían sucedido en los tres años de su ausencia; pero nunca tocó, ni por pienso, en las almadrabas" (2:143) ["Carriazo told his parents and everyone else a thousand magnificent long lies about the things that had happened to him during the three years of his absence, but never once did he touch upon, or even dream of mentioning, the tuna fisheries"]. Because the novella is not narrated in the first person, the reader need not rely on Carriazo's *luengas mentiras*, as do his naïve parents. Instead, the omniscient narrator relates the young man's actual experiences during his picaresque interlude and charts his lies. Yet given how volubly the narrator has already revealed his own penchant for the picaresque life, the alternative itself appears somewhat fishy.[13]

The emphasis on *gusto* as both a powerful determinant of self and as a counterexemplary force reappears when Carriazo ropes in his friend Avendaño for a renewed excursus into the picaresque life:

> Le contó punto por punto la vida de la jábega y cómo todas sus tristezas y pensamientos nacían del deseo que tenía de volver a ella; pintósela de modo que Avendaño, cuando le acabó de oir, antes alabó que vituperó su gusto. En fin, el de la plática fue disponer Carriazo la voluntad de Avendaño de manera que determinó de irse con él a gozar un verano de aquella felicísima vida que le había descrito, de lo cual quedó sobremodo contento Carriazo, por parecerle que había ganado un testigo de abono que calificase su baja determinación. (2:143)
>
> [He told him in great detail about the fishing/picaresque life and how all his sadness and pensiveness was born of his desire to return to it; he depicted it so that Avendaño, when he had heard him out, praised rather than condemned his desire. The end result was that Carriazo moved Avendaño's will so that he decided to go off with him to enjoy for a summer that most happy life he had described, which delighted Carriazo, for it seemed to him that he had gained a witness in his favor to validate his base decision.]

In mutually reinforced counterexemplarity, Avendaño decides to follow and imitate his slumming friend, while Carriazo finds validation in Avendaño's imitation of his actions.

To finance their expedition, they will loot the funds destined for Avendaño's education, as a new picaresque avocation replaces his earlier *gusto* for Greek and Latin (2:143). To get away, Carriazo tells his father "que tenía voluntad de irse con Avendaño a estudiar a Salamanca" (2:143–44) ["his wish was to go with Avendaño to study in Salamanca"], to which the unsuspecting father immediately accedes, in sincere pleasure at a pretended desire ("Vino su padre con tanto gusto en ello" ["His father responded with such pleasure"], 2:144). As with the unpredictable desire of the captive Madrigal for what the Ottoman world offers him, discussed in Chapter 2, *gusto* here undoes any predetermined sense of self, setting instead new trajectories and alternative itineraries.[14]

The two young men shake the bumbling *ayo* sent to accompany them to university by claiming that they wish to sightsee in Valladolid; "que querían estarse en aquel lugar dos días para verle, porque nunca le habían visto ni estado en él" (2:144) ["they wished to spend two days there to see the place, as they had never seen it nor been there"]. Yet a mere two pages earlier the narrator had specified Valladolid as the place where the prodigal Carriazo had stopped to restore his noble appearance (2:142). Even as the narrator conflates the two young men's experiences, his own voice echoes their excuses, suggesting how fragile is any distinction between his and their perspectives. As the narrator's voice collapses into the *pícaros*', he becomes ever less reliable. Although never as implicated as Delicado's Auctor, who actually enters the diegesis of *Lozana*, this narrator nonetheless endeavors to seduce the reader into adopting the *pícaros*' point of view.

Though the *ayo* demurs, the young men finally secure a day to see the famous fountain of Argales. This is simply a trick to shake off supervision, yet the narrator nonetheless dwells at great length on the fountain, "famosa por su antigüedad y sus aguas, a despecho del Caño Dorado y la reverenda Priora, con paz sea dicho de Leganitos y de la extremadísima fuente Castellana, en cuya competencia pueden callar Corpa y la Pizarra de la Mancha" (2:145) ["famous for its antiquity and its waters, much though it might pain the Golden Pipe and the reverend Priora, to say nothing of Leganitos and the most excellent Castellana fountain, which are enough to silence Corpa and the Pizarra fountain of La Mancha"]. Carried away on this itinerary of great fountains of Spain, and dwelling on their relative excellence and merit, the narrator effectively voices the young men's alibi, so that as the reader retraces the itinerary of watery excellence and comparative fountains she must remind herself: *this is not the point.* As a mise-en-abîme for the complex intersections of picaresque and exemplarity in the *Novelas*, the fountain may itself be exemplary, even inimitable, yet its role is to coopt or distract figures of authority—the narrator and the *ayo*—from what is really going on: the young men's ruse to avoid their supposed destination in Salamanca for their true, picaresque goal. Through a series of further unspecified complicities ("hubo quien les fiase . . . y aun quien les diese" ["there was someone to offer them credit . . . and even one to give them"], 2:145), the young men quickly shed horses, clothes, swords—the trappings of their aristocratic identities—as the narrator indulgently looks on: "Dejémoslos ir, por ahora, pues van contentos y alegres" (2:146) ["Let us let them go, for now, as they go so content and happy"].

The deceptions multiply as the two invoke the societal expectations for those of their class and gender simply in order to evade them. In a note, they instruct their minder to return home and tell their parents that they have decided to change course, claiming they have now decided to trade the university for the battlefield:

> Habiendo nosotros sus hijos, con madura consideración, considerado cuán más propias son de los caballeros las armas que las letras, habemos determinado de trocar a Salamanca por Bruselas y a España por Flandes. . . . Nuestra hidalga intención y el largo camino es bastante disculpa de nuestro yerro, aunque nadie le juzgará por tal, si no es cobarde. . . De la fuente de Argales, puesto ya el pie en el estribo para caminar a Flandes. (2:146)
>
> [We their sons, having with mature consideration considered how much more fitting for gentlemen are arms than letters, have decided to trade Salamanca for Brussels and Spain for Flanders. . . . Our noble intention and the long way ahead must suffice to excuse our error, although no one will judge it thus unless he is a coward. . . . From the fountain of Argales, with one foot on the stirrup on the way to Flanders.]

Considering with mature consideration, the young men protest too much. They sign off from Argales, recalling the place of that exemplary detour in their straying from their course. As though to underscore the protagonists' displacement and his own ambivalence at their behavior, the narrator bifurcates as soon as the *ayo* discovers the letter and the theft of the tuition, of which he must advise the boys' parents so they may pursue their sons:

> Pero destas cosas no dice nada el autor desta novela, porque así como dejó puesto a caballo a Pedro Alonso, volvió a contar de lo que les sucedió a Avendaño y a Carriazo a la entrada de Illescas, diciendo que al entrar de la puerta de la villa encontraron dos mozos de mulas, al parecer andaluces. (2:146)
>
> [But the author of this novella says nothing of these things, for as soon as he left Pedro Alonso on his mount, he returned to relating what had happened to Avendaño and Carriazo at the entrance to Illescas, telling how at the town gate they found two muleboys, who appeared to be Andalusian.]

The sudden irruption of a second narrator who identifies the path not taken only underscores the first narrator's unreliability: his picaresque enthusiasms, his contradictory account of Carriazo's acquaintance with Valladolid, his willingness to distract the reader with fluent alibis while his protagonists arrange their getaway. Of course such a narrator would choose the young men over their parents—as would the reader. Although the conceit of redoubled narration is not sustained as it is in the *Quijote*, it remains a powerful reminder of how the picaresque distorts the reliability of its narrators, even when, as in this case, it is not narrated in the first person.

At such moments, Cervantes ironizes exemplarity—all that "madura consideración" and "hidalga intención"—by not only presenting behavior that is far from exemplary, but emphasizing the idiosyncrasy of individual experience and taste, as well as the irrepressible nature of desire. The question that "La ilustre fregona" and other novellas marked by picaresque detours implicitly pose is not only who *should* follow such behavior but who *could* follow it, since it seems to correspond primarily to such idiosyncratic motives, however much the narrator claims to understand the protagonists. Thus Avendaño never really feels the pull of the picaresque life as does Carriazo—its appeal is not a generalizable principle. In fact, Avendaño will use sightseeing as a pretext of his own, in order to keep Carriazo in Toledo and delay their departure for the *almadrabas*, in the hope of seeing the *ilustre fregona* Costanza again: "pienso antes que desta ciudad me parta ver lo que dicen que hay famoso en ella, como es el Sagrario, el artificio de Juanelo, las Vistillas de San Agustín, la Huerta del Rey y la Vega" (2:151) ["before leaving this city I intend to see what they say is famous within it, such as the Sacred Tabernacle, Juanelo's device, the views of San Agustín, the King's Orchard and the fields"]—in none of which does he have any real interest. The itineraries of a novella like "La ilustre fregona" thus stand in an ironic relationship to forms that imply or invite imitation—not just moral exemplarity, but also emblems or travel literature, all of them characterized by generalizations and topoi. It is not actually possible to replicate these journeys, since they have so much to do with personal idiosyncrasy and the protagonists' own investments in the places they visit, or, as with the sightseeing in "La ilustre fregona," their dissimulation of their actual goals. *Lugares comunes*—commonplaces—do not apply when all places are experienced in individualized fashion.

As in the *Quijote*, many of the characters in the *Novelas* are most memorable for being out of place, or wanting what it is not their place to want. While in some cases, as with the title characters of "La gitanilla" or "La ilustre fregona," this being out of place replicates familiar romance structures of hidden identity or a child lost to aristocratic parents, the picaresque version also insistently questions the fixity of identity itself, whether for the male protagonists who choose less exalted versions of the self, or, more rarely, for a figure like Preciosa in "La gitanilla," who although she does not choose her alternate path finds much wider latitude within it for the construction of a three-dimensional self. In the moral and political realm, the male figures are at least temporarily counterexamples, in their avoidance of enlistment, university, or whatever might be for them the next step into adulthood. Recuperated by conservative endings that return them to their proper locations, the prodigal sons or lost daughters are gladly welcomed into the fold and returned to their "real" selves, as when the narrator in "La ilustre fregona" tells us that Tomás's father "le abrazó con grandísimo contento, a fuer del que tuvo el padre del Hijo Pródigo cuando le cobró de perdido" (2:196) ["embraced him with great joy, like that experienced by the father of the Prodigal Son when he recovered him after losing him"]. Yet reading for the end obviates the itineraries ardently desired and carefully mapped in the texts themselves: instead of forward movement and the teleological inevitability of the end, the novellas privilege wandering middles. Unlike in romance, however, this picaresque wandering is motivated, corresponding to subjectivity and agency rather than mysterious chance; indeed, subjectification involves taking a detour from the expected itinerary.

Beyond simply noting the destabilizing or ironizing force of these dubious journeys, we might therefore consider also their more positive dimension. What is the value of elsewhere, of a different perspective on things, of skepticism in relation to exemplarity? Does the actual value of these itineraries lie in trying out alternative selves, given the partiality and contingency of experience? The trenchant contribution of the novellas may be not simply to skewer the pieties of their culture, but to reflect on what postmoderns would call positionality, that is, on how class, lineage, social hierarchy, and geography fundamentally affect our perspective. Characters who explore alternative ways of being in the world, and hence of seeing the world, disrupt the fixity of identity on which the social and political hierarchies of the period are predicated. Thus fictional *gusto* takes on political and ideological significance as an alternative to conformism, and a reminder that it is possible to question the value of set models. Inexplicably personal and idiosyncratic, *gusto* might nonetheless prove exemplary as a model for seeing otherwise, whether by running away with the gypsies, trying out life as a *pícaro,* or whatever else catches one's particular fancy. Itineraries of the self link the various *Novelas* internally and also to *Don Quijote*, reconceived as not just one addled would-be hero whose *gusto* gets the better of him but a kaleidoscopic set of protagonists who attempt to live otherwise. The possibilities for experimentation or embarking on desired itineraries of the self are not distributed evenly across the *Novelas*—crucially, female characters, often captives of one sort or another, do not have the same agency as young, aristocratic men, and their return to their proper place (as with Preciosa or Isabela) often involves a diminution in agency. Nonetheless, the perverse itineraries followed by the male protagonists of so many of the novellas, who turn away, however momentarily, from their proper geographic and social place, the social ties that bind them, and their obligations, introduce a radical contingency into the world of the texts, suggesting the possibility of living otherwise and the paradoxical exemplarity of individual exploration.

Playing at Picaresque

While "La ilustre fregona" charts the powerful role of *gusto* in constructing itineraries of the self, "Rinconete y Cortadillo" explores how the perverse itineraries of its protagonists are pleasurably rendered for readers. The novella follows two young *pícaros* to Seville, where they join a criminal order—a *cofradía* of thieves, whores, and pimps—that slyly mirrors the hierarchies and pieties of mainstream society. At the thematic as at the formal level, the text plays constantly with the relationship between embeddedness and belief, foregrounding the narrative and authorial games of the picaresque even as it dismantles them.

From its first sentence, "Rinconete y Cortadillo" introduces the problem of perspective: "En la venta del Molinillo, que está puesta en los fines de los famosos campos de Alcudia, como vamos de Castilla a la Andalucía" (1:191) ["At the inn of the Small Mill, which is situated towards the end of the famous fields of Alcudia, as we head from Castile to Andalucía"]. Even something as ostensibly stable as geography depends on perspective—the inn lies at the far end of the fields when headed from Castile to Andalucía, but not if embarked on the reverse itinerary. In a genre typically associated with narration in the first-person singular, "como vamos" turns out to be a red herring, too, introducing a first-person plural that seems to correlate to two *pícaros*. But the inclusive verb leads nowhere: what follows is a third-person narrator who offers instead a precise description of the two characters.[15]

The narrator's account foregrounds the theatricality and even voyeurism of the narration as it describes the *pícaros*' visible clothes, those that can barely be seen, and those that will be seen only later: "Capa, no la tenían; los calzones eran de lienzo, y las medias, de carne . . . el otro venía escueto y sin alforjas, puesto que en el seno se le parecía un gran bulto, que, a lo que después pareció, era un cuello de los que llaman valones, almidonado con grasa, y tan deshilado de roto, que todo parecía hilachas" (1:191–92) ["They had no cape; their breeches were made of linen, and they had but flesh for their stockings . . . the other one was rather skimpily attired, and carried no bags, although there was a great lump on his chest that was later revealed as one of those collars they call *valones*, starched with grease, and so threadbare that it looked like a rag"]. Cervantes moves from the inclusiveness of a first-person plural that invites the reader into the text to a showy omniscience that even anticipates what will only happen later ("a lo que después pareció"). With remarkable economy, he thus marks the imbalance of knowledge between reader and narrator.

Narrative authority remains a central concern as the raggedy boys strike up a conversation. The older of the two asks the younger about his origins, only to have him deny any knowledge of them: "Mi tierra, señor caballero—respondió el preguntado—, no la sé, ni para dónde camino, tampoco" (1:193) ["'I know not from what land I come, sir,' answered the one who had been asked, 'nor where I am headed'"]. The echoes of the famous opening of *Don Quijote*—"En un lugar de la Mancha, de cuyo nombre no quiero acordarme" ["in a town in La Mancha whose name I do not wish to remember"]—and of the slippery, penniless squire in the third *tratado* of *Lazarillo* alert us to the heightened stakes in identifying origins for a subject being scrutinized. In an inquisitorial context, skepticism involves not just the questioning of truths *tout court*, but a recognition that negotiations of authority underlie negotiated truths.[16] After this false start, the boys quickly warm up and provide first-person picaresques in miniature, establishing their credentials as part of the tradition.[17] Both tales feature multiple elements associated with the picaresque, from fractured families to anticlerical satire to tangling with the law: Cortadillo's father disowns him, while his stepmother treats him ill; Rinconete's father sells indulgences, and the boy grows too fond of the money they collect, redirecting his affection from the familial to the material ("me abracé con un talego" ["I embraced a moneybag"], 1:195). Unlike the traditional picaresque, however, these accounts are punctuated by dialogue, with frequent interjections from each boy's interlocutor. Thus in a knowing wink to the legal analogues of the picaresque, Rincón declares, "Eso se borre" (1:198) ["Let that be erased"], when Cortado confesses his hasty escape from Toledo and the law.

After the two boys exchange their stories, each a mini-*Lazarillo* of sorts, we are quickly extruded from their narratives into the broader purview of third-person narration. That narrator, in turn, relays the external perspective of a listener who is somewhere between a voyeur and a theatergoer: the *ventera*, or innkeeper, "admirada de la buena crianza de los pícaros . . . les había estado oyendo su plática sin que ellos advirtiesen en ello" (1:198) ["surprised at the good breeding of the *pícaros*, . . . had been listening to their conversation without their noticing"]. Is the innkeeper surprised because *pícaros* speak so articulately, or is she too easily impressed, given that they are anything but well bred? The line thematizes the reception of the picaresque—not only are textual *pícaros* more articulate than one might expect (class does not reliably predict eloquence, especially when genre mediates), their narrative is crafted with an eye to the audience, so that it becomes anything but straightforwardly mimetic.

The *pícaros* do not even realize that anyone else is listening, and their increasingly frank confession of their origins and malfeasance does not really account for the eavesdropper. Yet the text balances three different audiences: the other *pícaro*, the naïve *ventera*, and the reader. At such moments, Cervantes explores how, instead of offering anything like an authentic voice from below, the picaresque in fact skirts the theatrical. The unknowing entertainment that the two boys provide for the innkeeper as they amuse each other anticipates the much more fulsome show provided by Monipodio's gang, which the boys and the reader will consume together. As Helen Reed notes, theatricality virtually makes the novella a "metapicaresque."[18] The back-and-forth between authoritative narrators and an absorbing theatricality makes for a constructive tension: fictionality lies somewhere in the discerning detachment of a skeptical reader who can tease them apart, weighing their various merits.

The novella explores this tension by submerging us into the tumultuous underworld of Seville. Once the pair join Monipodio's impious order, they are gradually incorporated into its rules and privileges. Beyond the local color, what is at stake in this enterprise is largely belief, a point that Cervantes makes as he slyly compares the gang to a religious institution, complete with hierarchies, initiation, and ordination to which all must subscribe. Belief in the laws of the *cofradía* contrasts comically with the general corruption that the novella portrays, from porters who are actually pickpockets to officers of the law in cahoots with the ruffians. As devout followers, the members of the *cofradía* must scrupulously observe its rules, even as they simultaneously participate in a broader urban drama where nothing is what it seems. As actors, they are also tremendously entertaining, given to outsize emotions, grandstanding, and swift scene changes from love to violence.[19]

After the highly theatrical suite of tricks, fights, and love quarrels that takes up most of the novella, the narrative returns to the playful perspectivism of the opening. The conclusion emphasizes skeptical distance over embeddedness, once again juxtaposing third-person narration and an absorbing theatricality. The third person simultaneously distances us from the spectacle that is Monipodio's gang and uncomfortably reminds us of our own pleasure in it. At this point, too, the text offers a distinction between the two *pícaros*, abandoning the pair to focus on one skeptical observer in the metaphorical corner (*rincón*).

The concluding paragraphs relay the perspective of Rinconete, who, taking his distance from what he has seen, questions the ruffians' all-encompassing belief system:

> Era Rinconete, aunque muchacho, de muy buen entendimiento, y tenía un buen natural; y como había andado con su padre en el ejercicio de las bulas, sabía algo de buen lenguaje, y dábale gran risa pensar en los vocablos que había oído a Monipodio y a los demás de su compañía y bendita comunidad . . . y, sobre todo, le admiraba la seguridad que tenían y la confianza de irse al cielo con no faltar a sus devociones, estando tan llenos de hurtos, y de homicidios, y de ofensas de Dios. Y reíase de la otra buena vieja de la Pipota, que dejaba la canasta de colar hurtada guardada en la casa y se iba a poner candelillas de cera a las imágenes y con ellos pensaba irse al cielo

calzada y vestida. No menos le suspendía la obediencia y respecto que todos tenían a Monipodio, siendo un hombre bárbaro, rústico y desalmado. (1:239–40)

[Although he was young, Rinconete was intelligent and had a good mind. Since he had often accompanied his father in the sale of his bulls, he knew something of good language, and laughed as he recalled the words of Monipodio and the other members in his company and blessed community . . . he was amazed to see how certain and confident they were of going to heaven as long as they did not skip their devotions, despite their many thefts, murders, and other offenses against God. He laughed also at the good old Pipota, who left the basket of stolen linen at home and then went to place little wax candles before the images of the saints, and so expected to go to heaven just as she was. He was no less amazed by the obedience and respect all had for Monipodio, given that he was a rude, barbarous, and soulless man.]

Ironically, Rinconete's skepticism is born of his experience with his father's "ejercicio de las bulas," or selling of indulgences—the phony métier teaches him to spot the ruffians' malapropisms and sharpens his eye for sanctimoniousness. The tension between belief and informed doubt here is palpable: the entire *ejercicio* depends on misplaced belief, as does Monipodio's criminal enterprise, yet it produces a skeptical result in a participant/witness who reflects on the limitations of the systems in which he is implicated. Behind the relatively easy targets—Monipodio, the seller of indulgences—lies a more devastating skeptical attack on the credulity of everyday religious practice, emptied of significance by the immorality of its practitioners.

However compromised his own moral position, Rinconete's background affords him the skeptical distance to suspend belief in the pieties of the *cofradía*, as well as the potential to remove himself from Monipodio's influence:

Propuso en sí de aconsejar a su compañero no durasen mucho en aquella vida tan perdida y tan mala, tan inquieta, y tan libre y disoluta. Pero, con todo esto, llevado de sus pocos años y de su poca experiencia, pasó con ella adelante algunos meses, en los cuales le sucedieron cosas que piden más luenga escritura, y así se deja para otra ocasión contar. (1:240)

> [He decided to dissuade his friend from continuing in that way of life, so hopeless and evil, so uneasy, so free and dissolute. And yet, despite all this, his youth and lack of experience led him to remain in it for some months longer, during which such things happened to him as deserve to be written of at greater length, so that I will leave them to tell on another occasion.]

Rinconete intends to advise his friend to leave, but then cannot quite extricate himself, at least for a few months. From his initial amazement ("no menos le suspendía"), he moves to suspended belief, and then to suspended judgment. The novella appears counterexemplary in two senses: on the one hand, the example of Monipodio's community must clearly be rejected, rather than followed, in some future time; on the other, this (counter)example does not result in an immediate spur to virtuous action. As the narrator tantalizes us with the thought of the additional adventures that will take place in the intervening time, the conclusion teeters between fugitive, embedded pleasures and retrospective telling once those pleasures are no more. Additional adventures will yield more fictions, as long as Rinconete eventually manages to take his leave of the corrupt community. Yet there is something uncontainable about the scene from which he cannot tear himself, and the concomitant text which we consume. Like Ginés's story, this one, too, is not quite done.

The negotiation of belief and text—that potential story yet to be written—in this concluding passage is palpable: without a skeptical distance, there can be no narrative. At the same time, Cervantes addresses our own readerly investment in the text, reminding us of the uncritical pleasures we have been experiencing throughout. Third-person narration corrects the first-person viewpoint of the *pícaro*, yet cannot completely contain the pleasures offered by the voyeuristic, theatrical text. These seduce the reader into a different kind of belief, too engrossing to allow for critical distance. For Rinconete to read skeptically—in this case, to produce a text out of his experience—he must resist a *cofradía* that would absorb him into belief, but also the theatricality that lulls him with its pleasures. Given the insistent pull of the picaresque on a figure such as Carriazo, who actually has a home to return to, we might be forgiven for wondering whether Rinconete will indeed ever achieve the necessary distance. Only the text before us confirms that he has, in at least some measure.

Moreover, as Rincón ponders what he has experienced and moves on to adventures "que piden más luenga escritura," we are reduced to his sole perspective. Having toyed with the reduplicated possibilities of two *pícaros*,

Cervantes underscores how stubbornly individualizing the genre is, how ready to privilege one perspective. This begs the question of the story that is never told: suspended, too, is Cortado's account, nipped in the bud before it can even begin. Our last glimpse of him is as Monipodio walks away, "dejando a los dos compañeros admirados de lo que habían visto" (1:239) ["leaving the two companions wondering at what they had seen"]. There is no room for this second opinion in the meta-narrative conclusion, yet its marked absence contributes to the construction of a skeptical reader. Like Rincón in his corner, we must take our distance. Once we notice the unceremonial banishment of Cortado, even the version that the narrator so tantalizingly promises in Rincón's name must be taken under advisement.

Doubting the Dogs

"El casamiento engañoso" and "El coloquio de los perros," the last two tales in Cervantes's collection, are actually frame and framed tale, and their duality returns us to the broader meditation on skepticism that underlies the *Novelas ejemplares*. Both frame and framed text explore alternative forms of picaresque, experimenting beyond first-person narration. In the frame narrative, Campuzano, a syphilitic soldier who has gotten more than he bargained for from his marriage to a woman of doubtful repute, tells his friend Peralta of his troubles. Campuzano and his bride engaged in a mutual con, both duped by carefully staged impersonations of wealth and personal worth: from a white hand artfully displayed, to jewels made of paste, to a borrowed house passed off as the "lady's" own.

Once the illusions dissolve, Campuzano is left with the reality of syphilis, which colors both frame and framed narrative, in a manner reminiscent of Delicado's *Lozana* in Chapter 1. When Peralta expresses his astonishment at Campuzano's story, the soldier reprises the tantalizing gesture that marks the end of "Rinconete and Cortadillo": "—Pues de poco se maravilla vuesa merced, señor Peralta—dijo el Alférez—; que otros sucesos me quedan por decir que exceden a toda imaginación, pues van fuera de todos los términos de naturaleza" (2:292) ["'Well, you are easily amazed, Master Peralta,' said the second lieutenant, 'for I have other things left to tell that exceed all imagination, for they lie beyond all bounds of nature'"]. Campuzano stokes Peralta's desire, while simultaneously reminding us of his impaired condition: "Doy por bien empleadas todas mis desgracias, por haber sido parte de haberme puesto en el hospital donde vi lo que ahora diré" (2:292) ["I consider all my misfortunes to have been worthwhile, as they put me in the hospital where I saw what I will now relate"]. Peralta's burning desire for the story sets the stage for the narrative to come (2:293).

As he finally delivers, Campuzano underscores his status as a near-eyewitness to what he relates:

> Vuesa merced se acomode a creerlo; y es que yo oí y casi vi con mis ojos a estos dos perros . . . estar una noche, que fue la penúltima que acabé de sudar, echados detrás de mi cama en unas esteras viejas, y a la mitad de aquella noche, estando a escuras y desvelado, pensando en mis pasados sucesos y presentes desgracias, oi hablar allí junto, y estuve con atento oído escuchando, por ver si podía venir en conocimiento de los que hablaban y de lo que hablaban, y a poco rato vine a conocer, por lo que hablaban, los que hablaban, y eran los dos perros Cipión y Berganza. (2:293)
>
> [Your worship had better prepare to believe it, for I heard and almost saw with my own eyes these two dogs . . . one night, and it was two nights before my sweating cure was done, lying behind my bed on some old mats, and in the middle of that night, when it was dark and I could not sleep, thinking of what had happened to me and my present misfortunes, I heard someone speak close by, and listened most attentively, to see whether I could figure out who was talking and what they were saying, and soon I realized, from what they said, who it was, and it was the two dogs Cipión and Berganza.]

Instead of the confident omniscient narrator of "Rinconete and Cortadillo," Cervantes here offers a paradoxically unreliable witness, who spins an amazing tale of talking dogs—a canine double-picaresque. Not only does Peralta not believe what Campuzano heard and "almost saw," he decides based on this new evidence not to believe what he has heard previously about Campuzano's deceitful marriage.

Campuzano acknowledges that a miracle would be required for the dogs to speak, yet insists that he did not dream the story. He offers his own self-doubt as reassurance, although Peralta is not appeased:

> Yo mismo no he querido dar crédito a mí mismo, y he querido tener por cosa soñada lo que realmente estando despierto, con todos mis

cinco sentidos, tales cuales nuestro Señor fue servido de dármelos, oí, escuché, noté y finalmente escribí, sin faltar palabra por su concierto; de donde se puede tomar indicio bastante que mueva y persuada a creer esta verdad que digo. (2:294)

[I haven't wanted to credit myself, and have wanted to take as a dream what, awake and with my five senses, as God saw fit to give them to me, I really heard, listened to, noted, and finally wrote down, with nary a word missing from the whole; which one may take as a sufficient sign to move and persuade one of this truth I tell.]

Campuzano trusts the evidence of his God-given senses, however dreamlike his experience. Anthony Cascardi explores the idea of truth revealed through dreams in the framing of the "Coloquio," yet Campuzano explicitly refuses that possibility here.[20] Fiction becomes the alternative to the dream vision. There is a humorous reflection here on the unreliability of the senses, a central obstacle to human knowledge noted by such key skeptics as Juan Luis Vives, Francisco Sánchez, and Juan Huarte de San Juan.[21] For his part, Campuzano doubts, yet allows his senses to reassure him.

The syphilitic braggart may be the most unreliable of narrators, but his story is ultimately irresistible, so that the question of truth is bracketed and judgment suspended. Although Campuzano first avers that he is prepared to swear to the truth of his story, he quickly changes tack, arguing for the pleasure it will provide even if it is not true:

—Pero puesto caso que me haya engañado, y que mi verdad sea sueño, y el porfiarla disparate, ¿no se holgará vuesa merced, señor Peralta, de ver escritas en un coloquio las cosas que estos perros, o sean quien fueren, hablaron?

—Como vuesa merced—replicó el Licenciado—no se canse más en persuadirme que oyó hablar a los perros, de muy buena gana oiré ese coloquio, que por ser escrito y notado del buen ingenio del señor Alférez, ya le juzgo por bueno. (2:294)

["And supposing I were mistaken, and that my truth were a dream, and it were nonsense to believe it, would you not take pleasure,

> Mr. Peralta, at seeing written in a colloquy the things that these dogs, or whoever they were, said?"
>
> "As long as you no longer insist on persuading me that you heard the dogs speak," answered the Licentiate, "I will gladly listen to that colloquy, which, written and noted by the good wit of Mr. Second-Lieutenant, I already judge worthy."]

Peralta finally relents, agreeing to read what Campuzano has written as long as the latter stops insisting on the truth of his narrative. Cervantes thus stages a pact of fictionality that anticipates Coleridge's notion of poetic or negative faith: Campuzano insists on the pleasure that the story provides, even if it should prove to be the product of his deluded brain, and his reader agrees with him, as long as the question of truth can be tabled and, once again, judgment suspended. Pleasure thus trumps verisimilitude and its mimetic—or exemplary—potential.[22]

As if to drive home the incommensurability of truth and fiction, Campuzano notes that while he remembered and wrote down exactly what he had heard, without adding or taking away "para hacerle gustoso" (2:294) ["to make it pleasurable"], he has only taken down half of what the dogs related, or one of the two nights' dialogue. The second half—the life of the second dog, Cipión—he will write "cuando viere, o que ésta se crea, o a lo menos no se desprecie" (2:295) ["when I see that this one is believed, or at least not scorned"]. In the best of cases, then, his version is but half the story. As with "Rinconete and Cortadillo," the reader is left longing for additional fictions, which here depend not on the ability of the narrator-protagonist to suspend belief and extricate himself, as in the case of Rinconete, but rather on the reader's ability to suspend disbelief at least long enough for the story to materialize. Yet even this suspension of disbelief occurs in a skeptical mode: the circumspect reader chooses, advisedly, to suspend judgment for the sake of pleasure, without conceding actual belief in the tale. The marked unreliability of the picaresque narrators in both cases—the trickster Rinconete, imperfectly reformed, and the addled Campuzano—makes the pact of fictionality all the more deliberate and counterintuitive: it is born not of belief, but of skepticism. Given the repeated allusions over the course of these novellas to texts that do not materialize, there is a suggestion that further skepticism might be in order about their very existence. The open-endedness of the tales—all those missing parts—strongly encourages suspended judgment.

The canine picaresque that Campuzano offers the reluctant Peralta provides several twists on the genre: although focused on one of the dog's stories, it is structured as a dialogue between them, ironizing the authority of the singular narrative voice much as the venal reception by Mátalas Callando and Juan de Voto a Dios does in the *Viaje de Turquía*, discussed in Chapter 2. What the dogs see behind the scenes not only satirizes social pieties, as did *Lazarillo*, but exposes the theatricality of a society built on deception. Their own impersonation is on a continuum with the various (mis)representations that surround them as people pretend to be what they are not, staging their own deceptions. These run the gamut from shepherds who kill sheep and blame the wolves, to sheriffs in cahoots with prostitutes who lure travelers into their traps. Cervantes explicitly invokes the theater, as Berganza tells of his corrupt master who "representaba su tragedia en el teatro de la . . . plaza" (2:331) ["presented his tragedy in the theater of the town square"].[23] In a rare move for the *Novelas*, Cervantes here explicitly connects the narrative to a previous story, as the dog Berganza follows his corrupt master the sheriff to Monipodio's lair, where the ruffians welcome their accomplice with open arms. This reminder of the shared theatricality that joins "Rinconete y Cortadillo" and "El coloquio de los perros" returns us to the vexed question of the relationship between belief, spectacle, and the consumption of fictions. In this vision, skepticism is born not only out of radical doubt, or a new empiricism, but from the concrete, experiential realization that things are not what they seem. Just as the *pícaro* crafts his narrative to present a particular version of events, society requires a series of fictions to be naïvely consumed by the uninitiated. In the face of such deception, skepticism appears as the prudent response, as both Rinconete and the dogs realize. In this sense, the texts internalize a vision of the disabused reader that they enable, in an unexpected dimension of their exemplarity.

There is yet another fascinating angle to skepticism in "Coloquio," as the dogs address the problem of their own origins and capacity for speech. As the colloquy begins, the dogs' perplexity about their ability to speak leads them to speculation, yet they quickly drop it in favor of a pragmatic decision to simply make the best of their situation. The suspension of judgment, as Jorge Checa rightly points out, aligns this moment with a skeptical stance.[24] Yet the reflection on skepticism continues as the dogs eventually learn more about their past. After Berganza himself takes up with performers, and is exhibited as a "wise dog" (2:333), he runs into Cañizares, an old woman accused of being a witch, who greets him warmly as her son. Actually born to her great comrade Montiela, another witch, the dogs were once twin boys who had been transformed into animals by the pair's jealous teacher, La Camacha. (Although Checa curiously refers to this passage as an investigation into paternity, he usefully notes the tremendous uncertainty that surrounds Cañizares's confession, so critical to the dogs' quest.)[25] The entire episode offers a fascinating skeptical meditation on witchcraft, as Cañizares describes her dealings with the devil while also offering a much more matter-of-fact account of the same events as born of her fantasy and delirium.

As critics have long recognized, at the heart of Cañizares's long narrative is a prophecy that takes on outsize importance. Cañizares explains that La Camacha had promised that the dogs would regain human form when the following prophecy came true:

> Volverán a su forma verdadera
> cuando vieren con presta diligencia
> derribar los soberbios levantados
> y alzar a los humildes abatidos
> por mano poderosa para hacello. (2:338)
>
> [They shall regain their true form
> When they see with swift diligence
> The lofty proud laid low
> And the abject poor raised
> By a hand powerful enough to do so.]

Consumed by distaste at this account from Cañizares, Berganza's response is violence, and he attacks the supposed witch as she lies in a drugged stupor. As Berganza tells the story to Cipión, the dogs puzzle over the prophecy, first dismissing it as an empty superstition, then reading it variously as a reference to everything from the wheel of fortune to the game of bowls, where those that stand fall and the lowly are raised. Cervantes questions the dogs' capacity as readers: they miss arguably the most significant dimension of meaning to the prophecy: the anagogical and eschatological reference to the Judgment Day, which links their fate to that of the larger society.[26] The episode thus collapses the relative distance that allows Berganza to comment on so many different aspects of his milieu. In those cases, he speaks from personal experience, balancing his proximity and his commentary, but when his own genealogy is at stake he breaks down and attacks his source, missing, in the process, the very link that connects him to those he surveys.

A central attack on the dogs' authority follows in the next episode, as Berganza proposes to reveal all about Spain's ostracized Moriscos, after having spent "over a month" with one of them: "Estuve con él más de un mes, no por el gusto de la vida que tenía, sino por el que me daba saber la de mi amo, y por ella la de todos cuantos moriscos viven en España" (2:349) ["I was with him for over a month, not for any pleasure in the life I led, but because of what I got from knowing about my master's, and through it that of all the Moriscos that live in Spain"]. As Checa notes, this moment exemplifies the risks of generalizing from our perceptions to broader convictions.[27] In the wake of the Morisco expulsions, the stereotyped, hateful account that Berganza provides, and his claims for its representativity, suggests the dangers of exemplarity without a corresponding skepticism. The partiality of Berganza's generalizing account, like his misreading of the prophecy, encourages readers to proceed advisedly, skeptically, even as they accept the conditions of fictionality.[28]

If the frame to Cervantes's last novella encourages the suspension of judgment, the *coloquio* itself models how partial and fragile knowledge remains, even when afforded by a first-person narrator presumably closest to the action. For every time when Berganza's behind-the-scenes perspective gives him greater insight, there is a moment when his own embeddedness, as well as his prejudice, clouds his judgment. The grand stakes of what he misses—a true understanding of where he comes from and what lies in store; the unexamined prejudice that condemned the Moriscos to expulsion from Spain—are much higher than what he understands about routine venality and insincerity. As Cervantes reiterates the incompleteness of Berganza's perspective—the dog's own failings, the fact that he provides but half the story that Cipión would complete—he moves further from exemplarity to a skeptical picaresque fictionality.

Cervantes's skepticism in the *Novelas ejemplares* eschews exemplarity for a series of experiments with picaresque fictions. Replacing the *exemplum* with an exploration of how we know and how we tell, the *Novelas* underscore the absolute interdependence of the two, thereby encouraging, and occasionally modeling, a skeptical readerly stance. Cervantes is not concerned here with verisimilitude—the resemblance to truth that so concerned Aristotelians, and which he explores so robustly in the *Quijote*. At key moments, such as Rincón's valediction or Campuzano's introduction of the "Coloquio" to his friend Peralta, the *Novelas* explicitly invite the reader to receive fiction on its own terms, without recourse to claims of truth or dogma. Thus the collection offers a version of the literary that requires the suspension of belief as much as the Coleridgean suspension of disbelief that we more commonly associate with fictionality. Both are necessary in order to distinguish fiction from lie or gospel, and theatrical spectacle from trap, enabling the middle distance that makes for critical reading and fiction itself.

Postscript

The Fact of Fiction

Having wandered across Spain, Italy, North Africa, and the Ottoman Empire, this book ends in classic picaresque form, perched on the voyage to a new world. Like Pablos in Quevedo's *Buscón*, or Loaysa in Cervantes's "El celoso extremeño," I want to *mudar mundo y tierra* (to change world and land, in Quevedo's phrase). Unlike them, I do so not to extricate myself from any unpleasantness, but to seek a more proximate contextualization of the picaresque's import. Whereas the early modern European encounter with a new world set the stage for the picaresque by casting authority into crisis and foregrounding the narrator-witness, our own new world of political and social turmoil calls for a reconsideration of knowing fictions.

The considerable popular and academic distress about insidious claims of "fake news," the end of truth, and other woes laid at the feet of postmodernism has produced an understandable desire to help orient citizens in relation to what they read. Journalists are often at the forefront of these efforts. In the United States, the News Literacy Project (NLP), founded by a former *Los Angeles Times* reporter, offers training in media literacy through a network of volunteer journalists. "Checkology," NLP's virtual curriculum, begins by asking, "Can your students tell the difference between fact and fiction?"[1]

In France, a leader in national efforts to promote media and internet literacy, the government offers schoolchildren training in identifying misinformation online, in collaboration with *Entre les lignes*, an organization of volunteer journalists and photographers.[2]

As writers attempt to make sense of our era, they often invoke the dyad of "fact versus fiction." Michiko Kakutani, to take one important example, opens her *The Death of Truth: Notes on Falsehood in the Age of Trump* by citing Hannah Arendt: "As Hannah Arendt wrote in her 1951 book *The Origins of*

Totalitarianism, 'The ideal subject of totalitarian rule is not the convinced Nazi or the convinced communist, but people for whom the distinction between fact and fiction (i.e., the reality of experience) and the distinction between true and false (i.e., the standards of thought) no longer exist.'"[3] To a literary critic, Arendt's monitory distinction, so frequently echoed in contemporary analyses, appears peculiarly reductive: the problem is not actually fiction but deliberate lies—a tendentious conflation that dates back to Plato.[4] To reduce fiction to the opposite of fact is to ignore its divergent epistemological status, to be sure, but also its potential as a tool for the kind of critical thinking that Arendt finds so urgent in the face of totalitarianism. Hence the important distinction between contemporary projects that promise to sift fact from fiction and those that encourage reading *entre les lignes*, especially if we recognize fiction as not the problem, but rather part of the solution.

My point here is not that fiction offers a different kind of truth, as so many writers have held for so long,[5] or, pace Salman Rushdie, that it helps us agree about what humans are really like,[6] or even that it helps "enlarge men's sympathies," as George Eliot noted long ago and the latest psychological studies confirm.[7] Instead, the knowing fictions on which I focus in this study—picaresques and para-picaresques alike—serve as guides to critical thinking, teaching how to read between the lines for intentionality, bad faith, internal contradictions, disavowals, or ambiguities. Crucially, knowing fictions such as *Lozana* and the *Viaje de Turquía* are not hoaxes: they include more than enough information to decode their status as fictional texts, and to trace within them the construction of a narrative stance that is less than forthcoming.[8] If anything, these texts show off their playfulness with narrative authority, their interestedness and partiality, as when Ginés de Pasamonte reminds us that his story—his life and thus his book—is not yet over. In Christopher L. Miller's useful formulation, fictions such as these, unlike hoaxes, "are at least partially transparent and purposefully so."[9]

Miller explores nineteenth- and twentieth-century texts; one of his key distinctions between hoaxes and "conventional devices" is that the latter operate "within a socially sanctioned implicit contract or pact with the reader" whose norms they do not violate.[10] Focusing on a particularly vibrant century of literary inventiveness in Spain, *Knowing Fictions* shows how the picaresque actually serves to establish that pact with readers, teaching them how to read in a particular mode texts marked by an interested and flawed narrator.[11] While *Lozana*, like *Lazarillo* and the *Guzmán* after it, all foreground the partiality and limitations of the witness-narrator, Cervantes's novellas proffer a pact of fictionality, encouraging the suspension of belief in order to receive fiction on its own terms.

In their self-consciousness as literary constructions, knowing fictions adumbrate the authority of nonfictional accounts, yet their skeptical stance is not one of radical doubt—trust no one, believe no official story, and so forth—of the kind Arendt finds terrifyingly compatible with gullibility.[12] Instead, they encourage the mode of critical reading that is essential if we are to discern which texts or voices we can trust, and on what we can or cannot trust them.[13] Knowing fictions offer specifically rhetorical, literary contributions to the toolkit of epistemology. As such, they complement the historiographical responses to the "crisis of history" of the 1980s and 1990s, or other discipline-specific responses to the most dizzying versions of postmodern relativism,[14] delineating a mode of critical inquiry on which we might base knowledge.

At the same time, picaresque reading offers a bridge across the divide between literature and history without negating its existence: my willfully perverse, skeptical framing of Miles Philips's narrative as a picaresque, for example, does not ignore that the text has a different ontological status than *Lazarillo*, but mobilizes the similarities between the two to reveal something about the fragility of the national and religious categories to which the narrator of the former appeals. In the same vein, to read between the lines of Columbus's letters or Alvar Núñez Cabeza de Vaca's *Naufragios*, even though their texts were not written as picaresques, complexifies our understanding of their disavowals and interestedness, even though they might not plant their clues as deliberately as Sigüenza's *Infortunios de Alonso Ramírez*. In the New World as in the Old, the picaresque is too valuable a tool for reading to confine it to the literary.

The long life of the picaresque as a broader mode of literary production suggests its purchase as a tool for reading well beyond the early modern moment at which it emerged. Even if the particular historical context that I explore here gave the picaresque its force as a locus of skepticism, it endures as a heuristic for critical reading. New experiments in autofiction and other contemporary forms that rework the distinctions between fiction and nonfiction, the self and the world, will doubtless necessitate their own hermeneutic and epistemological tools.[15] Yet as I hope *Knowing Fictions* has shown, fiction can be much more than the opposite of fact: in its exploration of what is knowable, of how we know, and of what is at stake in that knowledge, it can help us know better.

Notes

INTRODUCTION

1. The bibliography on the picaresque is extensive and often contentious in attempting to delimit the genre. Key studies include Alexander A. Parker, *Literature and the Delinquent: The Picaresque Novel in Spain and Europe, 1599–1753* (Edinburgh: Edinburgh University Press, 1967); Claudio Guillén, *Literature as System: Essays Toward the Theory of Literary History* (Princeton, NJ: Princeton University Press, 1971); Peter N. Dunn, *Spanish Picaresque Fiction: A New Literary History* (Ithaca, NY: Cornell University Press, 1993); and, in a sociohistorical vein, Juan Carlos Rodríguez, *La literatura del pobre* (Granada: Comares, 1994), and Anne J. Cruz, *Discourses of Poverty: Social Reform and the Picaresque Novel in Early Modern Spain* (Toronto: University of Toronto Press, 1999). For recent overviews, see Klaus Meyer-Minnemann and Sabine Schlickers, eds., *La novela picaresca: Concepto genérico y evolución del género (siglos XVI y XVII)* (Madrid: Iberoamericana, 2008), and J. A. Garrido Ardila, ed., *The Picaresque Novel in Western Literature: From the Sixteenth Century to the Neopicaresque* (Cambridge: Cambridge University Press, 2015).

2. Guillén, *Literature as System*, 72.

3. Guillén, *Literature as System*, 120.

4. Guillén, *Literature as System*, 41, 74.

5. John C. Parrack, "Reading the Silence: The Picaresque Game of *Lacunae* and Contradiction," *Revista Canadiense de Estudios Hispánicos* 32, no. 2 (2008): 291–314, citations on 291 and 292.

6. Parrack, "Reading the Silence," 293.

7. Barbara Fuchs, "An English Pícaro in New Spain: Miles Philips and the Framing of National Identity," *Early Modernities, CR: The New Centennial Review* 2, no. 1 (2002): 55–68.

8. Richard Helgerson, "'I Miles Philips': An Elizabethan Seaman Conscripted by History," *PMLA* 118, no. 3 (2003): 573–80.

9. Miles Philips, "A Discourse Written by one Miles Philips Englishman," in Richard Hakluyt, *The Principal Navigations, Voyages, Traffiques and Discoveries of the English Nation* (Glasgow: Maclehose and Sons, 1904), 9:398–445, citation on 425.

10. For a rich, related discussion that explores historicity in relation to the picaresque, see Aníbal González, "*Los infortunios de Alonso Ramírez*: Picaresca e historia," *Hispanic Review* 51, no. 2 (1983): 189–204.

11. Roberto González Echevarría, *Myth and Archive: A Theory of Latin American Narrative* (Cambridge: Cambridge University Press, 1990), 56.

12. "Los pícaros no creen en la sociedad que les rodea, pues 'todos roban' y 'todos mienten,'" observes Francisco Carrillo ("*La vida del pícaro* [1601]: Testimonio contextual de la

picaresca," *Actas del VIII Congreso de la Asociación Internacional de Hispanistas, I*, ed. A. David Kossoff et al. [Madrid: Ediciones Istmo, 1986], 357–66, citation on 361).

13. Miranda Fricker, *Epistemic Injustice: Power and the Ethics of Knowing* (Oxford: Oxford University Press, 2007).

14. For a suggestive account of verbal dissimulation as a historically specific phenomenon, see Perez Zagorin, *Ways of Lying: Dissimulation, Persecution, and Conformity in Early Modern Europe* (Cambridge, MA: Harvard University Press, 1990). Focusing on the challenge of religious persecution, Zagorin concludes by deeming the sixteenth and seventeenth centuries "the Age of Dissimulation" (330). Andrea Frisch, for her part, usefully historicizes the eyewitness: "the figure of the eyewitness is a historical construct rather than a philosophical abstraction" (*The Invention of the Eyewitness: Witnessing and Testimony in Early Modern France* [Chapel Hill: University of North Carolina Press, 2004], 13).

15. In Arndt Brendecke's formulation, "the process of European expansion produced knowledge problems of a special kind" (*The Empirical Empire: Spanish Colonial Rule and the Politics of Knowledge* [Berlin: Walter de Gruyter, 2016], 1).

16. On "Inner Worlds" in the picaresque, see Dunn's chapter of that title, *Spanish Picaresque Fiction,* 162–200.

17. On travel narratives and first-person authority, see Joan-Pau Rubiés, *Travel and Ethnology in the Renaissance: South India Through European Eyes, 1250–1625* (Cambridge: Cambridge University Press, 2000), xiii. See also Joan-Pau Rubiés, *Travellers and Cosmographers: Studies in the History of Early Modern Travel and Ethnology* (Burlington, VT: Ashgate, 2007). For the Spanish context, Brendecke is particularly helpful in identifying the gaps between the need to know and what was actually known as the empire grew, and in helping us recognize knowledge itself as less an absolute than a product of "political communication and social practice" (*The Empirical Empire*, 6).

18. Elizabeth Ross, *Picturing Experience in the Early Printed Book: Breydenbach's Peregrinatio from Venice to Jerusalem* (University Park: Penn State University Press, 2014).

19. Ross notes the tremendous pan-European popularity of the Breydenbach-Reuwich collaboration, with Latin, German, and Dutch editions in 1486 and 1488 and translations into French, Spanish, and Czech before 1500, for a total of thirteen editions before 1522, all closely associated with their images, "as the original woodcut blocks were passed from Mainz to Lyons to Speyer to Zaragoza, while also copied four times" (3). Pamela H. Smith also notes the key role of the artist as direct observer in the development of early modern European science, as "images came to play an integral part in the making of natural knowledge in the early modern period" and artists "helped change the view of what constitutes positive, certain knowledge" ("Art, Science, and Visual Culture in Early Modern Europe," *Isis* 97, no. 1 [2006]: 86–100, citations on 87 and 95).

20. Anthony Pagden, *European Encounters with the New World: From Renaissance to Romanticism* (New Haven, CT: Yale University Press, 1993), 51–56. Frisch complicates the notion of epistemic witnessing in relation to the New World by showing how uneven was the transition from medieval modes of testimony: "The eyewitness constituted but one subtype of witness among many in sixteenth-century Europe, and as such, was subject to the norms governing early modern witnessing and testimony quite broadly construed" (*The Invention of the Eyewitness,* 23).

21. Pagden, *European Encounters,* 55.

22. Gonzalo Fernandez de Oviedo, *Historia general y natural de Las Indias,* ed. Juan Pérez de Tudela Bueso, 5 vols., Biblioteca de Autores Españoles, vols. 117–121 (Madrid: Atlas, 1959), 117:39. All translations are my own unless otherwise noted.

23. Smith, "Art, Science, and Visual Culture," 89.

24. Oviedo, *Historia,* 118.8.

25. Ángel Rama, *La ciudad letrada* (Hanover, NH: Ediciones del Norte, 1984).

26. See Kathryn Burns, "Notaries, Truth, and Consequences," *American Historical Review* 110, no. 2 (2005): 350–79.

27. On Oviedo, see Kathleen Ann Myers, *Fernández de Oviedo's Chronicle of America: A New History for a New World* (Austin: University of Texas Press, 2007). On Garcilaso, see González Echevarría, *Myth and Archive,* 43–92.

28. Brendecke, *The Empirical Empire,* 11.

29. Mary M. Gaylord, "The True History of Early Modern Writing in Spanish: Some American Reflections," *MLQ* 57, no. 2 (1996): 213–25, citations on 217, 218.

30. Gaylord, "True History," 219–20.

31. Natalie Zemon Davis, *Fiction in the Archives: Pardon Tales and Their Tellers in Sixteenth-Century France* (Stanford, CA: Stanford University Press, 1987).

32. Burns, "Notaries," 355, 374.

33. Burns, "Notaries," 372.

34. Lisa Voigt, *Writing Captivity in the Early Modern Atlantic: Circulations of Knowledge and Authority in the Iberian and English Imperial Worlds* (Chapel Hill: University of North Carolina/Omohundro Institute, 2009), 48–49.

35. Voigt, *Writing Captivity,* 17 and passim.

36. González Echevarría, *Myth and Archive,* 55. See also his earlier review article, "The Life and Adventures of Cipión: Cervantes and the Picaresque," *Diacritics* 10, no. 3 (1980): 15–26.

37. Robert Folger, *Picaresque and Bureaucracy: Lazarillo de Tormes* (Newark, DE: Juan de la Cuesta, 2009), 17, and *Writing and Poaching: Interpellation and Self-Fashioning in Colonial relaciones de méritos y servicios* (Leiden: Brill, 2011).

38. David Gitlitz, "Inquisition Confessions and *Lazarillo de Tormes,*" *Hispanic Review* 68, no. 1 (2000): 53–74, citation on 54–55.

39. Gitlitz, "Inquisition Confessions," 60.

40. Gitlitz, "Inquisition Confessions," 71.

41. Dale Shuger, "The Language of Mysticism and the Language of Law in Early Modern Spain," *Renaissance Quarterly* 68, no. 3 (2015): 932–56, citation on 933.

42. Shuger, "Language of Mysticism," 940.

43. "External acts became insufficient as evidence, since there were no clearly reliable external signs that pointed toward Lutheran heresies or to the Catholic heterodoxies that, after Trent, made up the bulk of the Inquisitors' docket. In fact, many of the same practices—an intense spiritual relationship with God, supernatural or prophetic visions and miracles, extreme self-mortification and piety—could be indicative of Protestant heresy (a crime of faith), demonic possession (not a crime, unless it could be shown that an explicit pact had been made), illness, or true holiness" (Shuger, "Language of Mysticism," 938).

44. Paul Michael Johnson, "Feeling Certainty, Performing Sincerity: The Emotional Hermeneutics of Truth in Inquisitorial and Theatrical Practice," in *The Quest for Certainty in Early Modern Europe: From Inquisition to Inquiry, 1550–1700,* ed. Barbara Fuchs and Mercedes García-Arenal (Toronto: University of Toronto Press, 2020).

45. Johnson, "Feeling Certainty."

46. Enrique Fernández, *Anxieties of Interiority and Dissection in Early Modern Spain* (Toronto: University of Toronto Press, 2015), 8.

47. Nicholas D. Paige, *Being Interior: Autobiography and the Contradictions of Modernity in Seventeenth-Century France* (Philadelphia: University of Pennsylvania Press, 2001), 4, 10.

48. See Mercedes García-Arenal, ed., *After Conversion: Iberia and the Emergence of Modernity* (Leiden: Brill, 2018); Mercedes García-Arenal and Stefania Pastore, eds., *From Doubt to Unbelief: Forms of Scepticism in the Iberian World* (Cambridge: MHRA, 2019); and Fernando Rodríguez Mediano and Carlos Cañete, eds., "Interiority, Subject, Authority: Conversions and Counter-Reformation in the Construction of the Modern Subject (16th–17th Centuries)," special issue, *Culture and History* 6, no. 2 (2017).

49. Mercedes García-Arenal and Felipe Pereda, "On the Alumbrados: Confessionalism and Religious Dissidence in the Iberian World," in *The Early Modern Hispanic World: Transnational and Interdisciplinary Approaches,* ed. Kimberly Lynn and Erin Rowe (Cambridge: Cambridge University Press, 2017), 121–52, citation on 131, and García-Arenal, "A Catholic Muslim Prophet: Agustín de Ribera, 'The Boy Who Saw Angels,'" *Common Knowledge* 18, no. 2 (2012): 267–91.

50. Stefania Pastore, "From 'Marranos' to 'Unbelievers': The Spanish Peccadillo in Sixteenth-Century Italy," in *Dissimulation and Deceit in Early Modern Europe*, ed. Miriam Eliav-Felden and Tamar Herzig (New York: Springer, 2015), 80.

51. Marcel Bataillon, *Erasme et l'Espagne: Recherches sur l'histoire spirituelle du XVIe siècle* (Geneva: Droz, 1991 [1937]), 714.

CHAPTER 1

1. The critical tradition of reading *Lozana* in a documentary vein, for its depiction of the Rome of its time, ignores its ironic, tongue-in-cheek narration. See Folke Gernert and Jacques Joset, "¿Una obra realista?," in their edition, Francisco Delicado, *La Lozana andaluza* (Madrid: Real Academia Española, 2013), 440–63. On worldliness, see Israel Burshatin, "Rome as Andalusia: Bodies and Borders in Francisco Delicado's *Retrato de la Lozana Andaluza*," *MLN* 129, no. 2 (2014): 197–218, citation on 198.

2. Delicado, *La Lozana andaluza*, 331. Subsequent citations are to this edition, by page number only.

3. For the extensive bibliography on *Celestina* in Italy, see Margherita Morreale, "Apuntes bibliográficos para el estudio de la presencia de *La Celestina* en Italia," *Revista de Literatura* 52, no. 104 (1990): 539–43; Joseph Snow, "Historia de la recepción de *Celestina*: 1499–1822 II," *Celestinesca* 25, no. 1–2 (2001): 199–282; and Ottavio Di Camillo, "Algunas consideraciones sobre la Celestina italiana," *Rumbos del hispanismo en el umbral del Cincuentenario de la AIH*, ed. Patrizia Botta (Rome: Bagatto Libri, 2012), 2.216–26. On *Lozana* and *Celestina*, see Ronald Surtz, "Texto e imagen en el *Retrato de la Lozana andaluza*," *Nueva Revista de Filología Hispánica* 40, no. 1 (1992): 169–85, and Manuel da Costa Fontes, "Imitation, Banter, and Competition: Francisco Delicado and *Celestina*," *Romance Philology* 56 (2003): 293–305.

4. For "El modo de adoperare," I cite the critical transcription by Bruno Damiani, *Revista Hispánica Moderna* 36, no. 4 (1970–71): 251–71. On the probable first edition, see 252.

5. On the publication of Spanish-language books in various Italian contexts, see Augustus Pallotta, "Venetian Printers and Spanish Literature in Sixteenth-Century Italy," *Comparative Literature* 43, no. 1 (Winter 1991): 20–42, and Encarnación Sánchez García, "Sobre la princeps de la Propalladia (Nápoles, Ioan Pasqueto de Sallo, 1517): Los mecenas (Fernando D'Ávalos, Vittoria y Fabrizio Colonna, Belisario Acquaviva) y la epístola latina de Mesinerius I. Barberius," in *Lingua spagnola e cultura ispanica a Napoli fra Rinascimento e Barroco: Testimonianze a*

stampa (Naples: Tullio Pironti, 2013), 1–33. On Delicado in the print shop, see José Manuel Lucía Megías, *Imprenta y libros de caballerías* (Madrid: Ollero & Ramos, 2000), 375.

6. "Introducion del tercero libro," in *Los tres libros del muy esforzado caballero Primaleon et Polendos su hermano hijos del Emperador Palmerin de Oliva* [Venice, 1531] [no page number]. Burshatin deems this "a public confession of a linguistic transgression" ("Rome as Andalusia," 199).

7. Delicado's introduction to *Primaleón* attempts to position chivalric fiction as exemplary—"y fue tan maravillosamente fingida esta ystoria llena de doctrina para los caballeros y amadores de dueñas"—while also making the curious argument that the texts transpose to exotic Greeks what are actually the great feats of Spaniards, so that their descendants may best learn from them ("Introducion del primero libro de Primaleon fecha por el delicado en este dechado de Cavalleros corrigendolo en Venecia," in *Los tres libros del muy esforzado caballero Primaleon et Polendos su hermano hijos del Emperador Palmerin de Oliva* [Venice, 1531], iii).

8. On the role of the literary in the Hispanization of Naples in the early sixteenth century, see Sánchez García, "Sobre la princeps de la Propalladia."

9. Bruno Damiani, *Francisco Delicado* (New York: Twayne, 1974), 13–14. Federico Corriente argues instead for Delicado's possible Muslim origins, based on the presence of Arabic-derived forms in the text: "Los arabismos de *La Lozana andaluza*," *Estudis Romànics* 32 (2010): 51–72. For the vexed chronology, given how few documents exist, see Gernert and Joset, "Francisco Delicado y su circunstancia," in their edition, 371–76.

10. Tatiana Bubnova, *F. Delicado puesto en diálogo: Las claves bajtinianas de La Lozana andaluza* (Mexico City: Universidad Nacional Autónoma, 1987).

11. On the doubleness of language in *Lozana*, see Joachim Harst, "Making Love: Celestinesque Literature, Philology, and 'Marranism,'" *MLN* 127, no. 2 (2012): 169–89.

12. See Bruce Wardropper, "La novela como retrato: El arte de Francisco Delicado," *Nueva Revista de Filología Hispánica* 7 (1953): 475–88; the introduction by Claude Allaigre to his edition of *La Lozana Andaluza* (Madrid: Cátedra, 1985), 57; and Jorge Checa, "La Lozana Andaluza (o cómo se hace un retrato)," *Bulletin of Spanish Studies* 82 (2005): 1–18.

13. Covarrubias focuses on the reflexive in his definition of *retraer*, but links the two terms in his definition of *retrato*: "*Retraer:* Retraerse recogerse; retraído, el que está recogido en su casa. . . . *Retrato:* La figura contrahecha de alguna persona principal y de cuenta, cuya efigie y semejanza es justo quede por memoria a los siglos venideros. . . . Dixose a retrahendo, porque trae para sí la semejança y figura que se retrata" (Sebastián de Covarrubias, *Tesoro de la lengua castellana o española*, ed. Martín Riquer [Barcelona: Alta Fulla, 1998], 908b).

14. On Lozana in relation to migration, both early modern and contemporary, see Marta Albalá Pelegrín, "*La Lozana andaluza*: Migración y pluralismo religioso en el Mediterráneo," *Revista Canadiense de Estudios Hispánicos* 41, no. 1 (2016): 215–42.

15. Tatiana Bubnova notes, "Lo verdaderamente original en Delicado es que representa, incorpora temáticamente a la narración, el momento de la escritura, que, por supuesto, no coincide con la secuencia temporal de la historia" (*F. Delicado puesto en diálogo,* 105n36) ["What is truly original in Delicado is that he represents, he incorporates thematically in the narration, the moment of writing, which, of course, does not coincide with the temporal sequence of the story"].

16. Delicado plays with the metaphorics of *dechado* as exemplum, and the highly sexualized reference to needlework. Cf. Covarrubias: "*Dechado*: El exemplar de donde la labrandera saca alguna lavor, y por traslación decimos ser dechado de virtud el que da buen exemplo a los demás y ocasión para que lo imiten" (Covarrubias, *Tesoro*, 445a).

17. Louis Imperiale, "El marco dramático del *Retrato de la Lozana Andaluza*. Una lectura semiológica" (Ph.D. diss., Catholic University of America, 1980), 252.

18. On Julian propaganda, see Massimo Rospocher, "Print and Political Propaganda Under Pope Julius II (1503–13)," in *Authority in European Book Culture, 1400–1600*, ed. Polly Bromilow (Burlington, VT: Ashgate, 2013), 97–119.

19. Marga Cottino-Jones contrasts the positive representation of the city in Bibbiena's *Calandra*, represented in Rome in 1514 before Leo X and Isabella d'Este, with the emphasis on factionalism and corruption in Aretino's 1525 *Cortigiana*—itself influenced by *Celestina* and by *Lozana*—noting that the city appears in the latter as "a rather dismal and morally objectionable background against which the dramatic action of the plays unfolds" ("Rome and the Theatre in the Renaissance," in *Rome in the Renaissance: The City and the Myth*, ed. P. A. Ramsey [Binghamton, NY: Center for Medieval & Early Renaissance Studies, 1982], 237–45, citation on 239).

20. Imperiale, "El marco dramático," s 17.

21. Peter Partner, *Renaissance Rome, 1500–1559: A Portrait of a Society* (Berkeley: University of California Press, 1976), 117–18. As James Ackerman notes, "Every papal election brought in a horde of job-seekers from the victor's home territory and prompted the departure of another horde that had enjoyed the success of the predecessor." Moreover, because Rome lacked both "guild organizations built around industry and trade that were the core of civic enterprise in communal towns," and "the income that might have provided a tax base for the expenses of government and the costs of corruption," the Holy See encouraged prostitution instead ("The Planning of Renaissance Rome, 1450–1580," in Ramsey, *Rome in the Renaissance,* 3–17, citation on 6).

22. Pietro Aretino, *La cortigiana*, trans. J. Douglas Campbell and Leonard G. Sbrocchi, introduction by Raymond B. Waddington (Ottawa: Dovehouse, 2003), 14.

23. On Spanish exiles in Rome, see Marta Albalá Pelegrín, "Converso Migration and Social Stratification: Textual Representations of the Marrano from Iberia to Rome, 1480–1550," in *Exile and the Formation of Religious Identities in the Early Modern World*, ed. Gary Waite and Jesse Spohnholz (London: Pickering and Chatto, 2014), 141–55.

24. As Tatiana Bubnova has noted, Martos's connection to Hercules links it in turn to Charles V and the Spanish imperial project, both through the emperor's putative ancestry in Hercules himself and through his role as the "Spanish Mars." See Bubnova, "Delicado en la Peña de Martos," *Actas de la Asociación Internacional de Hispanistas* XII, vol. 2, ed. Jules Whicker (Birmingham, UK: University of Birmingham, 1998), 70–78.

25. On Egypt as a privileged source of civilization and a putative Spanish origin, see Mercedes García-Arenal and Fernando Rodríguez Mediano, *Un oriente español: Los moriscos y el Sacromonte en tiempos de Contrarreforma* (Madrid: Marcial Pons, 2010), 200.

26. On the erasure of the Muslim presence from a classicized landscape, see Javier Irigoyen-García, *The Spanish Arcadia: Sheep Herding, Pastoral Discourse, and Ethnicity in Early Modern Spain* (Toronto: University of Toronto Press, 2014), 113–21.

27. Under his entry for Martos, Covarrubias makes the brothers responsible for the name of the Peña: "La peña de Martos es un precipicio cerca deste lugar, al qual dieron nombre los dos hermanos dichos los Carvajales, a los cuales aviéndoles sido achacada la muerte de un otro cavallero, sin estar convencidos del delito ni averlo ellos confessado, el rey don Fernando el quarto los mandó precipitar de aquel peñasco altíssimo; y ellos, llevándolos a justiciar, dieron vozes, diziendo que, pues en la tierra no tenían tribunal para quien apelar, apelavan para el del cielo, y citavan al rey para que en él pareciesse dentro de treinta días. Estas palabras se tuvieron entonces por vanas; pero dentro del dicho término falleció el rey en Jaén. . . . Y en razón deste suceso le llamaron don Fernando el Emplaçado. Falleció de venticuatro años, el último día de los treinta

de la citación de los Carvajales" ["The Rock of Martos is a precipice near that place, named for two brothers known as the Carvajales, who, having been blamed for the death of another knight, without being convicted of the crime or having confessed to it, the king Fernando IV ordered them to be hurled from that highest rock; and they, as they were being led to their deaths, cried out that as they had no tribunal on earth to which they could appeal, they would appeal to that of heaven, and summon the king to appear there within thirty days. These words were taken as empty threats, but within the said term the king died in Jaén. . . . And for this event they called him don Fernando the Summoned. He died at twenty-four, on the last day of the summons by the Carvajales"] (Covarrubias, *Tesoro*, 792a).

28. In contradistinction to Lozana's canon here, Lucia Binotti notes the slightly later project by humanists such as Ambrosio de Morales of constructing a Spanish canon worthy of reflecting Spanish imperial ambitions. Referring to Morales's prologue to Pérez de Oliva's *Diálogo de la dignidad del hombre* (1546), which was published with a dedication to no other than Hernán Cortés, Binotti notes: "Hence Morales' emphatic disapproval of those contemporary authors who only wrote of vain love and vacuous fables: these lesser subjects could not make use of any of the prescribed styles, and they degraded the language so that it would be ever more difficult to raise it again to its proper dignity. Under so severe a judgment of the comprehensive worth of Spanish literature, there lies the desire to define a national identity for this literature suitable to the imperial aspirations of mid sixteenth-century Spain" (Lucia Binotti, "Alfonso de Ulloa's Editorial Project: Translating, Writing, and Marketing Spanish Best-Sellers in Venice," *Allegorica* 17 [1996]: 35–54, citation on 40).

29. *Carajicomedia*, ed. Alvaro Alonso (Málaga: Aljibe, 1995), 44.

30. *Carajicomedia*, 45.

31. The story comes from Valerius Maximus, *Facta et Dictia Memorabilia* 5.3.2b. See Valerius Maximus, *Memorable Doings and Sayings*, ed. D. R. Shackleton Bailey (Cambridge, MA: Harvard University Press, 2000), 477.

32. On the pun between *Coliseo* and *culi-seo*, which appears in both Italian and Spanish, see Alonso, *Carajicomedia*, 16. Rampín proudly shows off this same sexualized space to Lozana in Mamotreto XII, along with the Campo de Flor.

33. The name, with its echoes of Bacchus, also comes up in *Lozana*, where our heroine claims she will make Rampín "porquerón de Bacano" ["swineherd of Bacano"] (Delicado, *La Lozana andaluza*, 242). The editors gloss this as a Latian town famous for its bandits.

34. Bartolomé de Torres Naharro, "Introito y Argumento" to *Comedia Tinelaria*, in *Teatro completo*, ed. Julio Vélez-Sainz, 433–526, lines 30–54 (Madrid: Cátedra, 2013).

35. On the significance of *mancha* as a signifier for genealogical "impurity," see Irigoyen-García, *The Spanish Arcadia*, 59–67.

36. Torres Naharro's *Comedia Soldadesca*, lines 502–22, explains who the *bisoños* are, the origins of their name, and their needy behavior in Rome (*Teatro completo).*

37. Torres Naharro, *Tinelaria*, 1964–84.

38. Fernando de Rojas, *Tragicomedia de Calisto y Melibea en la qual se contiene de mas de su agradable & dulce estilo muchas sentencias filosofales y auissos muy necessarios para mancebos* (Venice: Stefano Nicolini da Sabio, 1534).

39. Emma Scoles, "Note sulla prima traduzione italiana della *Celestina*," *Studi Romanzi* 33 (1961): 158n2.

40. See Lucia Binotti, "*La Tragicomedia de Calisto y Melibea* and the 'Questione della Lingua' After Bembo's *Prose*," in *Actas del Simposio Internacional, 1502–2002: Five Hundred Years of Fernando de Rojas' Tragicomedia de Calisto y Melibea*, ed. Juan Carlos Conde (New York: Hispanic

Seminary of Medieval Studies, 2007), 310–33, and Kathleen Kish, "*Celestina* as Chameleon: The Early Translations," *Celestinesca* 33 (2009): 87–98.

41. Kish, "*Celestina* as Chameleon," 91.

42. Parrack notes the discrepancies between the "closed textuality" of the opening paratexts and the invitation at the end, ascribing them to "the growing instability of novelistic discourse" and the "instability of truth" ("Reading the Silence: The Picaresque Game of *Lacunae* and Contradiction," *Revista Canadiense de Estudios* Hispanicos 32, no. 2 [2008]: 291–314, citation on 300).

43. Delicado/Damiani, "El modo de adoperare," 256, 262.

44. Delicado/Damiani, "El modo de adoperare," 265.

45. Delicado/Damiani, "El modo de adoperare," 262.

46. John L. Flood and David J. Shaw, "The Price of the Pox in 1527: Johannes Sinapius and the Guaiac Cure," *Bibliothèque d'Humanisme et Renaissance*, 54, no. 3 (1992): 691–707, at 691–92.

47. Flood and Shaw, "The Price of the Pox," 693–94.

48. Delicado/Damiani, "El modo de adoperare," 257.

49. Agostino Giustiniani's *Castigatissimi annali della eccelsa et illustrissima republica di Genoa* (Genoa, 1537) mentions the historical events to which Divicia refers here, although with no particular connection to syphilis: "Hanno uno hospitale per gli infermi di S. Lazaro nelquale altre volte i Suizeri comissero quella gran crudelita al tempo delle guerre francese" ["They have a hospital of St. Lazarus for the sick where once the Swiss committed that great cruelty during the time of the French wars," 17b]. See https://books.google.com/books?id=wcZQAAAAcAAJ&pg.

50. Delicado/Damiani, "El modo de adoperare," 258.

51. Delicado/Damiani, "El modo de adoperare," 257.

52. Delicado/Damiani, "El modo de adoperare," 265.

53. On the author as a male version of Lozana, see Surtz, "Texto e imagen," 183–84.

54. On Delicado's immediate context in relation to war and the representation of Mars/Martos, see Bubnova, "Delicado en la Peña de Martos," 72.

55. Delicado/Damiani, "El modo de adoperare," 265.

56. Delicado/Damiani, "El modo de adoperare," 265.

57. There is no evidence either of the first edition to which Delicado refers here.

CHAPTER 2

Epigraph: "Dedicatoria," in *Viaje de Turquía: Diálogo de Hurdimalas y Juan de Voto a Dios y Mátalas Callando que trata de las miserias de los cautivos de turcos y de las costumbres y secta de los mismos haciendo la descripción de Turquía,* ed. Marie-Sol Ortola (Madrid: Castalia, 2000), 160–61. All subsequent references are to this edition, by page number only.

1. Fernand Braudel, *The Mediterranean and the Mediterranean World in the Age of Philip II*, Vol. 2, trans. Siân Reynolds (London: Collins, 1973), 865.

2. Daniel Hershenzon, *The Captive Sea: Slavery, Communication, and Commerce in Early Modern Spain and the Mediterranean* (Philadelphia: University of Pennsylvania Press, 2018), 18.

3. Hershenzon explains, "natal alienation—the deprivation of all ties to one's home community—did not define Mediterranean bondage as it defined some other slave systems" (*The Captive Sea*, 113).

4. Lisa Voigt, *Writing Captivity in the Early Modern Atlantic: Circulations of Knowledge and Authority in the Iberian and English Imperial Worlds* (Chapel Hill: University of North Carolina/ Omohundro Institute, 2009), 54.

5. Hershenzon, *The Captive Sea,* 146 ff.

6. Cervantes depicts a renegade's desperate attempts to secure these letters in *Los baños de Argel,* which I discuss below, and also in the Captive's Tale in *Don Quijote* I.

7. Hershenzon describes captives as "information entrepreneurs" (*The Captive Sea,* 140).

8. Florencio Sevilla Arroyo offers a cogent account of the *Viaje*'s reception, and the vexed attempts to classify it, in "Diálogo y novela en el *Viaje de Turquía,*" *Revista de Filología Española* 77, no. 1/2 (1997): 69–87. Jacqueline Ferreras reads it in the context of the humanist Renaissance dialogue in "Apuntes sobre la escritura del *Viaje de Turquía,*" in *El Siglo de Oro en escena: Homenaje a Mark Vitse,* ed. Odette Gorsse and Frédéric Serralta (Toulouse: Presses Universitaires du Mirail/Consejería de Educación de la Embajada Española en Francia, 2006), 297–309, although she focuses on how the conversational quality of the *Viaje* transcends the genre.

9. Ortola reviews the critical debate over the text's authorship: "Introducción," in *Viaje de Turquía,* 13–35.

10. On the *Palinodia,* see Ljiljana Pavlovic-Samurovic, "Los elementos renacentistas en la *Palinodia de los Turcos* (1547) de Vasco Díaz Tanco de Frejenal," *Estado actual de los estudios sobre el Siglo de Oro: Actas del II Congreso Internacional de Hispanistas del Siglo de Oro* (Salamanca: Ediciones Universidad de Salamanca, 1993), 753–59. On Mexía's attempts to foreground objectivity rather than insert himself into the text, see Isaías Lerner, "Acerca del texto de la primera edición de la *Silva* de Pedro Mexía," in *Actas del VII congreso de la Asociación Internacional de Hispanistas* (Rome: Bulzoni Editore, 1982), 677–84.

11. As Ortola notes, in Manuscript 3871 of the Biblioteca Nacional, Greek names have been added for the characters: "Apatilo. panurgo. Pollitropo" (185a). These foreground the *Viaje*'s connection to Rabelais, discussed by Marcel Bataillon (*Erasme et l'Espagne,* 3 vols. [1937; Geneva: Droz, 1991], 1.715), while also assigning to Pedro the Homeric epithet for Odysseus. In this version, Pollitropo is Pedro, and his voice is also conflated with the authorial voice of the dedication. See Christopher D. Johnson, "El Homero español: Translation and Shipwreck," *Translation and Literature* 20, no. 2 (2011): 157–74, at 160.

12. Bataillon, *Erasme et l'Espagne,* 714; *Le docteur Laguna auteur du* Voyage *en Turquie* (Paris: Librairie des Editions Espagnoles, 1958), 53.

13. Albert Mas, *Les Turcs dans la littérature espagnole du siècle d'or: Recherches sur l'évolution d'un thème littéraire,* 2 vols. (Paris: Centre de Recherches Hispaniques, 1967), 1:151.

14. Sevilla Arroyo, "Diálogo y novela en el *Viaje de Turquía,*" 81.

15. As Emilio Solá notes, "avisos" [warnings], depositions, or relations by a witness all claim the narrator as guarantor of truth and offer an important source for more elaborate narrations ("Los avisos de Levante: El nacimiento de una narración sobre Turquía," in *España y el Oriente Islámico entro los siglos XV y XVI,* ed. Encarnación Sánchez García, Pablo Martín Asuero, and Michele Bernardini [Istanbul: Editorial Isis, 2007], 207–30). At the same time, humanists such as Díaz Tanco, in his *Palinodia de los Turcos* or Pedro Mexía, in his *Silva de varia lección,* routinely repackaged early sources on the Ottomans. On the related question of the circulation and recycling of early modern images of "exotic" places, see Lisa Voigt and Elio Brancaforte, "The Traveling Illustrations of Sixteenth-Century Travel Narratives," *PMLA* 129, no. 3 (2014): 365–98.

16. Ortola, "Introducción," 13–14.

17. Bataillon, "Andrés Laguna, peregrinaciones de Pedro de Urdemalas: Una muestra de una edición comentada," *NRFH* 4 (1952): 127–37; Bataillon, *Le docteur Laguna,* 103–18.

18. "Peregrino," Covarrubias explains, is "el que sale de su tierra en romería a visitar alguna casa santa o lugar santo" ["he who leaves his country on pilgrimage to visit some sacred house or place"], while a "cosa peregrina" is a strange or rare thing (Sebastián de Covarrubias, *Tesoro de la lengua castellana o española*, ed. Martín Riquer [Barcelona: Alta Fulla, 1998], 863a).

19. Bataillon, *Le docteur Laguna*, 109.

20. On the *Odyssey* as a mirror for princes, see Juan Ramón Muñoz Sánchez, "'El mejor de los poetas' para 'el mejor de los príncipes': *La Ulixea de Homero, traducida de griego en lengua castellana por el secretario Gonzalo Pérez*, un tratado cortesano de educación principesca," *Calíope* 22, no. 1 (2017): 141–63. Johnson notes the midcentury translation into Spanish of the *Odyssey* by the court humanist Gonzalo Pérez, almost contemporary with the *Viaje*: "Pérez opens the door to a reading of Odysseus as a kind of noble pícaro who for all his vagabondage possesses prudence rather than cupidity" ("El Homero español," 168).

21. Thomas More, *Utopia*, ed. and with a revised translation by George M. Logan (New York: W. W. Norton, 2011), 130.

22. The *Palinodia* announces its instrumental goals very clearly: "Puseme en este trabajo: porque (mediante tal memoria) . . . se puedan hallar provechosos remedios contra las fuerças de aquellas abominables naciones. Donde con los enxemplos de las guerras passadas se puede tener mejor orden y mas provechosas maneras para poder señorearlos: y librar de sus manos y sujecion la gran christiandad que en su poder horrendo y cautividad esquiva esta" ["I wrought this so that (through such a remembrance) . . . there might be found profitable remedies against the forces of those abominable nations. For from the examples of past wars a better approach and more profitable methods to subdue them may be obtained, so as to free from their hands and their subjection the great part of Christendom that is in their horrid power and distant captivity"]. Vasco Díaz Tanco, *Palinodia de los Turcos* [1547], facsimile edition with an introduction by Antonio Rodríguez-Moñino (Badajoz: Diputación Provincial, 1947), iii.

23. Bataillon, *Le docteur Laguna,* 106–18.

24. John 18:15–16 (King James Version).

25. Marie-Sol Ortolá, *Un estudio del "Viaje de Turquía": Autobiografía o ficción* (London: Támesis, 1983), 53n25.

26. Miguel de Cervantes Saavedra, *Los trabajos de Persiles y Sigismunda*, ed. Juan Bautista Avalle-Arce (Madrid: Clásicos Castalia, 1969), Bk. 3, ch. 10.

27. Cf. Cervantes's novella of captivity, "El amante liberal." Edwin Williamson reads the protagonists' dissembling as justified in light of their larger goal of returning to Christianity ("Hacia la conciencia ideológica de Cervantes: Idealización y violencia en 'El amante liberal,'" in *Cervantes: Estudios en la víspera de su centenario* [Keissel: Reichenberger, 1994], 519–33).

28. Matthew 10:33 (King James Version).

29. Cf. the argument by the Morisco advocate Franciso Núñez Muley that Christianity may be practiced according to a variety of local customs. See K. Garrad, "The Original Memorial of Don Francisco Núñez Muley," *Atlante* 2 (1954): 199–226.

30. See Molly Greene, *A Shared World: Christians and Muslims in the Early Modern Mediterranean* (Princeton, NJ: Princeton University Press, 2002).

31. See Andrew Devereux, "The ruin and slaughter of . . . fellow Christians": The French as a Threat to Christendom in Spanish Assertions of Sovereignty in Italy, 1479–1516," in *Representing Imperial Rivalry in the Early Modern Mediterranean,* ed. Barbara Fuchs and Emily Weissbourd (Toronto: University of Toronto Press, 2015), 101–25.

32. Hershenzon, "The Captive Sea," 77–78.

33. Hershenzon, "The Captive Sea," 78.

34. Alban Forcione reads the episode in relation to Aristotelian questions of verisimilitude in *Cervantes, Aristotle, and the "Persiles"* (Princeton, NJ: Princeton University Press, 1970), 170–86. For readings that situate the episode in relation to the imperial project, see Barbara Fuchs, *Mimesis and Empire: The New World, Islam, and European Identities* (Cambridge: Cambridge University Press, 2001), 161–63, and Voigt, *Writing Captivity,* 68–77.

35. Marie-Blanche Requejo Carrió, "De como se guisa una fábula: El episodio de los falsos cautivos en el *Persiles* (III.X)," in Alicia Villar Lecumberri, ed., *Peregrinamente peregrinos: Actas del V Congreso Internacional de la Asociación de Cervantistas* (Alcalá de Henares: Asociación de Cervantistas, 2004), 861–79, 865. On beggars, see also the discussion of Guzmán de Alfarache in Chapter 3.

36. See Ángel Estévez Molinero, "La (re)escritura Cervantina de Pedro de Urdemalas," *Cervantes* 15, no. 1 (1995): 82–93.

37. Jean Canavaggio has argued that these Cervantine characters are more akin to court buffoons or *hombres de placer*, charged with entertaining those in power ("Sobre lo cómico en el teatro cervantino: Tristán y Madrigal, bufones in partibus," *Nueva Revista de Filología Hispánica* 34, no. 2 (1985/86): 538–47).

38. Aurelio González, "El gracioso de Cervantes, un modelo alternativo," *Teatro de Palabras: Revista sobre teatro áureo* 2 (2008): 29–44, citation at 32, 34.

39. On the tension between drama and narration, see Barbara Fuchs, "Ventriloquist Theater and the Omniscient Narrator: *Gatz* and *El pasado es un animal grotesco*," *Modern Drama* 57, no. 2 (2014): 165–86.

40. Miguel de Cervantes, *The Bagnios of Algiers and The Great Sultana: Two Plays of Captivity*, ed. and trans. Barbara Fuchs and Aaron Ilika (Philadelphia: University of Pennsylvania Press, 2009), lines 51–53. Subsequent citations are by line number and from this edition.

41. "Campana se toma algunas vezes por la iglesia o parrochia, y assí dezimos de ciertos diezmos deverse a la campana, conviene a saber a la parrochia donde nos administran los Sacramentos," Covarrubias, *Tesoro,* s.v. "campana," 279b.

42. Javier Irigoyen-García, "'La música ha sido hereje': Pastoral Performance, Moorishness, and Cultural Hybridity in *Los baños de Argel*," *Bulletin of the Comediantes* 62, no. 2 (2010): 45–62, at 52.

43. Although, as Ruth Fine has perceptively noted, Spanish orthodoxy often distinguishes biblical Hebrews—God's chosen people, a foreshadowing of the Christian people—from the pertinacious and disgraced Jews who refused to recognize Christ as the Messiah ("El entrecruzamiento de lo hebreo y lo converso en la obra de Cervantes: Un encuentro singular," in *Cervantes y las religions*, ed. Ruth Fine and Santiago López Navia [Madrid: Iberoamericana, 2008], 437–39), the two categories frequently collapse into each other.

44. The iteration goes beyond the redoubled Cervantine moments: Pedro Córdoba has discovered that these lines are not original to Cervantes, but appear in a manuscript miscellany of the humanist Alvar Gómez de Castro. Córdoba argues that the verses are unlikely to be Gómez de Castro's own, but are more probably part of the miscellany of verses, songs, and sayings that he collected ("Cita y autocita en Cervantes," in *La réception du texte littéraire*, ed. Jean-Pierre Étienvre and Leonardo Castro Tovar, vol. 7 [Zaragoza: Casa de Velázquez, 1988], 50). They thus suggest the much broader currency of such exogamous fantasies, which Cervantes merely replays. Although Cervantes frames the verses for great effect, then, their prehistory suggests that a Christian directing love poems to a Muslim was hardly an extraordinary occurrence.

45. Paul Lewis-Smith translates the term as indicating "guile or artfulness" in "*La gran sultana doña Catalina de Oviedo*: A Cervantine Practical Joke," *Forum for Modern Language Studies* 17, no. 1 (1981): 68–81, citation on 78.

46. On ventriloquist figures who undercut the official word, see Jacques Lezra, *Unspeakable Subjects: The Genealogy of the Event in Early Modern Europe* (Stanford, CA: Stanford University Press, 1997), 276–80.

47. In his erotic proclivities, Madrigal recalls the compromised figure of the servant Launcelot in Shakespeare's *Merchant of Venice*, who taunts Jessica about her imperfect conversion to Christianity—she will always be Shylock's daughter—while sleeping with a "blackamoor," whom he has impregnated (3.5.23–32). *The Merchant of Venice,* ed. M. Lindsay Kaplan (New York: Palgrave, 2002).

48. See Anson C. Piper, "The 'Breadly Paradise' of *Lazarillo de Tormes*," *Hispania* 44, no. 2 (1961): 269–71, and Benjamín Torrico, "Retorno al 'paraíso panal': Derecho civil y canónico como claves eucarísticas en el Tratado segundo de *Lazarillo de Tormes*," *Hispanic Review* 74, no. 4 (2006): 419–35.

49. Although Fine notes that commentators and lexicographers have missed the Hebrew origins of *trefe* (443), she does not bring out the deliberate erasure of what was surely a widely recognized etymology, at least in some quarters. Francisco del Rosal, in his unpublished *Diccionario etimológico* (licensed in 1601), gives not one but two Greek etymologies: "Trefe: cosa sin jugo. Del griego *terphos* que es la corteza y cáscara de cualquiera cosa, porque ésta no participa del jugo y virtud de la planta. Y asimesmo *trefe de livianos*, enfermedad que dicen *tísica*. Pero de aquí infiero que debe decirse de *Atrophe*, que del griego será lo que no sustenta, nutre o mantiene" (293r). Covarrubias gives as the definition "cosa ligera que facilmente se dobla, se ensancha, y encoge, por ser de cuerpo delgado y floxo: y assí el que está flaco y enfermo, dizé estar deble y trefe. Antonio Nebrisense dize assí: trefe de *livianos pulmunarius, a, um, phthisicus, a, um.* Trefedad, dolencia, *phtisis is.*" (Covarrubias, *Tesoro,* s.v. "trefe," 976b). These Greek and Latin references classicize a term that has a very different origin, recognized, though only partially, by the *Diccionario de Autoridades* (1739): "TREFE. Lo que es ligero, delgado, y floxo, por lo qual facilmente se ensancha, dobla, y encoge. Usase algunas veces por falso, o falto de ley. Es voz Hebrea, que significa enfermo, o dañado. Lat. *Levis. Spongiosus*," (http://web.frl.es/DA.html). Del Rosal and Covarrubias thus perform the etymological cleansing of what was surely a widely recognized term in early modern Iberia, given its frequency in accusations to the Inquisition and depositions before it, as historians and linguists have documented (see Mary Elizabeth Perry and Anne J. Cruz, *Cultural Encounters: The Impact of the Inquisition in Spain and the New World* [Berkeley: University of California Press, 1991], 183–84; Steven N. Dworkin, *A History of the Spanish Lexicon: A Linguistic Perspective* [Oxford: Oxford University Press, 2012], 115; Rolf Eberenz and Mariela de La Torre, *Conversaciones estrechamente vigiladas: Interacción coloquial y español oral en las actas inquisitoriales de los siglos XV a XVII* [Zaragoza: Libros Pórticos, 2003], 246–47).

50. Or Hasson, "*Los baños de Argel*: Un análisis del tratamiento cervantino de lo hebreo y lo judío desde un punto de vista kleiniano," in *Cervantes y las religiones,* ed. Ruth Fine and Santiago López Navia (Madrid: Iberoamericana, 2008), 473–502, citation at 495. On antisemitic prejudice in Spain in relation to the figure of the *converso*, see Barbara F. Weissberger, "Motherhood and Ritual Murder in Medieval Spain and England," *Journal of Medieval and Early Modern Studies* 39, no. 1 (2009): 7–30.

51. The scene also obliquely references the contemporary debates over how to deal with Morisco children and their religious education, from the aftermath of the uprising in the Alpujarras (1568–71) to the decrees of expulsion contemporary with the publication of Cervantes's *comedias* (1609–14). See Stephanie M. Cavanaugh, "Litigating for Liberty: Enslaved Morisco Children in Sixteenth-Century Valladolid," *Renaissance Quarterly* 70, no. 4 (2017): 1282–1320,

and Georgina Dopico Black, "Ghostly Remains: Valencia, 1609," *Arizona Journal of Hispanic Cultural Studies* 7 (2003): 91–100.

52. Hasson, "*Los baños*," 497.

53. Javier Irigoyen-García notes that the bones of the martyred boy become his father's own testimony to his enduring Christianity in captivity ("El problema morisco en *Los baños de Argel*, de Miguel de Cervantes: De renegados a mártires cristianos," *Revista Canadiense de Estudios Hispánicos* 32, no. 3 [2008]: 421–38, 429).

54. George Mariscal, "*La gran sultana* and the Issue of Cervantes's Modernity," *Revista de Estudios Hispánicos* 28, no. 2 (1994): 185–211, 204.

CHAPTER 3

1. Michel Cavillac, one of the foremost critics of the *Guzmán* and one to whom this chapter owes much, demurs. In his view, categorizing Alemán's text as a picaresque diminishes it: it should be considered simply a novel, with no reductive qualifier. Although I fully concur with Cavillac's account of the complexity of the text, my own study proposes a richer understanding of the picaresque, so that including *Guzmán* in this category no longer implies a simplistic reading. See Cavillac, Guzmán de Alfarache *y la novela moderna* (Madrid: Casa de Velázquez, 2010), especially 197–215.

2. For influential readings that question Guzmán's reformation, see Joan Arias, *Guzmán de Alfarache: The Unrepentant Narrator* (London: Támesis, 1977); Benito Brancaforte, *Guzmán de Alfarache: ¿Conversión o proceso de degradación?* (Madison, WI: Hispanic Seminary of Medieval Studies, 1980); Judith Whitenack, *The Impenitent Confession of Guzmán de Alfarache* (Madison, WI: Hispanic Seminary of Medieval Studies, 1985); Carlos Antonio Rodríguez Matos, *El narrador pícaro: Guzmán de Alfarache* (Madison, WI: Hispanic Seminary of Medieval Studies, 1985); and John C. Parrack, "Reading the Silence: The Picaresque Game of *Lacunae* and Contradiction," *Revista Canadiense de Estudios Hispanicos* 32, no. 2 (2008): 291–314.

3. Katharina Niemeyer, "'. . . el ser de un pícaro el sujeto deste libro': La *Primera parte de Guzmán de Alfarache*," in *La novela picaresca: Concepto genérico y evolución del género (siglos XVI y XVII)*, ed. Klaus Meyer-Minnemann and Sabine Schlickers (Madrid: Iberoamericana, 2008), 77–116, at 98. See also Michel Cavillac, *Gueux et marchands dans le* Guzmán de Alfarache (Bordeaux: Bière, 1983), and Francisco Márquez Villanueva, "Sobre el lanzamiento y recepción del *Guzmán de Alfarache*," *Bulletin Hispanique* 92 (1990): 549–77.

4. See the important theoretical intervention by Paul Julian Smith, "The Rhetoric of Representation in Writers and Critics of Picaresque Narrative: *Lazarillo de Tormes, Guzmán de Alfarache, El Buscón*," *Modern Language Review* 82, no. 1 (1987): 88–108.

5. Américo Castro, *Cervantes y los casticismos españoles* (Madrid: Alfaguara, 1966). The evidence on Alemán is inconclusive. More important, the epistemological uncertainty of his text does not depend on, or even reflect, the author's identitarian condition. See Cavillac, Guzmán de Alfarache *y la novela moderna*, 30–35.

6. Baltasar Cuart Moner, "El juego de la memoria: Manipulaciones, reconstrucciones y reinvenciones de linajes en los Colegio Mayores salmantinos durante el siglo XVI," in *Cultura, política y práctica del derecho: Juristas de Salamanca, siglos XV–XX*, ed. S. de Dios and E. Torijano (Salamanca: Universidad de Salamanca, 2012), 71–142.

7. Cuart Moner, "El juego de la memoria," 74, 78.

8. See also the classic of *limpieza* and its blind spots. Albert Sicroff, *Les controverses des statuts de "pureté de sang" en Espagne du XVe au XVIIe siècles* (Paris: Didier, 1960), and Robert Folger's more recent exploration of the connections between bureaucratic structures and fiction in *Writing and Poaching: Interpellation and Self-Fashioning in Colonial* relaciones de méritos y servicios (Leiden: Brill, 2011).

9. Cuart Moner, "El juego de la memoria," 80.

10. Mateo Alemán, *Guzmán de Alfarache*, ed. José María Micó, 2 vols. (Madrid: Cátedra, 1994), 1:107. Subsequent references are in the text by volume and page number.

11. Ulrich Wicks suggests that all readers automatically choose *not* to be the *vulgo*, but the discreet readers who look down upon it: "This flattery aimed at the self-images of readers makes them paradoxically both willing and wary participants in a narrative confidence game that enables picaresque narration to function between author and reader" (*Picaresque Narrative, Picaresque Fictions: A Theory and Research Guide* [New York: Greenwood, 1989], 7).

12. Although Niemeyer unproblematically aligns the moralizing narrator with the "implied author" against the *pícaro*, I concur with Whitenack in finding this identification far less stable; that is, the reliability of the reformed narrator is consistently undercut by his own narrative. Cf. Niemeyer, "'. . . el ser de un pícaro el sujeto de este libro,'" and Whitenack, *The Impenitent Confession*.

13. It is perhaps worth noting that the very organization of the text into chapters complicates the question of Guzmán's authority over his story. Although the text is consistently narrated in the first person, the chapter headings all refer to Guzmán in the third person, granting his actions a definitiveness—Guzmán actually does such and such—beyond what they have in the text itself. I am grateful to Allison Collins for pointing out this discrepancy between the title chapters and the text.

14. Anne Cruz, *Discourses of Poverty: Social Reform and the Picaresque Novel in Early Modern Spain* (Toronto: University of Toronto Press, 1999), 100.

15. As Micó reminds us in his edition, the name Guzmán was perhaps the one most often selected by those who wanted to invent an ancient and distinguished lineage for themselves (1:161, n. 90).

16. Guzmán invokes his own direct witnessing as he describes the abuses that occur in inns and hostels ("ventas y posadas" 1:272). Yet direct observation leads only to *occupatio*, and whatever effect it might have immediately pales before the mediating force of habit: "Soy testigo de haber visto cosas que en mucho tiempo no podría decir de aquestas insolencias, que si las oyéramos pasar entre bárbaros, como a tales los culpáramos y, tratándolas a los ojos, no hacemos caso dellas" (1:272) ["I have witnessed such things as I could not relate their insolence in a long while, and if we heard of their occurring among barbarians, we would condemn them as such, yet when we see them with our very eyes we pay them no heed"]. Alemán's narrator here seems to invoke the complex negotiation of geographical distance, narrative authority, and social critique that animates the *Viaje de Turquía*, as discussed in Chapter 2.

17. As economic historians have shown, this international circuit of credit enriched Italian creditors while destroying small-scale commerce within Spain. See Felipe Ruiz Martín, *Las finanzas de la Monarquía Hispánica en tiempos de Felipe IV* (Madrid: Real Academia de la Historia, 1990) and *Pequeño capitalismo, gran capitalismo* (Barcelona: Crítica, 1990), and Pedro Tedde de Lorca, ed., *Las finanzas de Castilla y la Monarquía Hispánica (siglos xvi–xvii): homenaje a Felipe Ruiz Martín* (Valladolid: Universidad de Valladolid, 2008).

18. On the ideology of Gothicism, see Francisco Márquez Villanueva, "Trasfondos de 'La profecía del Tajo': Goticismo y profetismo," in *Fray Luis de León: Historia, humanismo y letras,*

ed. Víctor García de la Concha and Javier San José Lera (Salamanca: Universidad de Salamanca, 1996), and Patricia Grieve, *The Eve of Spain: Myths of Origin in the History of Christian, Muslim, and Jewish Conflict* (Baltimore: Johns Hopkins University Press, 2009). Micó notes that "es de los Guzmanes" has the same valence.

19. On Italian constructions of Spain, see Arturo Farinelli, *Marrano (storia di un vituperio)* (Geneva: Olschki, 1925); Benedetto Croce, *España en la vida italiana del Renacimiento*, trans. Franscisco González Ríos (Buenos Aires: Imán, 1945); Sverker Arnoldsson, *La leyenda negra: Estudios sobre sus orígenes* (Göteborg: Göteborgs Universitets Arsskrift, 1960).

20. For the broader context of proposed programs, see Cruz, *Discourses of Poverty*.

21. The moral appended to an emblem of justice in the treatise claims: "El atajar que no pida / Quien mendiga con malicia / Es administrar justicia" ["To prevent those who beg with cunning is to administer justice"], thus connecting the proper workings of justice in the state with the ability to distinguish between legitimate and illegitimate claims on charity. Reproduced in Cristóbal Pérez de Herrera, *Amparo de pobres*, ed. Michel Cavillac (Madrid: Espasa-Calpe, 1975), 17.

22. Cruz, *Discourses of Poverty*, 76–77; Cavillac, "Alemán y Guzmán ante la reforma de la mendicidad," in his *Guzmán de Alfarache y la novela moderna*, 73–92.

23. Pérez de Herrera, *Amparo de pobres*, 33. Cf. the noble *pícaros* in Cervantes's "La ilustre fregona," which I discuss in Chapter 4.

24. Cavillac, "Alemán y Guzmán ante la reforma de la mendicidad," 77.

25. The term *galeote* refers to the galleys on which these criminals usually served out their cruel sentences. In this case, the Crown had been persuaded to provide condemned criminals to work in the mines, hence *galeotes* on land. See Germán Bleiberg, *El "Informe secreto" de Mateo Alemán sobre el trabajo forzoso en las minas de Almadén* (London: Támesis, 1985). See also Juan Carlos Rodríguez, *La literatura del pobre* (Granada: Comares, 1994), 220.

26. Bleiberg, *"Informe secreto,"* 23.

27. See Michele L. Clouse, *Medicine, Government, and Public Health in Philip II's Spain: Shared Interests, Competing Authorities* (Burlington, VT: Ashgate, 2013).

28. Cavillac, "Alemán y Guzmán ante la reforma de la mendicidad," 82–91.

29. See Chapter 1 for Torres Naharro's account of "soldados bisoños"—needy Spanish soldiers in Italy.

30. See Laurence Fontaine, *The Moral Economy: Poverty, Credit, and Trust in Early Modern Europe* (Cambridge: Cambridge University Press, 2014). On the negotiation of trust in cross-cultural trade, see Francesca Trivellato, *The Familiarity of Strangers: The Sephardic Diaspora, Livorno, and Cross-Cultural Trade in the Early Modern Period* (New Haven, CT: Yale University Press, 2009).

31. Covarrubias, *Tesoro*, s.v. "crédito," 368b. Cf. the three linked definitions of *crédit* in Antoine Furetière's *Dictionnaire universel* (The Hague and Rotterdam, 1690): "Crédit: croyance, estime qu'on s'acquiert dans le public par sa vertu, sa probité, sa bonne foy & son mérite. . . . Crédit, se dit aussi de la puissance, de l'autorité, des richesses qu'on s'acquiert par le moyen de cette réputation qu'on a acquise. . . . Crédit, se dit plus ordinnairement dans le commerce de ce prest mutuel qui se fait d'argent et de marchandises, sur la réputation de la probité & solvabilité d'un négociant" (Vvv3).

32. Cavillac, *Pícaros y mercaderes en el* Guzmán de Alfarache*: Reformismo burgués y mentalidad aristocrática en la España del Siglo de Oro*, trans. Juan M. Azpitarte Almagro (Granada: Universidad de Granada, 1994), especially 193–251, and "La figura bifronte del mercader en el *Guzmán de Alfarache*," in his Guzmán de Alfarache *y la novela moderna*.

33. Covarrubias, *Tesoro*, s.v. "mohatra," 809b.

34. Francisco Javier Jiménez Muñoz, *La usura: Evolución histórica y patología de los intereses* (Madrid: Librería Editorial Dykinson, 2010).

35. Miguel de Cervantes Saavedra, *Don Quijote de la Mancha*, ed. Martín de Riquer (Barcelona: Planeta, 1997), 790.

36. The English version of the proverb is "to throw out a sprat to catch a mackerel."

37. This merchant, described as "hombre del más mal nombre que tiene toda la ciudad, y el peor quisto de toda ella" (2:239) ["the man with the worst reputation in the entire city, and the worst liked within it"], anticipates Guzmán's own exploits back in Madrid (Rodríguez Matos, *El narrador pícaro*, 37).

38. Rodríguez Matos, *El narrador pícaro*, 37–39.

39. On early modern account books of the period, see Fernando Ramos González, "Libros de contabilidad" (Alicante: Biblioteca Virtual Miguel de Cervantes, 2014), http://www.cervantesvirtual.com/obra-visor/libros-de-contabilidad/html/db70e24c-51e9-4cab-8180-66c44e91b2ae_2.html#I_0_. On the suggestive relation between the *libro de memoria* and Guzmán's story, see Rodríguez Matos, *El narrador pícaro*, 37–38.

40. On the long-term, interest-bearing bonds or annuities known as *juros*, see I. A. A. Thompson, "Castile: Polity, Fiscality, and Fiscal Crisis," in *Fiscal Crises, Liberty, and Representative Government, 1450–1789*, ed. Philip T. Hoffman and Kathryn Nohrberg (Stanford, CA: Stanford University Press, 2002).

41. Thompson, "Castile," 159. Thompson's description of a financial pyramid scheme is uncannily reminiscent of subprime lending and the financial crisis of 2008.

42. Covarrubias, *Tesoro*, s.v. "cambio," 276a.

43. Miguel de Cervantes, "La española inglesa," in *Novelas ejemplares*, 2 vols., ed. Harry Sieber (Madrid: Cátedra, 1997), 2:272. The transaction requires three separate merchants, based in London, Paris, and Seville.

44. The episode anticipates in fascinating ways the remarkable scene in "La española inglesa," in which the recusant Englishman privateer Ricaredo, riven by national, religious, and romantic obligations, faces the crux of whether to attack Spanish ships. Ricaredo is saved by the appearance of a Turkish ship, which provides an uncomplicated prey (Cervantes, *Novelas ejemplares*, 1:252–53).

45. On the relation between the novella and the broader text, see Hortensia Morell, "La deformación picaresca del mundo ideal en *Ozmín y Daraja* del *Guzmán de Alfarache*," *La Torre* 13, no. 87–88 (1975): 101–25, and Judith Whitenack, "The *alma diferente* of Mateo Alemán's 'Ozmín y Daraja,'" *Romance Quarterly* 38, no. 1 (1991): 59–71.

46. Manuel Montalvo, "La crisis del siglo XVII desde la atalaya de Mateo Alemán," *Revista de Occidente* 112 (1990): 116–35, citation on 135. Cavillac, *Guzmán de Alfarache y la novela moderna*, 112–13. This charged open-endedness anticipates the unresolved condition of the *Moriscos* Ricote and Ana Félix in the second part of *Don Quijote*, whose fate remains similarly undecided by the authorities.

CHAPTER 4

Epigraph: Miguel de Cervantes Saavedra, *Don Quijote de la Mancha*, ed. Martín de Riquer (Barcelona: Planeta, 1997), 224.

1. Roberto González Echevarría, *Myth and Archive: A Theory of Latin American Narrative* (Cambridge: Cambridge University Press, 1990), and "The Life and Adventures of Cipión:

Cervantes and the Picaresque," *Diacritics* 10, no. 3 (1980): 15–26; David Gitlitz, "Inquisition Confessions and Lazarillo de Tormes," *Hispanic Review* 68, no. 1 (2000): 53–74.

2. Cf. John C. Parrack, who focuses on lacunae as sites of productive picaresque contradiction, attributing the increased need for a reader to interpret these lacunae to the development of private reading ("Reading the Silence: The Picaresque Game of *Lacunae* and Contradiction," *Revista Canadiense de Estudios* Hispanicos 32, no. 2 [2008]: 291–314).

3. See, for example, Mercedes García-Arenal, "A Catholic Muslim Prophet: Agustín de Ribera, 'the Boy Who Saw Angels,'" *Common Knowledge* 18, no. 2 (2012): 267–91, and Mercedes García-Arenal and Felipe Pereda, "A propósito de los Alumbrados: Confesionalidad y disidencia en el mundo ibérico," *La Corónica* 41, no. 1 (2012): 109–48. See also the collection edited by García-Arenal and Barbara Fuchs, *The Quest for Certainty in Early Modern Europe: From Inquisition to Inquiry, 1550–1700* (2020).

4. The classic account of Cervantes's perspectivism is Leo Spitzer's "Linguistic Perspectivism in the Don Quijote," in *Linguistics and Literary History: Essays in Stylistics* (New York: Russel and Russel, 1972), 223–71. After a general introduction to skepticism in early modern Spain, Maureen Ihrie (*Skepticism in Cervantes* [London: Tamesis Books, 1982]) focuses almost exclusively on *Don Quijote* and the *Persiles*. Daniel Lorca ("The Function of Skepticism in Part I of Don Quijote," *Cervantes* 30, no. 2 [2010]: 115–48) assesses how skepticism structures the *Quijote*, while Anthony Cascardi ("Cervantes and Skepticism: The Vanishing of the Body," in *Essays on Hispanic Literature in Honor of Edmund L. King*, ed. Sylvia Molloy and Luis Fernández Cifuentes [London: Tamesis Books, 1983], 23–29), focuses on "El licenciado Vidriera" and Descartes. More recently, Jorge Checa has examined the interplay of skepticism and language in "El coloquio de los perros" ("Cervantes y la cuestión de los orígenes: escepticismo y lenguaje en *El coloquio de los perros*," *Hispanic Review* 68, no. 3 [2000]: 295–317).

5. Miguel de Cervantes Saavedra, *Novelas ejemplares*, 2 vols., ed. Harry Charles Sieber (Madrid: Cátedra, 1980 [1613]), citation on 1:52. Subsequent references are in the text and to this edition, by volume and page number only.

6. See, for example, Carroll Johnson, *Cervantes and the Material World*, Hispanisms (Urbana: University of Illinois Press, 2000); Julio Baena, "Novela señoresca: *La Señora Cornelia* o señorial monumento agrietado," *Romance Quarterly* 61, no. 2 (2014): 100–10; and Javier Irigoyen-García, "'Si no es adivinando la mitad del pergamino': Discurso y realidad en 'La ilustre fregona,'" in *Novelas ejemplares: Las grietas de la ejemplaridad*, Juan de La Cuesta Hispanic Monographs no. 31, ed. Julio Baena (Newark, DE: Juan de la Cuesta, 2008), 227–49.

7. On exemplarity in the Renaissance, see John D. Lyons, *Exemplum: The Rhetoric of Example in Early Modern France and Italy* (Princeton, NJ: Princeton University Press, 1989), and Timothy Hampton, *Writing from History: The Rhetoric of Exemplarity in Renaissance Literature* (Ithaca, NY: Cornell University Press, 1990). François Rigolot notes the tension between the dialogue and exemplarity in "Problematizing Renaissance Exemplarity: The Inward Turn of Dialogue from Petrarch to Montaigne," in *Printed Voices: The Renaissance Culture of Dialogue*, ed. Dorothea Heitsch and Jean-François Vallée (Toronto: University of Toronto Press, 2004), 3–24. On early modern alternatives to exemplarity, see Parrack, "Reading the Silence," 293–94.

8. Coleridge makes his famous point in *Biographia Literaria* (1817), 2 vols., ed. J. Shawcross (London: Oxford University Press, 1939), relating a conversation with Wordsworth about supernatural versus ordinary subjects: "It was agreed, that my endeavors should be directed to persons and characters supernatural, or at least romantic; yet so as to transfer from our inward nature a human interest and a semblance of truth sufficient to procure for these shadows of imagination that willing suspension of disbelief for the moment, which constitutes poetic faith" (2:5).

9. Edwin Williamson suggests that the prologue to the *Novelas* and the linked novellas "El casamiento engañoso" and "El coloquio de los perros," to which I turn below, are in fact the occasion for "Cervantes' extended meditation on didacticism" ("El juego de la verdad en 'El casamiento engañoso' y 'El coloquio de los perros,'" *Actas del II Coloquio Internacional de Cervantistas* [Barcelona: Anthropos, 1990], 183–99, citation on 185).

10. *La vida de Lazarillo de Tormes y de sus fortunas y adversidades*, ed. Alberto Blecua (Madrid: Clásicos Castalia, 1984), 89.

11. Juan Bautista Avalle-Arce suggests that the reference to Guzmán reveals Carriazo's picaresque condition as a literary predilection rather than an inherited condition ("Cervantes entre pícaros," *Nueva Revista de Filología Hispánica* 38, no. 2 [1990]: 591–603, at 595).

12. On the presence of noble *pícaros* in the *almadrabas*, see the remarkable account in Pedro Herrera Puga, *Sociedad y delincuencia en el Siglo del Oro* (Madrid: La Editorial Católica, 1974), 416–23. See also Francisco Carrillo, "La vida del pícaro (1601): Testimonio contextual de la picaresca," in *Actas del VIII Congreso de la Asociación Internacional de Hispanistas* 22–27, ed. A. David Kossoff, Ruth H. Kossoff, Geoffrey Ribbans, José Amor y Vázquez (1986), 357–66, and Enrique García-Santo Tomás, "Outside Bets: Disciplining Gamblers in Early Modern Spain," *Hispanic Review* 77, no. 1 (2010): 147–64, on nobles who behave like *pícaros* in gambling houses.

13. In her reading of the *almadrabas*, Jannine Montauban recalls that the protagonist of *Segunda parte del Lazarillo de Tormes* is actually transformed into a tuna (*El ajuar de la vida picaresca: Reproducción, genealogía y sexualidad en la novela picaresca española* [Madrid: Visor Libros, 2003], 114).

14. Montauban emphasizes the sense of many possible stories in the novella: "Se puede afirmar que el texto de 'La ilustre fregona' se propone a sí mismo como una suerte de máquina de producir historias; una máquina que, una vez en funcionamiento, se aleja lo más posible de su origen hasta el punto de ejercer sobre él una voluntaria borradura" (*El ajuar*, 113).

15. Montauban notes how "Rinconete y Cortadillo" systematically challenges picaresque commonplaces: rather than being marked by heredity or birth the two young men decide to go off to Seville on a whim; the focus is on two protagonists; the narration is in the third person; and it is sustained rather than episodic (*El ajuar*, 109).

16. On the theatricality of inquisitional testimony, see Paul Michael Johnson, "Feeling Certainty, Performing Sincerity: The Emotional Hermeneutics of Truth in Inquisitorial and Theatrical Practice" in Fuchs and García-Arenal, *The Quest for Certainty.*

17. Jorge García López notes that their self-presentations are "carefully identical" ("Rinconete y Cortadillo y la novela picaresca," *Cervantes* 19, no. 2 [1999]: 113–24, citation on 115).

18. Helen Reed, "Theatricality in the Picaresque of Cervantes," *Cervantes* 7, no. 2 (1987): 71–84, citation on 72.

19. As Reed notes, "The scenes in Monipodio's house form something like a play within a play in that they are presented for Rinconete and Cortadillo, who are more spectators than actors in that scene" ("Theatricality," 75). Francisco J. Sánchez further notes the similarities between these scenes and the entremés or interlude, "where the audience laughs at the usurpation of signs and words of social prestige by people of lower social status," in "Theater Within the Novel: 'Mass' Audience and Individual Reader in *La Gitanilla* and *Rinconete y Cortadillo*," in *Cervantes's "Exemplary Novels" and the Adventure of Writing*, Hispanic Issues 6, ed. Michael Nerlich and Nicholas Spadaccini (Minneapolis: Prisma Institute, 1989), 23–98, citation on 91.

20. Cascardi, "¿Qué es filosofar?: A Dog's Eye View," *Cervantes* 34, no. 1 (2014): 77–95.

21. See Ihrie, *Skepticism*, 21–22, 25.

22. Montauban suggests that, in a line of valorizing fictions that extends from *Celestina* to *Lazarillo*, the dogs, too, "expresan su preferencia por lo textual hasta el extremo de no importarles demasiado la precisión de sus relatos" (*El ajuar de la vida picaresca*, 115). Cf. Katharina Niemeyer, who writes of the *Guzmán*: "Aceptar el carácter ficticio del discurso narrativo es la clave para poder entrar en el juego entre la conciencia de saber que se está leyendo una ficción y la postura imaginaria de credulidad ilimitada que caracteriza el pacto novelístico" (". . . el ser de un pícaro el sujeto deste libro: La *Primera parte de Guzmán de Alfarache* [Madrid, 1599]," in *La novela picaresca: Concepto genérico y evolución del género [siglos XVI y XVII]*, ed. Klaus Meyer-Minnemann and Sabine Schlickers [Madrid: Iberoamericana, 2008], 87).

23. Before his story is over, Berganza will both be exhibited as an entertainer himself and serve a poet who writes plays.

24. Checa, "Cervantes y la cuestión de los orígenes," 296–97.

25. Checa, "Cervantes y la cuestión de los orígenes," 304–7.

26. See Edward Riley, "La profecía de la bruja (El coloquio de los perros)," *Actas del Primer Coloquio Internacional de Cervantistas* (Barcelona: Anthropos, 1989), 83–94, and Williamson, "El juego de la verdad."

27. Checa, "Cervantes y la cuestión de los orígenes," 301.

28. Cascardi ignores this blatantly prejudiced account in his exploration of the dogs as Cynics, concerned with questioning "the assumptions, beliefs, and practices of the established world" ("¿Qué es filosofar?," citation on 91).

POSTSCRIPT

1. "Checkology," *The News Literacy Project*, accessed January 10, 2019, https://newslit.org/educators/checkology/.

2. Adam Satariano and Elian Peltier, "In France, School Lessons Ask: Which Twitter Post Should You Trust?," *New York Times*, December 13, 2018, https://www.nytimes.com/2018/12/13/technology/france-internet-literacy-school.html.

New strategies continue to emerge, such as NewsGuard's effort to label online news organizations for their reliability (Edmund Lee, "Veterans of the News Media Are Now Fighting Fakes," *New York Times*, January 16, 2018, https://www.nytimes.com/2019/01/16/business/media/media-steve-brill-fake-news.html).

3. Michiko Kakutani, *The Death of Truth: Notes on Falsehood in the Age of Trump* (New York: Tim Duggan Books, 2018), 11.

4. In their coverage of French efforts in the *New York Times*, Adam Satariano and Elian Peltier are careful to specify "online misinformation" or "junk information online" as the target of media literacy efforts (Satariano and Peltier, "In France, School Lessons Ask: Which Twitter Post Should You Trust?"). Yet "fact versus fiction" appears with remarkable regularity, often in relation to the teaching of critical thinking. In addition to NLP's Checkology, see, for example, Jennifer LaGarde and Darren Hudgins, *Fact vs. Fiction: Teaching Critical Thinking Skills in the Age of Fake News* (Portland, OR: International Society for Technology in Education, 2018).

5. A representative example is Doris Lessing, "There is no doubt fiction makes a better job of the truth," in her *Under My Skin: Volume One of My Autobiography to 1949* (New York: HarperCollins, 1994), 314.

6. Salman Rushdie, "Truth, Lies, and Literature," *New Yorker*, May 31, 2018, https://www.newyorker.com/culture/cultural-comment/truth-lies-and-literature.

7. *The George Eliot Letters*, 9 vols., ed. Gordon S. Haight (New Haven, CT: Yale University Press, 1954–78), 3:111. See also Keith Oatley, "Fiction: Simulation of Social Worlds," *Trends in Cognitive Sciences* 20, no. 8 (2016): 618–28.

8. Cf. the exploration of deliberate hoaxes by Christopher L. Miller, *Impostors: Literary Hoaxes and Cultural Authenticity* (Chicago: University of Chicago Press, 2018), which focuses on authors who attempt to trick readers by writing as another. Miller usefully surveys Platonic versus Aristotelian approaches to fiction (4ff.).

9. Miller, *Impostors*, 8.

10. Miller, *Impostors*, 8.

11. As Aníbal González puts it, these are "las indiscreciones de un 'Yo' hipercrítico que termina por desautorizar su propio discurso" ["the indiscretions of a hypercritical 'I' that ultimately deauthorizes his own discourse"], "*Los infortunios de Alonso Ramírez*: Picaresca e historia." *Hispanic Review* 51, no. 2 (1983): 198.

12. "In an ever-changing, incomprehensible, world the masses had reached the point where they would, at the same time, believe everything and nothing, think that everything is possible and that nothing was true. . . . Mass propaganda discovered that its audience was ready at all times to believe the worst, no matter how absurd, and did not particularly object to being deceived because it held every statement to be a lie anyhow. The totalitarian mass leaders based their propaganda on the correct psychological assumption that, under such conditions, one could make people believe the most fantastic statements one day, and trust if the next day they were given irrefutable proof of their falsehood, they would take refuge in cynicism; instead of deserting the leaders who had lied to them, they would protest that they had known all along the statement was a lie and would admire the leaders for their superior tactical cleverness." Hannah Arendt, *Totalitarianism: Part Three of The Origins of Totalitarianism* (San Diego, CA: Harcourt, 1976), 80.

13. Cf. Paul Veyne's useful formulation for productive skepticism in historiographical inquiry: "I believe that this document teaches me this: may I trust it to do that?" (*Writing History: Essay on Epistemology*, trans. Mina Moore-Rinvolucri [Middletown, CT: Wesleyan University Press, 1984], 12).

14. For a useful review of the debates, see Roger Chartier, "History, Time, and Space," *Republics of Letters: A Journal for the Study of Knowledge, Politics, and the Arts* 2, no. 2 (June 1, 2011), http://arcade.stanford.edu/sites/default/files/article_pdfs/roflv02i02_Chartier_060111_0.pdf.

15. See David Shields, *Reality Hunger: A Manifesto* (New York: Vintage, 2010). Jonathan Sturgeon offers a more recent account: "What's happening is that new novels . . . are redistributing the relation between the self and fiction. Fiction is no longer seen as 'false' or 'lies' or 'make-believe.' Instead it is more like Kenneth Burke's definition of literature as 'equipment for living.' Fiction includes the narratives we tell ourselves, and the stories we're told, on the path between birth and death" ("2014: The Death of the Postmodern Novel and the Rise of Autofiction," *Flavorwire*, December 31, 2014, http://flavorwire.com/496570/2014–the-death-of-the-postmodern-novel-and-the-rise-of-autofiction, consulted January 13, 2019).

Bibliography

Ackerman, James. "The Planning of Renaissance Rome, 1450–1580." In *Rome in the Renaissance: The City and the Myth*, edited by P. A. Ramsey, 3–17. Binghamton, NY: Center for Medieval and Early Renaissance Studies, 1982.

Albalá Pelegrín, Marta. "Converso Migration and Social Stratification: Textual Representations of the Marrano from Iberia to Rome, 1480–1550." In *Exile and the Formation of Religious Identities in the Early Modern World*, edited by Gary Waite and Jesse Spohnholz, 141–55. London: Pickering and Chatto, 2014.

———. "*La Lozana andaluza*: Migración y pluralismo religioso en el Mediterráneo." *Revista Canadiense de Estudios Hispánicos* 41, no. 1 (2016): 215–42.

Alemán, Mateo. *Guzmán de Alfarache*. Edited by José María Micó. 2 vols. Madrid: Cátedra, 1994.

Allan, Madera. "Food Fight: Taste in the Inquisitorial Trials of Ciudad Real." Ph.D. diss., University of Pennsylvania, 2009.

Alvar, Carlos. "Cervantes y los judíos." In *Cervantes y las religiones,* edited by Ruth Fine and Santiago López Navia, 29–54. Madrid: Iberoamericana, 2008.

Arendt, Hannah. *Totalitarianism: Part Three of The Origins of Totalitarianism.* San Diego, CA: Harcourt, 1976.

Aretino, Pietro. *La cortigiana.* Translated by J. Douglas Campbell and Leonard G. Sbrocchi. Introduction by Raymond B. Waddington. Ottawa: Dovehouse, 2003.

Arias, Joan. *Guzmán de Alfarache: The Unrepentant Narrator.* Colección Támesis: Serie A—Monografías 58. London: Tamesis, 1977.

Arnoldsson, Sverker. *La leyenda negra: Estudios sobre sus orígenes.* Göteborg: Göteborgs Universitets Arsskrift, 1960.

Baena, Julio. "Novela señoresca: *La Señora Cornelia* o sensorial monumento agrietado." *Romance Quarterly* 61, no. 2 (2014): 100–110.

———, ed. *Novelas ejemplares: Las grietas de la ejemplaridad,* Newark, DE: Juan de la Cuesta, 2008.

Bataillon, Marcel. "Andrés Laguna, peregrinaciones de Pedro de Urdemalas: Una muestra de una edición comentada." *Nueva Revista de Filología Hispánica* 4 (1952): 127–37.

———. *Le docteur Laguna auteur du Voyage en Turquie*. Paris: Libraries des Éditions Espagnoles, 1958.

———. *Erasmo y España: Recherches sur l'histoire spirituelle du xvie siècle.* 1937; Geneva: Droz, 1991.

Bautista Avalle-Arce, Juan. "Cervantes entre pícaros." *Nueva Revista de Filología Hispánica* 38, no. 2 (1990): 591–603.

Binotti, Lucia. "Alfonso de Ulloa's Editorial Project: Translating, Writing, and Marketing Spanish Best-Sellers in Venice." *Allegorica* 17 (1996): 35–54.

———. "*La Tragicomedia de Calisto y Melibea* and the 'Questione della Lingua' After Bembo's *Prose*." In *Actas del Simposio Internacional, 1502–2002: Five Hundred Years of Fernando de Rojas' Tragicomedia de Calisto y Melibea*, edited by Juan Carlos Conde, 310–39. New York: Hispanic Seminary of Medieval Studies, 2007.

Blecua, Alberto, ed. *La vida de Lazarillo de Tormes y de sus fortunas y adversidades.* Madrid: Clásicos Castalia, 1984.

Bleiberg, Germán. *El "Informe secreto" de Mateo Alemán sobre el trabajo forzoso en las minas de Almadén.* Colección Támesis: Serie A—Monografías, 107. London: Tamesis, 1985.

Brancaforte, Benito. *Guzmán de Alfarache: ¿Conversión o proceso de degradación?* Madison, WI: Hispanic Seminary of Medieval Studies, 1980.

Braudel, Fernand. *The Mediterranean and the Mediterranean World in the Age of Philip II.* Translated by Siân Reynolds. London: Collins, 1973.

Brendecke, Arndt. *The Empirical Empire: Spanish Colonial Rule and the Politics of Knowledge.* Berlin: Walter de Gruyter, 2016.

Bubnova, Tatiana. "Delicado en la Peña de Martos." *Actas de la Asociación Internacional de Hispanistas* 12 (1995): 70–78.

———. *F. Delicado puesto en diálogo: Las claves bajtinianas de* La Lozana andaluza. Mexico City: Universidad Nacional Autónoma, 1987.

Burns, Kathryn. "Notaries, Truth, and Consequences." *American Historical Review* 110, no. 2 (2005): 350–79.

Burshatin, Israel. "Rome as Andalusia: Bodies and Borders in Francisco Delicado's *Retrato de la Lozana Andaluza*." *MLN* 129, no. 2 (2014): 197–218.

Canavaggio, Jean. "Sobre lo cómico en el teatro cervantino: Tristán y Madrigal, bufones in partibus." *Nueva Revista de Filología Hispánica* 34, no. 2 (1985/86): 538–47.

Carajicomedia. Edited by Alvaro Alonso. Málaga: Aljibe, 1995.

Carrillo, Francisco. "La vida del pícaro (1601): Testimonio contextual de la picaresca." In *Actas del VIII Congreso de la Asociación Internacional de Hispanistas,* edited by A. David Kossoff, Ruth H. Kossoff, Geoffrey Ribbans, and José Amor y Vázquez, 357–66. Madrid: Ediciones Istmo, 1986.

Cascardi, Anthony. "Cervantes and Skepticism: The Vanishing of the Body." In *Essays on Hispanic Literature in Honor of Edmund L. King,* edited by Sylvia Molloy and Luis Fernández Cifuentes, 23–29. Colección Támesis: Serie A—Monografías, 48. London: Tamesis Books, 1983.

———. "¿Qué es filosofar? A Dog's Eye View." *Cervantes* 34, no. 1 (2014): 77–95.

Castillo, Moisés R. "¿Ortodoxia cervantina? Un análisis de *La gran sultana, El trato de Argel* y *Los baños de Argel*." *Bulletin of the Comediantes* 56, no. 2 (2004): 219–40.

Castro, Americo. *Cervantes y los casticismos españoles.* Madrid: Alfaguara, 1966.

Cavanaugh, Stephanie M. "Litigating for Liberty: Enslaved Morisco Children in Sixteenth-Century Valladolid." *Renaissance Quarterly* 70, no. 4 (2017): 1282–1320.

Cavillac, Michel. *Guex et marchands dans le Guzmán de Alfarache (1599–1605): Roman picaresque et mentalité bourgeoise dans l'Espagne du Siècle d'Or.* Bordeaux: Institut d'études ibériques et ibéro-américaines de l'Université de Bordeaux, 1983.

———. Guzmán de Alfarache *y la novela moderna.* Madrid: Casa de Velázquez, 2010.

———. *Pícaros y mercaderes en el* Guzmán de Alfarache*: Reformismo burgués y mentalidad aristocrática en la España del Siglo de Oro.* Translated by Juan M. Azpitarte Almagro. Granada: Universidad de Granada, 1994.

Cervantes Saavedra, Miguel de. *"The Bagnios of Algiers" and "The Great Sultana": Two Plays of Captivity.* Edited and translated by Barbara Fuchs and Aaron Ilika. Philadelphia: University of Pennsylvania Press, 2009.

———. *Don Quijote de la Mancha.* Edited by Martín de Riquer. Barcelona: Planeta, 1997.

———. *Los trabajos de Persiles y Sigismunda.* Edited by Juan Bautista Avalle-Arce. Madrid: Clásicos Castalia, 1969.

———. *Novelas ejemplares.* Edited by Harry Charles Sieber. 2 vols. Letras Hispánicas, vols. 105–6. Madrid: Cátedra, 1980.

———. *Teatro completo.* Edited by Florencio Sevilla Arroyo and Antonio Rey Hazas. Barcelona: Planeta, 1987.

Chartier, Roger. "History, Time, and Space." *Republics of Letters: A Journal for the Study of Knowledge, Politics, and the Arts* 2, no. 2 (June 1, 2011). http://arcade.stanford.edu/sites/default/files/article_pdfs/roflv02i02_Chartier_060111_0.pdf.

Checa, Jorge. "Cervantes y la cuestión de los orígenes: Escepticismo y lenguaje en *El coloquio de Los Perros." Hispanic Review* 68, no. 3 (2000): 295–317.

———. "La Lozana Andaluza (o cómo se hace un retrato)." *Bulletin of Spanish Studies* 82 (2005): 1–18.

Clouse, Michele L. *Medicine, Government, and Public Health in Philip II's Spain: Shared Interests, Competing Authorities.* Burlington, VT: Ashgate, 2013.

Coleridge, Samuel T. *Biographia Literaria.* Edited by J. Shawcross. 2 vols. London: Oxford University Press, 1939.

Córdoba, Pedro. "Cita y autocita en Cervantes." In *La réception du texte littéraire,* edited by Jean-Pierre Étienvre and Leonardo Castro Tovar, vol. 7, 39–50. Zaragoza: Casa de Velázquez, 1988.

Corriente, Federico. "Los arabismos de *La Lozana andaluza." Estudis Romànics* 32 (2010): 51–72.

Costa Fontes, Manuel da. "Imitation, Banter, and Competition: Francisco Delicado and *Celestina." Romance Philology* 56 (2003): 293–305.

Cottino-Jones, Marga. "Rome and the Theatre in the Renaissance." In *Rome in the Renaissance: The City and the Myth,* edited by P. A. Ramsey, 237–45. Binghamton, NY: Center for Medieval & Early Renaissance Studies, 1982.

Covarrubias, Sebastián de. *Tesoro de la lengua castellana o española.* Edited by Martín Riquer. Barcelona: Alta Fulla, 1998.

Croce, Benedetto. *España en la vida italiana del Renacimiento.* Translated by Franscisco González Ríos. Buenos Aires: Imán, 1945.

Cruz, Anne J. *Discourses of Poverty: Social Reform and the Picaresque Novel in Early Modern Spain.* Toronto: University of Toronto Press, 1999.

Cuart Moner, Baltasar. "El juego de la memoria: Manipulaciones, reconstrucciones y reinvenciones de linajes en los Colegio Mayores salmantinos durante el siglo XVI." In *Cultura, política y práctica del derecho: Juristas de Salamanca, siglos XV–XX,* edited by S. de Dios and E. Torijano, 71–142. Salamanca: Universidad de Salamanca, 2012.

Damiani, Bruno. *Francisco Delicado.* New York: Twayne, 1974.

———. "Text: Francisco Delicado. 'El modo de adoperare el legno de India occidentale.' A Critical Transcription." *Revista Hispánica Moderna* 36 (1970–71): 251–71.

Davis, Natalie Zemon. *Fiction in the Archives: Pardon Tales and Their Tellers in Sixteenth-Century France.* Stanford, CA: Stanford University Press, 1987.

Delicado, Francisco. *La Lozana andaluza.* Edited by Folke Gernert and Jacques Joset. Madrid: Real Academia Española, 2013.

———. *La Lozana Andaluza*. Edited by Claude Allaigre. Madrid: Cátedra, 1985.
———. "El modo de adoperare el legno de India Occidentale." Venice, 1529.
Devereux, Andrew. "'[T]he ruin and slaughter of . . . fellow Christians': The French as a Threat to Christendom in Spanish Assertions of Sovereignty in Italy, 1479–1516." In *Representing Imperial Rivalry in the Early Modern Mediterranean*, edited by Barbara Fuchs and Emily Weissbourd, 101–25. Toronto: University of Toronto Press, 2015.
Díaz Tanco, Vasco. *Palinodia de los Turcos* [1547]. Facsimile with an introduction by Antonio Rodríguez-Moñino. Badajoz: Diputación Provincial, 1947.
Di Camillo, Ottavio. "Algunas consideraciones sobre la Celestina italiana." In *Rumbos del hispanismo en el umbral del Cincuentenario de la AIH*, edited by Patrizia Botta, 2:216–26. Rome: Bagatto Libri, 2012.
Dopico Black, Georgina. "Ghostly Remains: Valencia, 1609." *Arizona Journal of Hispanic Cultural Studies* 7 (2003): 91–100.
Dunn, Peter N. *Spanish Picaresque Fiction: A New Literary History.* Ithaca, NY: Cornell University Press, 1993.
Dworkin, Steven N. *A History of the Spanish Lexicon: A Linguistic Perspective.* Oxford: Oxford University Press, 2012.
Eberenz, Rolf, and Mariela de la Torre. *Conversaciones estrechamente vigiladas: Interacción coloquial y español oral en las actas inquisitoriales de los siglos XV a XVII.* Zaragoza: Libros Pórticos, 2003.
Eliot, George. *The George Eliot Letters.* 9 vols. Edited by Gordon S. Haight. New Haven, CT: Yale University Press, 1954–78.
Estévez Molinero, Ángel. "La (re)escritura Cervantina de Pedro de Urdemalas." *Cervantes* 15, no. 1 (1995): 82–93.
Farinelli, Arturo. *Marrano (storia di un vituperio).* Geneva: Olschki, 1925.
Fernández, Enrique. *Anxieties of Interiority and Dissection in Early Modern Spain.* Toronto: University of Toronto Press, 2015.
Fernandez de Oviedo, Gonzalo. *Historia general y natural de Las Indias.* Edited by Juan Pérez de Tudela Bueso. 5 vols. Biblioteca de Autores Españoles, vols. 117–21. Madrid: Atlas, 1959.
Ferreras, Jacqueline. "Apuntes sobre la escritura del *Viaje de Turquía.*" In *El Siglo de Oro en escena: Homenaje a Mark Vitse,* edited by Odette Gorsse and Frédéric Serralta, 297–309. Toulouse: Presses Universitaires du Mirail/Consejería de Educación de la Embajada Española en Francia, 2006.
Fine, Ruth. "El entrecruzamiento de lo hebreo y lo converso en la obra de Cervantes: Un encuentro singular." In *Cervantes y las religiones,* edited by Ruth Fine and Santiago López Navia, 435–51. Madrid: Iberoamericana, 2008.
Flood, John L., and David J. Shaw. "The Price of the Pox in 1527: Johannes Sinapius and the Guaiac Cure." *Bibliothèque d'Humanisme et Renaissance* 54, no. 3 (1992): 691–707.
Folger, Robert. *Picaresque and Bureaucracy: Lazarillo de Tormes.* Newark, DE: Juan de la Cuesta, 2009.
———. *Writing and Poaching: Interpellation and Self-Fashioning in Colonial* relaciones de méritos y servicios. Leiden: Brill, 2011.
Fontaine, Laurence. *The Moral Economy: Poverty, Credit, and Trust in Early Modern Europe.* Cambridge: Cambridge University Press, 2014.
Forcione, Alban. *Cervantes, Aristotle, and the "Persiles."* Princeton, NJ: Princeton University Press, 1970.

Fricker, Miranda. *Epistemic Injustice: Power and the Ethics of Knowing*. Oxford: Oxford University Press, 2007.

Frisch, Andrea. *The Invention of the Eyewitness: Witnessing and Testimony in Early Modern France*. Chapel Hill: University of North Carolina Press, 2004.

Fuchs, Barbara. "An English Pícaro in New Spain: Miles Philips and the Framing of National Identity." *CR: The New Centennial Review* 2, no. 1 (2002): 55–68.

———. *Exotic Nation: Maurophilia and the Construction of Early Modern Spain.* Philadelphia: University of Pennsylvania Press, 2009.

———. *Mimesis and Empire: The New World, Islam, and European Identities.* Cambridge: Cambridge University Press, 2001.

———. "Ventriloquist Theater and the Omniscient Narrator: *Gatz* and *El pasado es un animal grotesco*." *Modern Drama* 57, no. 2 (2014): 165–86.

Fuchs, Barbara, and Mercedes García-Arenal. *The Quest for Certainty in Early Modern Europe: From Inquisition to Inquiry, 1550–1700.* Toronto: University of Toronto Press, 2020.

Furetière, Antoione. *Dictionnaire universel.* The Hague and Rotterdam, 1690.

Garcés, María Antonia. *Cervantes in Algiers: A Captive's Tale.* Nashville: Vanderbilt University Press, 2002.

García-Arenal, Mercedes. "A Catholic Muslim Prophet: Agustín de Ribera, the Boy Who Saw Angels." *Common Knowledge* 18, no. 2 (2012): 267–91.

———. *After Conversion: Iberia and the Emergence of Modernity.* Leiden: Brill, 2018.

García-Arenal, Mercedes, and Stefania Pastore, eds. *From Doubt to Unbelief: Forms of Scepticism in the Iberian World.* Cambridge: MHRA, 2019.

García-Arenal, Mercedes, and Felipe Pereda. "A propósito de los Alumbrados: Confesionalidad y disidencia en el mundo ibérico." *La Corónica* 41, no. 1 (2012): 109–48.

———. "On the Alumbrados: Confessionalism and Religious Dissidence in the Iberian World." In *The Early Modern Hispanic World: Transnational and Interdisciplinary Approaches,* edited by Kimberly Lynn and Erin Rowe, 121–52. Cambridge: Cambridge University Press, 2017.

García-Arenal, Mercedes, and Fernando Rodríguez Mediano. *Un oriente español: Los moriscos y el Sacromonte en tiempos de Contrarreforma.* Madrid: Marcial Pons, 2010.

García López, Jorge. "*Rinconete y Cortadillo* y la novela picaresca." *Cervantes* 19, no. 2 (1999): 113–24.

García-Santo Tomás, Enrique. "Outside Bets: Disciplining Gamblers in Early Modern Spain." *Hispanic Review* 77, no. 1 (2010): 147–64.

Garrad, K. "The Original Memorial of Don Francisco Núñez Muley." *Atlante* 2 (1954): 199–226.

Garrido Ardila, J. A., ed. *The Picaresque Novel in Western Literature: From the Sixteenth Century to the Neopicaresque.* Cambridge: Cambridge University Press, 2015.

Gaylord, Mary M. "The True History of Early Modern Writing in Spanish: Some American Reflections." *Modern Language Quarterly* 57, no. 2 (1996): 213–25.

Gernert, Folke, and Jacques Joset, "¿Una obra realista?" In Francisco Delicado, *La Lozana andaluza,* edited by Folke Gernert and Jacques Joset, 440–63. Madrid: Real Academia Española, 2013.

Gitlitz, David. "Inquisition Confessions and *Lazarillo de Tormes*." *Hispanic Review* 68, no. 1 (2000): 53–74.

Giustiniani, Agostino. *Castigatissimi annali della eccelsa et illustrissima republica di Genoa.* Genoa, 1537. Available at https://books.google.com/books?id=wcZQAAAAcAAJ&pg.

González, Aníbal. "*Los infortunios de Alonso Ramírez*: Picaresca e historia." *Hispanic Review* 51, no. 2 (1983): 189–204.
González, Aurelio. "El gracioso de Cervantes, un modelo alternativo." *Teatro de Palabras: Revista sobre teatro áureo* 2 (2008): 29–44.
González Echevarría, Roberto. *Myth and Archive: A Theory of Latin American Narrative*. Cambridge: Cambridge University Press, 1990.
———. "The Life and Adventures of Cipión: Cervantes and the Picaresque." *Diacritics* 10, no. 3 (1980): 15–26.
Greene, Molly. *A Shared World: Christians and Muslims in the Early Modern Mediterranean.* Princeton, NJ: Princeton University Press, 2002.
Grieve, Patricia. *The Eve of Spain: Myths of Origin in the History of Christian, Muslim, and Jewish Conflict.* Baltimore: Johns Hopkins University Press, 2009.
Guillén, Claudio. *Literature as System: Essays Toward the Theory of Literary History*. Princeton, NJ: Princeton University Press, 1971.
Hampton, Timothy. *Writing from History: The Rhetoric of Exemplarity in Renaissance Literature.* Ithaca, NY: Cornell University Press, 1990.
Harst, Joachim. "Making Love: Celestinesque Literature, Philology, and 'Marranism.'" *MLN* 127, no. 2 (2012): 169–89.
Hasson, Or. "*Los baños de Argel:* Un análisis del tratamiento cervantino de lo hebreo y lo judío desde un punto de vista kleiniano." In *Cervantes y las religiones,* edited by Ruth Fine and Santiago López Navia, 473–502. Madrid: Iberoamericana, 2008.
Helgerson, Richard. "'I Miles Philips': An Elizabethan Seaman Conscripted by History." *PMLA* 118, no. 3 (2003): 573–80.
Herrera Puga, Pedro. *Sociedad y delincuencia en el Siglo del Oro.* Madrid: La Editorial Católica, 1974.
Hershenzon, Daniel. *The Captive Sea: Slavery, Communication, and Commerce in Early Modern Spain and the Mediterranean.* Philadelphia: University of Pennsylvania Press, 2018.
Ihrie, Maureen. *Skepticism in Cervantes.* Colección Támesis: Serie A—Monografías, 86. London: Tamesis Books, 1982.
Imperiale, Louis. "El marco dramático del *Retrato de la Lozana Andaluza*: Una lectura semiológica." Ph.D. diss., Catholic University of America, 1980.
Irigoyen-García, Javier. "El problema morisco en *Los baños de Argel*, de Miguel de Cervantes: De renegados a mártires cristianos." *Revista Canadiense de Estudios Hispánicos* 32, no. 3 (2008): 421–38.
———. "'La música ha sido hereje': Pastoral Performance, Moorishness, and Cultural Hybridity in *Los baños de Argel*." *Bulletin of the Comediantes* 62, no. 2 (2010): 45–62.
———. *The Spanish Arcadia: Sheep Herding, Pastoral Discourse, and Ethnicity in Early Modern Spain.* Toronto: University of Toronto Press, 2014.
———. "'Si no es adivinando la mitad del pergamino': Discurso y realidad en *La ilustre fregona.*" In *Novelas ejemplares: Las grietas de la ejemplaridad,* edited by Julio Baena, 227–49. Newark, DE: Juan de la Cuesta, 2008.
Jiménez Muñoz, Francisco Javier. *La usura: Evolución histórica y patología de los intereses*. Madrid: Librería Editorial Dykinson, 2010.
Johnson, Carroll B. *Cervantes and the Material World.* Urbana: University of Illinois Press, 2000.
Johnson, Christopher D. "El Homero español: Translation and Shipwreck." *Translation and Literature* 20, no. 2 (2011): 157–74.

Johnson, Paul Michael. "Feeling Certainty, Performing Sincerity: The Emotional Hermeneutics of Truth in Inquisitorial and Theatrical Practice." In *The Quest for Certainty in Early Modern Europe: From Inquisition to Inquiry, 1550–1700,* edited by Barbara Fuchs and Mercedes García-Arenal. Toronto: University of Toronto Press, 2020.

Kakutani, Michiko. *The Death of Truth: Notes on Falsehood in the Age of Trump.* New York: Tim Duggan Books, 2018.

Kanellos, Nicolas. "The Anti-Semitism of Cervantes' *Los baños de Argel* and *La gran sultana:* A Reappraisal." *Bulletin of the Comediantes* 27 (1975): 48–52.

Kish, Kathleen. "*Celestina* as Chameleon: The Early Translations." *Celestinesca* 33 (2009): 87–98.

LaGarde, Jennifer, and Darren Hudgins. *Fact vs. Fiction: Teaching Critical Thinking Skills in the Age of Fake News.* Portland, OR: International Society for Technology in Education, 2018.

Lasso de la Vega, Gabriel. *Manojuelo de romances.* Madrid: Sueta, 1942.

Lerner, Isaías. "Acerca del texto de la primera edición de la *Silva* de Pedro Mexía." *Actas del VII congreso de la Asociación Internacional de Hispanistas* (Rome: Bulzoni Editore, 1982), 677–84.

Lessing, Doris. *Under My Skin: Volume One of My Autobiography to 1949.* New York: HarperCollins, 1994.

Lewis-Smith, Paul. "La gran sultana doña Catalina de Oviedo: A Cervantine Practical Joke." *Forum for Modern Language Studies* 17, no. 1 (1981): 68–81.

Lezra, Jacques. "Translated Turks on the Early Modern Stage." In *Transnational Exchange in Early Modern Theater,* edited by Robert Henke and Eric Nicholson, 159–78. Burlington, VT: Ashgate, 2008.

———. *Unspeakable Subjects: The Genealogy of the Event in Early Modern Europe.* Stanford, CA: Stanford University Press, 1997.

Lorca, Daniel. "The Function of Skepticism in Part I of *Don Quijote.*" *Cervantes* 30, no. 2 (2010): 115–48.

Lucía Megías, José Manuel. *Imprenta y libros de caballerías.* Madrid: Ollero & Ramos, 2000.

Lyons, John D. *Exemplum: The Rhetoric of Example in Early Modern France and Italy.* Princeton, NJ: Princeton University Press, 1989.

Mariscal, George. "*La gran sultana* and the Issue of Cervantes's Modernity." *Revista de Estudios Hispánicos* 28, no. 2 (1994): 185–211.

Márquez Villanueva, Francisco. "Sobre el lanzamiento y recepción del *Guzmán de Alfarache.*" *Bulletin Hispanique* 92 (1990): 549–77.

———. "Trasfondos de 'La profecía del Tajo': Goticismo y profetismo." In *Fray Luis de León: Historia, humanismo y letras,* edited by Víctor García de la Concha and Javier San José Lera, 423–40. Salamanca: Universidad de Salamanca, 1996.

Mas, Albert. *Les Turcs dans la littérature espagnole du siècle d'or: Recherches sur l'évolution d'un thème littéraire,* 2 vols. Paris: Centre de recherches hispaniques, 1967.

Maximus, Valerius. *Memorable Doings and Sayings.* Edited by D. R. Shackleton Bailey. Cambridge, MA: Harvard University Press, 2000.

Meyer-Minnemann, Klaus, and Sabine Schlickers, eds. *La novela picaresca: Concepto genérico y evolución del género (siglos XVI y XVII).* Madrid: Iberoamericana, 2008.

Miller, Christopher L. *Impostors: Literary Hoaxes and Cultural Authenticity.* Chicago: University of Chicago Press, 2018.

Montalvo, Manuel. "La crisis del siglo XVII desde la atalaya de Mateo Alemán." *Revista de Occidente* 112 (1990): 116–35.

Montauban, Jannine. *El ajuar de la vida picaresca: Reproducción, genealogía y sexualidad en la novela picaresca Española.* Madrid: Visor Libros, 2003.

More, Thomas. *Utopia*. Edited and translated by George M. Logan. New York: W. W. Norton, 2011.

Morell, Hortensia. "La deformación picaresca del mundo ideal en *Ozmín y Daraja* del *Guzmán de Alfarache*." *La Torre* 13, no. 87–88 (1975): 101–25.

Morreale, Margherita. "Apuntes bibliográficos para el estudio de la presencia de *La Celestina* en Italia." *Revista de Literatura* 52, no. 104 (1990): 539–43.

Muñoz Sánchez, Juan Ramón. "'El mejor de los poetas' para 'el mejor de los príncipes': *La Ulixea de Homero, traducida de griego en lengua castellana por el secretario Gonzalo Pérez,* un tratado cortesano de educación principesca." *Calíope* 22, no. 1 (2017): 141–63.

Myers, Kathleen Ann. *Fernández de Oviedo's Chronicle of America: A New History for a New World.* Austin: University of Texas Press, 2007.

Niemeyer, Katharina. "'. . . El ser de un pícaro el sujeto deste libro': La *Primera parte de Guzmán de Alfarache*." In *La novela picaresca: concepto genérico y evolución del género (siglos XVI y XVII),* edited by Klaus Meyer-Minnemann and Sabine Schlickers, 77–116. Madrid: Iberoamericana, 2008.

Oatley, Keith. "Fiction: Simulation of Social Worlds." *Trends in Cognitive Sciences* 20, no. 8 (2016): 618–28.

Ortiz Lottman, Mayrica. "*La gran sultana:* Transformations in Secret Speech." *Cervantes: Bulletin of the Cervantes Society of America* 16, no. 1 (1996): 74–90.

Ortolá, Marie-Sol. *Un estudio del "Viaje de Turquía": Autobiografía o ficción.* Colección Támesis: Serie A—Monografías, 87. London: Tamesis, 1983.

———, ed. *Viaje de Turquía.* Madrid: Castalia, 2000.

Pagden, Anthony. *European Encounters with the New World: From Renaissance to Romanticism.* New Haven, CT: Yale University Press, 1993.

Paige, Nicholas D. *Being Interior: Autobiography and the Contradictions of Modernity in Seventeenth-Century France.* Philadelphia: University of Pennsylvania Press, 2001.

Pallotta, Augustus. "Venetian Printers and Spanish Literature in Sixteenth-Century Italy." *Comparative Literature* 43, no. 1 (1991): 20–42.

Parker, Alexander A. *Literature and the Delinquent: The Picaresque Novel in Spain and Europe, 1599–1753.* Edinburgh: Edinburgh University Press, 1967.

Parrack, John C. "Reading the Silence: The Picaresque Game of *Lacunae* and Contradiction." *Revista Canadiense de Estudios Hispanicos* 32, no. 2 (2008): 291–314.

Partner, Peter. *Renaissance Rome, 1500–1559: A Portrait of a Society.* Berkeley: University of California Press, 1976.

Pastore, Stefania. "From 'Marranos' to 'Unbelievers': The Spanish Peccadillo in Sixteenth-Century Italy." In *Dissimulation and Deceit in Early Modern Europe,* edited by Miriam Eliav-Felden and Tamar Herzig, 79–93. New York: Springer, 2015.

Pavlovic-Samurovic, Ljiljana. "Los elementos renacentistas en la *Palinodia de los Turcos* (1547) de Vasco Díaz Tanco de Frejenal." *Estado actual de los estudios sobre el Siglo de Oro: Actas del II Congreso Internacional de Hispanistas del Siglo de Oro* (1993): 753–59.

Pérez de Herrera, Cristóbal. *Amparo de pobres.* Edited by Michel Cavillac. Madrid: Espasa-Calpe, 1975.

Perry, Mary Elizabeth, and Anne J. Cruz. *Cultural Encounters: The Impact of the Inquisition in Spain and the New World.* Berkeley: University of California Press, 1991.

Philips, Miles. "A Discourse Written by one Miles Philips Englishman." In Richard Hakluyt, *The Principal Navigations, Voyages, Traffiques and Discoveries of the English Nation*, 12 vols., 9:398–445. Glasgow: Maclehose and Sons, 1904.

Piper, Anson C. "The 'Breadly Paradise' of *Lazarillo de Tormes*." *Hispania* 44, no. 2 (1961): 269–71.

Rama, Ángel. *La ciudad letrada*. Hanover, NH: Ediciones del Norte, 1984.

Ramos González, Fernando. "Libros de contabilidad." Alicante: Biblioteca Virtual Miguel de Cervantes, 2014. http://www.cervantesvirtual.com/obra-visor/libros-de-contabilidad/html/db70e24c-51e9-4cab-8180–66c44e91b2ae_2.html#I_0_.

Reed, Helen. "Theatricality in the Picaresque of Cervantes." *Cervantes* 7, no. 2 (1987): 71–84.

Requejo Carrió, Marie-Blanche. "De como se guisa una fábula: El episodio de los falsos cautivos en el *Persiles* (III.X)." In Alicia Villar Lecumberri, ed., *Peregrinamente peregrinos: Actas del V Congreso Internacional de la Asociación de Cervantistas*, 861–79. Alcalá de Henares: Asociación de Cervantistas, 2004.

Rico, Francisco, ed. *Lazarillo de Tormes*. Letras Hispánicas 44. Madrid: Cátedra, 1987.

Rigolot, François. "Problematizing Renaissance Exemplarity: The Inward Turn of Dialogue from Petrarch to Montaigne." In *Printed Voices: The Renaissance Culture of Dialogue*, edited by Dorothea Heitsch and Jean-François Vallée, 3–24. Toronto: University of Toronto Press, 2004.

Riley, Edward. "La profecía de la bruja (*El coloquio de los perros*)." In *Actas del Primer Coloquio Internacional de Cervantistas*, 83–94. Barcelona: Anthropos, 1990.

Rodríguez, Juan Carlos. *La literatura del pobre*. Granada: Comares, 1994.

Rodríguez Matos, Carlos Antonio. *El narrador pícaro: Guzmán de Alfarache*. Madison, WI: Hispanic Seminary of Medieval Studies, 1985.

Rodríguez Mediano, Fernando, and Carlos Cañete, eds. "Interiority, Subject, Authority: Conversions and Counter-Reformation in the Construction of the Modern Subject (16th–17th Centuries)." Special issue, *Culture and History* 6, no. 2 (2017).

Rojas, Fernando de. *Tragicomedia de Calisto y Melibea en la qual se contiene de mas de su agradable & dulce estilo muchas sentencias filosofales y auissos muy necessarios para mancebos*. Venice: Stefano Nicolini da Sabio, 1534.

———. *La Celestina*. Edited by Bruno Mario Damiani. Letras Hispánicas 4. Madrid: Cátedra, 1979.

Rosal, Francisco del. *Diccionario etimológico. Alfabeto primero de Origen y Etimología de todos los vocablos originales de la Lengua Castellana*. Facsimile edited by Enrique Gómez Aguado. Madrid: CSIC, 1992.

Rospocher, Massimo. "Print and Political Propaganda under Pope Julius II (1503–13)." In *Authority in European Book Culture, 1400–1600*, edited by Polly Bromilow, 97–119. Burlington, VT: Ashgate, 2013.

Ross, Elizabeth. *Picturing Experience in the Early Printed Book: Breydenbach's Peregrinatio from Venice to Jerusalem*. University Park: Penn State Press, 2014.

Rubiés, Joan-Pau. *Travel and Ethnology in the Renaissance: South India Through European Eyes, 1250–1625*. Cambridge: Cambridge University Press, 2000.

———. *Travellers and Cosmographers: Studies in the History of Early Modern Travel and Ethnology*. Burlington, VT: Ashgate, 2007.

Ruiz Martín, Felipe. *Las finanzas de la Monarquía Hispánica en tiempos de Felipe IV*. Madrid: Real Academia de la Historia, 1990.

———. *Pequeño capitalismo, gran capitalism*. Barcelona: Crítica, 1990.

Sánchez, Francisco. *Quod nihil scitur*. Edited and translated by Sergio Rábade Rabade, José María Artola, and M. Francisco Pérez López. Madrid: CSIC, 1984.
Sánchez, Francisco J. "Theater Within the Novel: 'Mass' Audience and Individual Reader in *La Gitanilla* and *Rinconete y Cortadillo.*" In *Cervantes' "Exemplary Novels" and the Adventure of Writing,* edited by Michael Nerlich and Nicholas Spadaccini, 23–98. Hispanic Issues 6. Minneapolis: Prisma Institute, 1989.
Sánchez García, Encarnación. "Sobre la princeps de la Propalladia (Nápoles, Ioan Pasqueto de Sallo, 1517): Los mecenas (Fernando D'Ávalos, Vittoria y Fabrizio Colonna, Belisario Acquaviva) y la epístola latina de Mesinerius I. Barberius." In *Lingua spagnola e cultura ispanica a Napoli fra Rinascimento e Barroco: Testimonianze a stampa,* edited by Encarnación Sánchez García, 1–33. Naples: Tullio Pironti, 2013.
Scoles, Emma. "Note sulla prima traduzione italiana della *Celestina.*" *Studi Romanzi* 33 (1961): 157–217.
Sevilla Arroyo, Florencio. "Diálogo y novela en el *Viaje de Turquía.*" *Revista de Filología Española* 77, no. 1/2 (1997): 69–87.
Shakespeare, William. *The Merchant of Venice.* Edited by M. Lindsay Kaplan. New York: Palgrave, 2002.
Shields, David. *Reality Hunger: A Manifesto.* New York: Vintage, 2010.
Shuger, Dale. "The Language of Mysticism and the Language of Law in Early Modern Spain." *Renaissance Quarterly* 68, no. 3 (2015): 932–56.
Sicroff, Albert. *Les controverses des statuts de "pureté de sang" en Espagne du XVe au XVIIe siècles.* Paris: Didier, 1960.
Smith, Pamela H. "Art, Science, and Visual Culture in Early Modern Europe." *Isis* 97, no. 1 (2006): 86–100.
Smith, Paul Julian. "The Rhetoric of Representation in Writers and Critics of Picaresque Narrative: *Lazarillo de Tormes, Guzmán de Alfarache, El Buscón.*" *Modern Language Review* 82, no. 1 (1987): 88–108.
Snow, Joseph. "Historia de la recepción de *Celestina*: 1499–1822 II." *Celestinesca* 25, no. 1–2 (2001): 199–282.
Solá, Emilio. "Los avisos de Levante: El nacimiento de una narración sobre Turquía." In *España y el Oriente Islámico entro los siglos XV y XVI,* edited by Encarnación Sánchez García, Pablo Martín Asuero, and Michele Bernardini, 207–30. Istanbul: Isis, 2007.
Spitzer, Leo. *Linguistics and Literary History: Essays in Stylistics.* New York: Russel and Russel, 1972.
Surtz, Ronald. "Texto e imagen en el *Retrato de la Lozana andaluza.*" *Nueva Revista de Filología Hispánica* 40, no. 1 (1992): 169–85.
Tedde de Lorca, Pedro, ed. *Las finanzas de Castilla y la Monarquía Hispánica (siglos xvi–xvii): homenaje a Felipe Ruiz Martín.* Valladolid: Universidad de Valladolid, 2008.
Thompson, I. A. A. "Castile: Polity, Fiscality, and Fiscal Crisis." In *Fiscal Crises, Liberty, and Representative Government, 1450–1789,* edited by Philip T. Hoffman and Kathryn Nohrberg, 140–80. Stanford, CA: Stanford University Press, 2002.
Torres Naharro, Bartolomé de. "Introito y Argumento" to *Comedia Tinelaria.* In *Teatro completo,* edited by Julio Vélez-Sainz, 433–526. Madrid: Cátedra, 2013.
———. *Comedia Soldadesca.* In *Teatro completo,* edited by Julio Vélez-Sainz, 371–432. Madrid: Cátedra, 2013.
Torrico, Benjamín. "Retorno al 'paraíso panal': Derecho civil y canónico como claves eucarísticas en el Tratado segundo de *Lazarillo de Tormes.*" *Hispanic Review* 74, no. 4 (2006): 419–35.

Los tres libros del muy esforzado caballero Primaleon et Polendos su hermano hijos del Emperador Palmerin de Oliva. Venice, 1531.

Trivellato, Francesca. *The Familiarity of Strangers: The Sephardic Diaspora, Livorno, and Cross-Cultural Trade in the Early Modern Period.* New Haven, CT: Yale University Press, 2009.

Veyne, Paul. *Writing History: Essay on Epistemology.* Translated by Mina Moore-Rinvolucri. Middletown, CT: Wesleyan University Press, 1984.

Voigt, Lisa. *Writing Captivity in the Early Modern Atlantic: Circulations of Knowledge and Authority in the Iberian and English Imperial Worlds.* Chapel Hill: University of North Carolina/ Omohundro Institute, 2009.

Voigt, Lisa, and Elio Brancaforte. "The Traveling Illustrations of Sixteenth-Century Travel Narratives." *PMLA* 129, no. 3 (2014): 365–98.

Wardropper, Bruce. "La novela como retrato: El arte de Francisco Delicado." *Nueva Revista de Filología Hispánica* 7 (1953): 475–88.

Weissberger, Barbara F. "Motherhood and Ritual Murder in Medieval Spain and England." *Journal of Medieval and Early Modern Studies* 39, no. 1 (2009): 7–30.

Whitenack, Judith. "The *alma diferente* of Mateo Alemán's 'Ozmín y Daraja.'" *Romance Quarterly* 38, no. 1 (1991): 59–71.

———. *The Impenitent Confession of Guzmán de Alfarache.* Madison, WI: Hispanic Seminary of Medieval Studies, 1985.

Wicks, Ulrich. *Picaresque Narrative, Picaresque Fictions: A Theory and Research Guide.* New York: Greenwood, 1989.

Williamson, Edwin. "El juego de la verdad en 'El casamiento engañoso' y 'El coloquio de los perros.'" *Actas del II Coloquio Internacional de Cervantistas,* 183–99. Barcelona: Anthropos, 1990.

———. "Hacia la conciencia ideológica de Cervantes: Idealización y violencia en 'El amante liberal.'" In *Cervantes: Estudios en la víspera de su Centenario,* edited by Kurt Reichenberger, 519–33. Kassel: Reichenberger, 1994.

Zagorin, Perez. *Ways of Lying: Dissimulation, Persecution, and Conformity in Early Modern Europe.* Cambridge, MA: Harvard University Press, 1990.

Index

Acknowledgments

As is so often the case, I developed many of the ideas in this book in the classroom, thinking with both my graduate and my undergraduate students at UCLA. Their curiosity and enthusiasm are always a delight. I am grateful to the many audiences who heard portions of this work and helped me sharpen and refine the arguments, including at UCLA, Harvard, Colorado, Minnesota, Princeton, Duke, Michigan, Johns Hopkins, Brown, and the CSIC. Encountering the work of the CORPI project was crucial for the conceptualization of this book. I thank Mercedes García-Arenal for her generous friendship and intellectual stimulation over the past few years. Marta Albalá Pelegrín, whose own work on Spain and Italy is a great inspiration, offered invaluable comments on *La Lozana andaluza*, as did Pablo García Pinar. My stalwart works-in-progress group—Christine Chism, Hannah Landecker, Carla Pestana, and Sarah Stein—read every chapter and made them all stronger. I would also like to thank the research assistants who helped me on this project: Paul Cella, Allison Collins, Laura Muñoz, Payton Phillips Quintanilla, and Rhonda Sharrah all offered invaluable assistance.

Preliminary versions of portions of Chapters 2, 3, and 4 appeared previously as the following essays: "Trusting the 'I': The Uncertainty of Picaresque Confession in *Guzmán de Alfarache*," in *The Quest for Certainty in Early Modern Europe: From Inquisition to Inquiry (1550–1700)*, edited by myself and Mercedes García-Arenal (Toronto: University of Toronto Press, 2020); "Intimate Strangers: Humor and the Representation of Difference in Cervantes's Drama of Captivity," in *In and Of the Mediterranean: Medieval and Early Modern Iberian Studies*, Hispanic Issues 41, edited by Michelle Hamilton and Núria Silleras-Fernández (Nashville, TN: Vanderbilt University Press, 2015); and "Suspended Judgments: Scepticism and the Pact of Fictionality in Cervantes's Picaresque Novellas," *Modern Language Quarterly* 76, no. 4 (December 2015): 447–63. I am grateful for the permissions granted to republish.